TOP 100 INDIAN INNOVATIONS (2023)

INDIAN INNOVATORS ASSOCIATION

Copyright © Indian Innovators Association 2023
All Rights Reserved.

ISBN 979-8-89133-723-7

This book has been published with all efforts taken to make the material error-free after the consent of the author. However, the author and the publisher do not assume and hereby disclaim any liability to any party for any loss, damage, or disruption caused by errors or omissions, whether such errors or omissions result from negligence, accident, or any other cause.

While every effort has been made to avoid any mistake or omission, this publication is being sold on the condition and understanding that neither the author nor the publishers or printers would be liable in any manner to any person by reason of any mistake or omission in this publication or for any action taken or omitted to be taken or advice rendered or accepted on the basis of this work. For any defect in printing or binding the publishers will be liable only to replace the defective copy by another copy of this work then available.

Contents

Contents

■ Contents ■

Acknowledgement

This is the fifth publication of Indian Innovators Association. Earlier publications; *Creating Demand for Local Innovations*, *Andhra Entrepreneurs-past, present and future*, *Patent IPR Licensing – Technology Commercialisation-Innovation Marketing* and **Top 100 Indian Innovations (2022)** were well received by the innovator community (www.motguru.com)

Every publication is intended to fill a gap in the learning space. Here the gap is information on product innovations from India. Aiming that we excluded innovations in Software, E-Commerce, Financial innovations, *juggad* etc and targeted physical, embodied, systematic innovation, for this compilation. We received nearly 1000 nominations, directly or indirectly and thank all innovators & stakeholders for helping us in this task. Hundred innovations are selected from out of the sourced documents. For selection, equal weight is given to '*innovator profile*' and '*innovation merit*'.

To give a global perspective, we included Global innovators of Indian origin and provided technology history & key patents along with profiles of resident Indian innovators. To supplement information furnished along with nomination, additional details are collected from publicly available documents on the net. Photos of inventors/ founders are taken from their LinkedIn profiles which are also cited in select cases.

Editors
– Aynampudi. Subbarao Rao,
– Dr Sreeram Dhurjaty,
– KVSP Rao,
– Pravin Rajpal,
– Poorvi Pawar

Foreword

(Ashok Atluri is a graduate in Commerce from Osmania University and a PG Diploma holder in Applied Computer Science from CMC. He is a first generation Entrepreneur who along with his partners stared Zen Technologies, which was one of the pioneers in the field of Simulation in India)

In the department of economy, an act, a habit, an institution, a law, gives birth not only to an effect, but to a series of effects. Of these effects, the first only is immediate; it manifests itself simultaneously with its cause – it is seen. The others unfold in succession – they are not seen: it is well for us if they are foreseen. Between a good and a bad economist this constitutes the whole difference — the one takes account of the visible effect; the other takes account both of the effects which are seen and also of those which it is necessary to foresee. The parable of the broken window was introduced by French economist Frédéric Bastiat in his 1850 essay *"That Which We See and That Which We Do Not See"* ("Ce qu'on voit et ce qu'on ne voit pas"). The parable seeks to show how opportunity costs, as well as the law of unintended consequences, affect economic activity in ways that are unseen or ignored. Bastiat says … *it follows that the bad economist pursues a small present good, which will be followed by a great evil to come, while the true economist pursues a great good to come, at the risk of a small present evil."*

True innovators, whether companies or individuals, are willing to put in the resources and efforts for the *"small present evil"*, that may cost lots in terms of money and time, for some future uncertain benefit. While success, which is dependent on many factors including luck, is not guaranteed, innovators don't know any other way to live. They have to create something that will make their lives worthwhile. Innovation is almost like an addiction, a healthy one, that can help us create great solutions to world's biggest problems. R&D, the key to innovation, is almost built into the DNA of a person or company, and either propels them to extreme heights or can destroy them. While failure is at the level of individuals and corporations, as a whole the society benefits tremendously from innovation, we should learn to celebrate failure, esp of the experiments, if we want to succeed as a nation.

Preface

Governments around the world have recognized the importance of new technologies to their economies and have encouraged public-private partnerships to develop and anchor them within their national economies. The long-term goal of these programs is to achieve greater productivity growth through the creation of knowledge that can be applied to industrial processes, products, and services.

Whilst previous investment in knowledge can stimulate more creation and stock of it, knowledge can also spill over from organisations (such as the firms in a cluster or a university) so that it can be appropriated by others to enhance their own productivity. This is especially the case with knowledge generated from universities that both academics and policymakers have identified as a key contributor to national and regional competitiveness. As a result, universities have become increasingly engaged in using knowledge generated to support economic and entrepreneurial development rather than focusing their mission exclusively on teaching and research. Towards this objectives, governments around the world have encouraged public-private partnerships. The long-term goal of these programs is to achieve greater productivity growth in an economy through the creation of knowledge that may become incorporated in industrial processes, products and services.

China and India are technology powerhouses in the horizon and studies increasingly focus on these countries. The evolution of Chinese policies and institutions related to innovation and to the role of the government has been researched in several studies. The focus was on how S&T and industrial policy-centered innovation strategy have become strengthened through a departure from top-down approach driven by a single government agency, and also by broad-basing through financial, tax, and fiscal incentives. The trajectory and evolution of technological catch-up are examined in multiple studies on China and Scholars have studied the role of technology assimilation, new product development performance, firm diversification and innovation performance in enabling spate of secondary innovations.

Studies on India present a mixed picture of uniqueness and successes of Indian innovation efforts, as well as deep concerns. Earlier, Technology denials, catching up with import substitution, Impact of TRIPs were analyzed in detail and now there are scattered studies on impact of Venture Capital, emergence of Unicorns, Startup boom etc. There is need for more studies to develop deeper historical and contextual understanding of innovation-related institution-building in the Indian context.

This publication shares several cases of industry-academia linkages, technology spill over startups and technology licensing opportunities. Talking to computers is the norm these days, from digital assistants in smartphones and smart devices to translation applications that break down language barriers. But 50 years ago, when Carnegie Mellon University began its work in speech understanding, all that was a pipe dream. The knowledge accumulations started 50 years back with Raj Reddy founder of the speech recognition research efforts at CMU. Jaswinder Singh Sandhu spent all his life working on Acoustagraphy a NDT method. Similarly Dr. Hardarshan Singh Valia name is associated with Coal, Anil Jha's name with water, Sumita Mitra's name with nanocompisite dental material and Sanjay Mehrotra's name with flash memory. Our global innovators of Indian origin are pioneers in their chosen field.

Several innovations selected in Agriculture group had their knowledge base in Research and Technical Institutes.

CSIR-Central Salt and Marine Chemicals Research Institute (CSIR-CSMCRI) has been actively pursuing the seaweed research for nearly half a century. This institute takes pride in being first for pioneering seaweed cultivation, heralding an era of commercial seaweed farming in India. Scientists Dr M Ganesan and Dr Vibhav Matri made it top 100. Stem cell research has progressed at a phenomenal pace and is rapidly contributing to providing new avenues to prevent and cure many currently untreatable diseases. The Institute for Stem Cell Science and Regenerative Medicine (DBT-InStem) located Bangalore Life Sciences Cluster (BLiSC) has pioneered translation research. Several inventions and innovations have led to seed-funding for startups, or have been transferred to industry partners. Famer special sunscreen developed at Praveen Kumar Vemula lab of InStem made it top 100.

Healthcare innovations take lion's share of the top 100. As can be expected, many innovators are practicing medical professionals and others in bio-technology have strong linkages with research institutions. Dr Sudhir Srivastava designed, developed, trained and made in India Surgical Robot. Dr. Kumaresh Krishnamoorthy a Practicing Surgeon developed Video Laryngoscope and Dr.Vishal Rao, oncology surgeon have voice to cancer patients with voice prosthesis.

Our research labs and technical institutes are active in water & sanitation and their presence is significant in this group. NEERI established Water Technology & Management Division (WTMD) to carry out research and development activities pertaining to water quality monitoring and surveillance, water treatment, water safety plan, water security plan, contaminant transport studies, hydrogeological investigations and water audits. WTMD has a history of various technology/processes development in the field of surface and ground water treatment for providing potable drinking water to large and small communities with constant efficiency and at an affordable price. EDF technique of NEERI, HeloBorne

TEM technology of NGRI bring water technologies to the group. Sanitation, Environment, Circular economy are equally important and the group covers oil spill recovery, Hydrogen bus, energy from plastic waste, textile waste water treatment – all based on research funded by Government of India.

Governments inclusive policy to encourage participation of private sector in strategic areas of defense and space is paying dividends with significant innovations in this group of Defense & Aerospace. Ankit Mehta has made history with his startup incubated at SINE going public with shares(IPO). Subbaro of Anath technologies, partner with every ISRO launch is now preferred global partner for international players. Development of Air Independent Propulsion (AIP) by Dr. Suman Roy Choudhury and his team for submarines is a landmark achievement for DRDO's Naval Materials Research Laboratory (NMRL).

Indian industry hungry for new technologies to meet global competitions has started knocking the doors of research institutes with the result technology transfer agreements have come into force with increased vigour as is evident in this group on Industrial products. IITs have strong connections with industry leaders and investors, which allows them to bring cutting-edge technologies and innovations to market. These connections also provide entrepreneurs with access to mentorship, funding, and other resources that can help them grow their businesses. Profiles of Prof Kothandaraman Ramanujam, Prof Krishnan Balasubramanian, Prof Sathyan S, Prof. Krishna Moorthy Sivalingam Prof Madhav Desai, Prof Ashwin Gumaste from IITM & IITB are covered in this group.

– A.S. Rao
Indian Innovators Association

Past Publications of Indian Innovators Association

Buy online:

https://notionpress.com/read/top-100-indian-innovations-2022

Buy online:

https://notionpress.com/read/creating-demand-for-local-innovations

Buy online:

https://notionpress.com/read/patent-ipr-licensing-technology-commercialisation-innovation-marketing

Buy online:

https://notionpress.com/read/andhra-entrepreneurs

Buy online:

https://www.amazon.in/gp/product/1482710684/

Papers of A. S. Rao on SSRN

1. Change Management by Patanjali, (pages: 8 Posted: 22 Aug 2007)
2. Technology Acceptance Model for Complex Technologies in a Period of Rapid Catching-Up, (pages: 9 Posted: 21 Sep 2007)
3. Financing Innovations for the Bottom of the Pyramid Market, (pages: 12 Posted: 19 Sep 2007)
4. Covering Patent Infringement Risks in Technology Transfer Agreements, (pages: 10 Posted: 17 Apr 2008)
5. Minimum Viable Product (MVP) for Product Startup: An Indian Perspective – Forum for Knowledge Sharing IX Annual Conference: October 27-29, 2014, (pages: 10 Posted: 06 Apr 2019)
6. Technopreneur Promotion Programme (TePP): Investing in Innovation Biotechnews, August 2008, (pages: 4 Posted: 21 Dec 2008)
7. Sub-National Innovation Networks in India – an Emerging Scenario, (pages: 14 Posted: 20 Sep 2007)
8. Rising Creative Class in India, (pages: 7 Posted: 09 Jul 2008)
9. Timing it Right with Technology Forecasting, (pages: 50 Posted: 18 Feb 2010)
10. Stage Gate Model of Innovation – Indian Version 1.0, (pages: 9 Posted: 31 May 2011)
11. White Spaces in Building Innovation Clusters, (pages: 20 Posted: 26 Aug 2011)
12. Who is Creative? (pages: 5 Posted: 09 Jun 2008)

Follow Indian Innovators Association on Social Media

 http://www.indiainvents.in/home.html

 http://indiainvents.blogspot.com/

Linked https://www.linkedin.com/in/indiainvents/

https://twitter.com/IndiaInvents

facebook https://www.facebook.com/aynampudi.subbarao

https://www.instagram.com/aynampudisubbarao/

Why We Must Design and Develop in India, Not Just 'Make' – Ashok Atluri

A teardown report on the Apple iPhone 6 claimed that the bill of material for the smartphone was $200 and the gross margin was around $450. And the major part of this gross margin is captured by Apple. This is what happens when you design and develop – – you capture the major part of the value add. In manufacturing, one barely makes any money and capturing may be at most 2-3% per piece.

So, it was surprising that the game-changing announcement from Defence Minister Manohar Parrikar that indigenously designed and developed products are being given top priority and "will form a vital part of DPP (defence procurement procedure) 2015" went almost unnoticed. This announcement indicates that significant money will now be poured into indigenous R&D and focus will shift to designing and developing defence technologies rather than putting significant efforts in having "strategic" tie-ups with foreign vendors and setting up and managing dumb built-to-print facilities in India.

Self-reliance in defence is a strategic necessity, and countries like the US give outright preference to domestic companies while making procurements for their armed forces. And that is one of the major reasons that these countries have such vast and deep capabilities.

This policy announcement will ensure that Indian companies, in consultation with the armed forces, will proactively identify products that have market potential in defence – – both Indian and overseas – – and start designing and developing equipment to address defence needs. Such focused development efforts, benchmarking the existing market leading products as the base, will ensure that Indian firms make products that not only meet Indian needs but also are export-worthy. Such encouragement will create global champions. Taking a cue from the US, the Indian government can also insist on such products being procured as part of offsets and should also be promoted in government to government (G2G) deals.

The Make in India (#MakeinIndia) campaign that lays so much stress on manufacturing needs to be expanded to include the design and development phases of product manufacturing too. The major objective of the Make in India campaign has been to generate jobs. But the reality is that manufacturing is moving more and more towards automation, and low-level jobs are being replaced with robots. Further, robots can work three shifts a day, don't need breaks, "love" to do repetitive work, and they never go on strike. The process of automating and other breakthroughs will be relentless and, by one estimate, will endanger 47% of the jobs in the US, where the number of manufacturing jobs are already few and far between. For India, it is going to be much larger. The new factories being set up are expected to be mostly automated, as the prices of robots continue to plummet rapidly.

In addition, for defence, designing and developing are strategic imperatives. Benefits include that the IPR remains within India, the effects of sanctions during war are neutralised, more jobs are generated (especially for R&D talent), the defence ecosystem is rejuvenated, global leadership in certain defence segments leads to export growth, and, finally, the growth in pride and self-esteem in using indigenous defence products.

Therefore, unless we focus on the design and development phase, we will not be able to shed our dependence on defence imports. More generally, unless we focus on design and development and capture significant value, we will not be able to generate the surplus needed to sustain the deluge of unemployment and to retrain redundant workers for jobs that may still be available after robots take over "easy" jobs.

There is a need to expand the #MakeInIndia campaign to #DesignDevelop&MakeInIndia.

(The complete article was published on Huffingtonpost.in, 22/12/2015

How Can You Use Gamification to Boost Innovation?

Companies are becoming increasingly aware of the benefits of gamification. It promotes disinhibition, reduces prejudice, encourages cross-disciplinary teamwork and co-creation, helps groups with very different profiles to speak the same language and achieves a level of engagement that drives participants to go one step further. These benefits are particularly important when it comes to ensuring success in creative thinking and innovation. Gartner studies highlight that 70% of companies on the Forbes Global 2000 list are currently using gamification techniques and that 50% of innovation processes will be gamified in the coming years. In countries where companies have already made gamification part of their day-to-day, they know that it can bring specific benefits beyond having a bit of fun and improving teambuilding.

At what stage in an innovation process can you bring in gamification?

To optimise problem solving. You can find different sets of idea generation cards, like IDEO Method Cards, or a game like Binnakle the Expedition, covering not only idea generation but all phases of the creative process (from Reframing the problem to defining experiments)

To optimise co-creation. Playing is a tool that lets you eliminate hierarchies and foster collaboration between very different profiles. Serious games use the universal language of playing and methodologies that allow people with various profiles to collaborate and understand each other.

To start an innovation project. Gamification can be used to kick off a project by identifying, defining, and agreeing on challenges. It also helps players find new avenues to explore.

To improve a Design Thinking process. We use it to begin each phase of the process, to bring more disruption, more fun and to fill in the pipeline to start on a good base.

To improve innovation hackathons. Nothing motivates members of a group more than getting them to play with a shared challenge. And if they are competing, the results will be even better. A serious game for a kick-off activity with a group will also generate the balance you need between motivation and practical results.

For an innovative training format. People are tired of classic training formats. Including a serious game for innovation to train people on creativity and innovation makes them more motivated to learn the methodology and helps them better assimilate the concepts involved.

– Philippe Delespesse
Founder and CEO Binnakle Serious Games to Innovate
(www.binnakle.com/en/)
Founder and CEO Inteligencia Creativa

Global Innovators of Indian Origin

1. Acoustography – Dr. Jaswinder Singh Sandhu, USA
2. Bio surfactants – TeeGene Biotech, UK
3. Coal Science – Dr. Hardarshan Singh Valia, USA
4. Carrier Gas Extraction technology – Gradiant corporation, USA
5. Computer Science – Raj Reddy, USA
6. Flash memory – Micron Technology, USA
7. Green Steel – Veena Sahazwalla, Australia
8. Nanocomposite Dental Materials – Sumita Mitra, USA
9. Regrowth of Bones – Nina Tandon, EpiBone, USA
10. Rotimatic – Zimplistic Pte, Singapore
11. Tiny Robots – Prof Vijay Kumar, USA
12. Water Technology Visionary – Anil Jha, USA
13. Wearable Sweat sensor – EnLiSense, USA
14. Wearable and reusable outpatient ambulatory ECG monitoring products – NimbleHeart, USA

Acoustography – Dr. Jaswinder Singh Sandhu, USA

Dr. Jas Sandhu received a B.Sc (honors) in Physics from the University of Sussex (UK) in 1975 and M.Sc. in Solid State Physics from the University of London (UK) in 1976. He then went on to do research work in the field of Ultrasonics and received his Ph.D. degree in Physics from the University of London in 1980. After graduate school, Dr. Sandhu joined ITT Corporation and in 1989 he decided to start his own company Santec Systems, Inc to develop and commercialize Acoustography. Dr. Sandhu is the President & Founder of Santec Systems, Inc

He is best known for his pioneering work in developing "Acoustography," a novel ultrasound imaging method. Jas has dedicated most of his professional career to developing Acoustography for various industrial and medical applications. He is currently collaborating with various aerospace companies to develop Acoustography to provide dramatically faster NDI (Non Destructive Inspection) of composites. Jas's dedicated effort earned him the Best Paper Award in 2001 by SPIE-The International Society for Optical Engineering. He also received the prestigious *"Award for Innovation,"* in 2010 from the American Society for Nondestructive Testing (NDT) the world largest organization in the NDT field. Jas is the recipient of more than 15 patents and has authored over 100 papers, presentations and reports in the field of Acoustography.

LinkedIn Profile – https://www.linkedin.com/in/jaswinder-singh-sandhu-08b1048/

Technology

Acoustic microscopy employs very high or ultrahigh frequency ultrasound. Acoustic microscopes operate non-destructively and penetrate most solid materials to make visible images of internal features, including defects such as cracks, delamination and voids. The notion of acoustic microscopy dates back to 1936 when S. Ya. Sokolov proposed a device for producing magnified views of structure with 3-GHz sound waves. However, due to technological limitations at the time, no such instrument could be constructed, and it was not until 1959 that Dunn and Fry performed the first acoustic microscopy experiments, though not at very high frequencies. Today, Acoustography is a broad-area, near real-time ultrasonic imaging technique that provides an alternative to point-by-point UT.

Innovation

Acoustography differs from conventional ultrasonic testing in that test objects are inspected in full field, analogously to real time x-ray imaging. The approach uses a novel, super high resolution large area acousto-optic (AO) sensor, which allows image formation through simple ultrasound shadow casting, analogous to x-ray image formation. This NDE approach offers significant inspection speed advantage over conventional point-by-point ultrasonic scanning procedures and is well-suited for high volume production. ACOUSTOGRAPHY developed by Dr Sandu is an ultrasound imaging method where a novel, super high-resolution 2D ultrasound detector (AO sensor) is used to produce instant x-ray-like ultrasound images.

Patent

Optical imager for birefringent detector acoustic imaging systems-https://patents.google.com/patent/WO2000022478A1/en

Acoustic imaging systems – United States Patent 5796003

Commercialisation

Santec systems is promoted by Dr Sandu. http://www.santecsystems.com/

The basic components needed to perform Acoustography NDE are: 1) AO-Sensor (Imaging Screen); 2) Wand Transducer (ultrasound emitter); 3) Optical imager Detector. The Wand Transducer is swept across the part held over the AO sensor to form instant x-ray like ultrasound images of the part revealing anomalies in the test part. The image formed on the AO sensor is viewed and digitally recorded using the Optical Imager.

The company offers ACOUSTOGRAPHY NDE as a standalone system, or as an add-on ACOUSTOGRAPHY NDE capability to existing C-scan systems. The small Table-Top system is perfect for the NDE researcher, providing a simple, practical tool for quick evaluation of composite parts and for providing near real-time monitoring of damage growth in coupons subject to load. And retrofit system package is perfect for providing add-on Acoustography NDE capability to customers with existing C-scan systems. Further fully-automated systems are perfect for the manufacturing floor, capable of enhancing inspection throughput by up to 10 times. In addition, ACOUSTOGRAPHY components can also be purchased, along with data electronics and software package, by customers desiring to build their own systems or wanting to retrofit components to have add-on ACOUSTOGRAPHY NDE capability to their C-scan systems.

Biosurfactants – TeeGene Biotech Ltd. UK

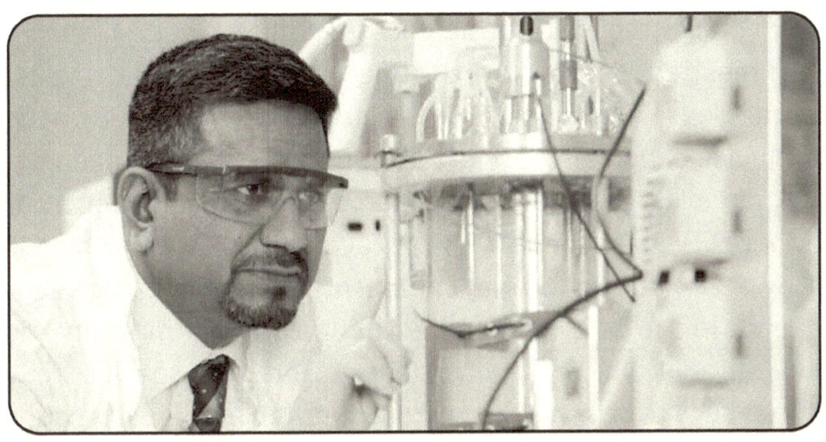

Dr Pattanthu Rahman completed his Bachelor degree at PSG College, Coimbatore, Master and Doctorate degrees in Environmental Microbiology at Bharathiar University (Coimbatore) and Advanced Biomanufacturing of Biopharmaceuticals Course at the University of Cambridge. He then started his career as a postdoctoral researcher in the University of Ulster (2000-01) with subsequent roles as a research Scientist at the Brookhaven National Laboratory, New York, USA (2001-02), an academic and enterprise researcher at Teesside University (2003-2018) and University of Portsmouth (2018 – 2020). Dr Rahman is now a Senior Lecturer at Liverpool John Moores University and Founder of TeeGene & TARA Biologics.

He has 25 years of academic experience in research, innovation, management, and commercialization. He has discovered novel bio surfactant producing bacteria and is the author of 70+ peer-reviewed journal articles and editor of three books on the topic of

Bio surfactants. He is a winner of Teesside University's Enterprise Project of the year award.

https://www.linkedin.com/in/prahman/

Technology

Biosurfactants refers to surfactants from microbial origin and can be synthesized by several identified microorganisms including bacteria, yeast and fungi. They display excellent surface activity and emulsification properties with very low toxicity and higher biodegradability features as compared to chemical counterparts. They have also been found to be very effective at low concentrations and over a wide range of environmental conditions such as pH, temperature and salinity; better environmental compatibility, lower critical micelle concentration, higher selectivity, specific activity and the ability to be synthesized from renewable low cost resources. There are five major categories of bio surfactants viz. glycolipids, phospholipids and fatty acids, lipopeptides and lipoproteins. Polymeric biosurfactants, particulate biosurfactants have found applications in agricultural, pharmaceutical, food, cosmetics, and detergent industries.

Innovation

Among the various categories of biosurfactants the glycolipid biosurfactants "*rhamnolipids*" stand apart. Rhamnolipids are highly applicable in various activities with some researchers advancing the technology from laboratory to higher scale. However, there still are very limited companies in the field which are producing biosurfactants at a marketable scale. TeeGene Biotech produces Rhamnolipids and Lipopeptides for Pharmaceuticals, cosmetics, antimicrobials and anti-cancer ingredients.

Patents

In 1984, the first patent for the production of rhamnolipids was filed by Kaeppeli and Guerra-Santos (US 4628030) and obtained in 1986 for their work on Pseudomonas aeruginosa DSM 2659. Subsequently, Wagner et al. filed a patent (US 4814272) in 1985 for the biotechnical production of rhamnolipids from Pseudomonas sp. DSM 2874 and obtained the same in 1989.

Commercialisation

In 2013, the European Commission launched Bio Base NWE, a three-year and €6,2 million project to support the development of the biobased economy in North West Europe (NWE). Bio Base NWE successfully implemented an Innovation Coupon Scheme. A coupon represented a value of maximum €30.000 for feasibility studies and scale-up work undertaken at the Bio Base Europe Pilot Plant (BBEPP), an independent, flexible, state-of–the-art demonstration facility in Ghent, Belgium, to validate innovative biobased technologies and scale them up to an industrial level.

TeeGene Biotech Ltd. (UK), a Teesside University spin-out venture, received a coupon to conduct feasibility studies to prove the technology platform. With insights from experts at Bio Base Europe Pilot Plant the biosurfactant scale-up work was successful, and the startup can manufacture biosurfactants at an industrial level.

Link: https://www.teegene.co.uk/

Coal Science – Dr. Hardarshan Singh Valia, USA

Dr. Harshan Singh Valia received his Masters in Applied Geology from Nagpur University and Masters in Geology from Bryn Mawr College and Ph.D.in Geology from Boston University. Dr. Valia has published 85 articles, contributed to 5 books (including Making, Shaping, and Treating of Steel), chaired 30 National/International conferences, taught 20 courses worldwide, authored two patents, consulted to many industries around the world (especially extensively in China), and presently is a contributor to American Iron & Steel Institute's web site www.steel.org under *How Steel is Made*?

He is the First Ever Indian and Second Ever Asian person to receive Iron & Steel Society's Joseph Becker Award in 1991 (for distinguished achievement in Coal Technology) for his work on Coal Usage in Steel Industry. Dr. Valia was awarded Joseph Kapitan Award in 2006 (best paper) from the Association for Iron & Steel Technology on his work regarding unique properties of Indiana coals. He is also a recipient of the American Iron & Institute President's Medal in 1990. These honors have brought him the distinction of the only Coal Scientist in the world to have received all the three awards offered by American Steel Industry related organizations.

Research

He entered the industrial world in 1979 as a research engineer at Inland Steel Co.'s research and development laboratories, East Chicago, Ind., USA. His initial work began with improving blast furnace performance/operation by finding ways to improve Coke Strength after Reaction (CSR) with CO2, which resulted in the development of a CSR predictive model. The model is successfully used to predict CSR from coal properties and helped increase CSR that resulted in performance and operation improvements at No. 7 blast furnace. During his career, Valia worked on a wide range of projects: coke behavior in the blast furnace utilizing blast furnace tuyere sampling; modification of Chinese beehive cokes for blast furnace usability; coal selection and blend design for heat recovery/non-recovery and slot oven coke making; research on carbonization behavior of coal in heat recovery/non-recovery and slot oven coke making; use of poor-quality (low-rank) coals in coke making; prediction of coking quality of coal reserves; effect of oxidation on coke quality; new coke making technologies; coal selection and coal behavior in blast furnace pulverized coal injection; and the use of additives in coke making, ironmaking and steelmaking.

Patents

Utilizing certain unique properties of Indiana coals, Dr. Valia, in collaboration with Allen Ellis and other scientists from Purdue University, earned a patent entitled *"Multipurpose Coke Plant for Synthetic Fuel Production."* Such a process would result in not only production of coke for the steel industry but can also produce diesel oil, methane gas, hydrogen, fertilizer, and power.

Publication number: 20130008771, Filed: Sep 14, 2012, Publication Date: Jan 10, 2013, Patent Grant number: 9068123, Applicant: PURDUE RESEARCH FOUNDATION (West Lafayette, IN), Inventors: Robert A. Kramer (Crown Point, IN), Libbie S.W. Pelter (Schererville, IN), Harvey Abramowitz (Chicago, IL), Hardarshan S. Valia (Highland, IN), Allen Ellis (Crown Point, IN)

https://patents.justia.com/patent/20130008771

Consultancy

Dr. Valia, after retiring as a Staff Scientist from Arcelor Mittal (formerly Inland Steel Company), started his own consulting firm Coal Science Inc. and also jointly owns Coal science Laboratory in Gary, Indiana.

https://www.purdue.edu/discoverypark/energy/assets/pdfs/cctr/presentations/RKramer-CCTR-09-06-07.pdf

Carrier Gas Extraction Technology- Gradiant Corporation, USA

Prakash Govindan is the Co-Founder and COO of Gradiant. Prakash earned his Ph.D. in Mechanical Engineering from MIT, where he co-developed the Carrier Gas Extraction (CGE) system, which remains a flagship Gradiant product. He continues to innovate prolifically, with over 100 patents, including Gradiant's Counter-flow Reverse Osmosis (CFRO) and Selective Chemical Extraction (SCE) technologies. Prakash earned a master's degree from IIT Madras.

Anurag Bajpayee is the Co-Founder and CEO of Gradiant. Anurag earned his Ph.D. in Mechanical Engineering from MIT, focusing on industrial desalination and water treatment. Scientific American recognized his doctoral work as a "Top 10 World Changing Idea" and it remains a foundation for Gradiant's proprietary technology stack. Anurag has co-authored several seminal journal articles and received patents in the water treatment field. Anurag holds a bachelor's degree in Mechanical Engineering from the University of Missouri and a master's degree and doctorate from MIT.

https://www.linkedin.com/in/anurag-bajpayee-82068b6/

https://www.linkedin.com/in/prakash-govindan-87168310/

Technology

OPW (Oilfield Produced Water) contains a mixture of suspended solids and dissolved organic and inorganic compounds. Various treatment technologies are needed to reduce the level of toxic contaminants or improve OPW quality. RO is best used for tertiary treatment because ultra-small droplets of oil removal, turbidity, contaminant ions and most dissolved non-ions are removed.

Innovation

Carrier gas extraction (CGE), a humidification and dehumidification (HDH) technique developed by the Gradiant co-founders at MIT, heats OPW into vapor, and condenses it back into water, without contaminants. This yields freshwater and saturated brine, commonly used in drilling and completion processes.

HDH is a decades-old concept: Water is vaporized and condensed on a cold metallic surface to remove salts. But commercial-scale systems have always been too energy-intensive, because water must be boiled while condensing surfaces must be kept very cold. But Gradiant's system designed by Govindan and colleagues in the lab of Gradiant co-founder John H. Lienhard, (the Abdul Latif Jameel World Water and Food Security Professor at MIT) scaled well by using a readily available carrier gas (dry air) that vaporizes water below boiling temperatures, and incorporating a column with microbubbles that optimizes condensing surfaces. In the Gradiant system's humidifier chamber, briny water drops through packing material and mixes with dry air to produce a hot and humid vapor stripped of contaminants such as salts that forms at the top of the chamber. This "raining" happens in a bubble column, which has several levels of perforated trays, each containing a shallow pool of freshwater. As vapor rises through the bubble column, it passes through the plates' holes, causing an extremely rapid mixing process that cools and condenses the water within the pools. As levels rise, the water overflows and is captured in a tray as fresh, nearly distilled water. The temperature difference between the warm and cool water is much less than in a conventional dehumidifying system, using less energy, and the surface area provided by the microbubbles in the trays offers a more efficient heat-transfer ratio than a flat, metallic condenser surface. Not using expensive materials, such as titanium, in the heat exchanger also reduces the capital costs.

(https://news.mit.edu/2015/cheaper-fracking-water-treatment-0716)

(https://startupexchange.mit.edu/startup-features/gradiant)

Patents

WATER TREATMENT SYSTEMS AND ASSOCIATED METHODS, Publication number: 20150060286, 2014 and many more – https://patents.justia.com/assignee/gradiant-corporation

Commercialisation

https://www.gradiant.com/solutions-and-industries/

This MIT spin off offers solutions across the world – Industrial Wastewater & Recycling, Industrial Process Water, Minimum & Zero Liquid Discharge, Resource Recovery & Lithium, Ultrapure Water, PFAS & Emerging Contaminants.

Dabbala Rajagopal ("RAJ") Reddy is renowned for his work in computer speech recognition, robotics, human-computer interaction, innovations in higher education, and efforts to bring digital technology to people on the other side of the "digital divide." He received his Bachelor's degree in civil engineering from Guindy College of Engineering, Madras, moved to Australia as an exchange student and received a Master's degree in technology in 1960 from the University of New South Wales in Sydney, Australia, came to Stanford University as a PhD student. In early 1964, completed his PhD dissertation in 1966, stayed at Stanford as an assistant professor, doing and directing work on speech recognition, image processing, and face recognition. In 1969, attracted by Allen Newell, Herbert Simon and Alan Perlis (all three are also Turing Award recipients), he accepted a position as an associate professor at Carnegie Mellon University, where he continued his research on speech recognition and image processing. He became a Full Professor in 1973, and a University Professor in 1984. He served as the founding Director of the Robotics Institute from 1980 to 1992 and as the Dean of the School of Computer Science from 1991 to 1999. He became the Founding Director of Carnegie Mellon's West Coast Campus in 2001.

He is the chairman of the Governing Council of the International Institute of Information Technology, Hyderabad. Reddy was awarded the Padma Bhushan. Reddy's accomplishments have led to many awards and honors. In addition to being a co-recipient with Ed Feigenbaum of the ACM Turing Award in 1994, he is a member of the National Academy of Engineering and the American Academy of Arts and Sciences. He was awarded the Legion d'Honneur, by French President Francois Mitterrand in 1984 for his work in developing countries; the Okawa Prize in 2004 for "pioneering researches of large scale artificial intelligence system, human-computer interaction… outstanding contributions to information and telecommunications policy", the Honda Prize in 2005 for his "outstanding achievements in computer science and robotics," the 2005 IJCAI Donald E. Walker Distinguished Service Award for "his outstanding service to the AI community," and the Vannevar Bush Award in 2006 for his "pioneering research in robotics and intelligent systems, and his significant contributions in the formulation of national information and telecommunications policy."

https://amturing.acm.org/award_winners/reddy_9634208.cfm

https://en.wikipedia.org/wiki/Raj_Reddy

Technology

Reddy pioneered AI research, concentrated on perceptual and motor aspect of intelligence such as speech, language, vision and robotics. Over a span of five decades, Reddy and his colleagues created several historic demonstrations of spoken language systems, e.g., voice control of a robot, large vocabulary connected speech recognition, speaker independent speech recognition and unrestricted vocabulary dictation.

Innovation

Raj Reddy pioneered the construction of systems for recognizing continuous speech. He developed the first system, Hearsay I, capable of continuous speech recognition. In this system and subsequent systems like Hearsay II, Harpy, and Dragon, he and his students developed most of the ideas underlying modern commercial speech recognition technology. Some of these ideas most notably the "blackboard model" for coordinating multiple knowledge sources have been adopted across the spectrum of applied artificial intelligence. Together, the joint Turing Award recipients in 1994, Edward Feigenbaum and Raj Reddy, have been seminal leaders in defining the emerging field of applied artificial intelligence and demonstrating its technological significance.

Patents

Few patents assigned to CMU – https://patents.justia.com/inventor/d-raj-reddy

Commercialization

A visionary in artificial intelligence and robotics, Reddy has focused his career on how technology can serve society, particularly in education and in developing societies.

Flash Memory-Micron Technology, USA

Sanjay Mehrotra was born in 1958 in Kanpur, India. His father was a liaison officer in the cotton industry, who later moved the family to New Delhi when Mehrotra was 10 years old. At an early age, Mehrotra began expressing interest in math and science, and eventually transferred over to Sardar Patel Vidyalaya, a top-ranking high school in New Delhi. Mehrotra has said that it was his father's dream to see him continue his education in the U.S., so he committed himself to applying to American universities. At the age of 18, Mehrotra moved to the U.S., transferring from BITS Pilani to attend the University of California, Berkeley, where he earned his bachelor's degree and master's degree in Electrical Engineering and Computer Science. He graduated in 2009 from Stanford University Graduate School of Business Executive Education Program.

Mehrotra co-founded SanDisk in 1988, the company that helped popularize flash storage. and served as president and CEO from

2011 until 2016. Current President and CEO of Micron, an iconic memory and storage company with a long history of innovation and creative technology breakthroughs.

https://www.linkedin.com/in/sanjay-mehrotra/

Technology

Flash memory, a type of floating-gate memory, was invented at Toshiba in 1980 and is based on EEPROM technology. Toshiba began marketing flash memory in 1987. EPROMs had to be erased completely before they could be rewritten. NAND flash memory, however, may be erased, written, and read in blocks (or pages), which generally are much smaller than the entire device. NOR flash memory allows a single machine word to be written to an erased location or read independently. A flash memory device typically consists of one or more flash memory chips (each holding many flash memory cells), along with a separate flash memory controller chip.

Innovation

Sanjay began his career in 1980 by designing EPROMs at Intel. This job allowed him to work with George Perlegos and to meet Eli Harari (George received the 2017 Lifetime Achievement Award, and Eli received the 2012 Lifetime Achievement Award). After Intel, Dr, Mehrotra designed memory devices at SEEQ, Integrated Device Technologies, and ATMEL. During this time, he created the first five-volt CMOS EEPROM with integrated error correction. In 1988, Eli Harari recruited Sanjay Mehrotra and Jack Yuan to start a new company with a vision to build solid-state drives from flash memory, which at the time was a fledgling laboratory technology. The three immigrants (from Israel, India, and China, respectively) formed a start-up named SunDisk (later renamed SanDisk).

Patents

The initial SunDisk design was based on a unique triple-poly NOR technology, and this led to the first system-level flash design which used a processor to manage the flash in order to deal with flash's wear-out characteristic. The founders spent their initial months securing multiple patents which would ultimately shape the future of the flash industry. Most critical amongst these patents was U.S. Patent No. 5,297,148 (the '148 patent), whose inventors were Sanjay Mehrotra, Eli Harari, and Bob Norman. This was the first of a large family of patents that encompassed this system-level approach, and these are amongst over 70 patents that include Mehrotra as an inventor.

During the early days at SunDisk, Dr. Mehrotra was co-inventor of an important patent (U.S. Patent No. 5,172,338), along with Eli Harari and Winston Lee, on multi-level cell (MLC) technology, which described how more than one bit could be stored in a flash memory cell. Mehrotra also led the SanDisk engineering teams that drove innovation in controller and firmware technology based on the '148 patent. These innovations spurred the exponential cost declines that allowed flash memory to be a key enabler of the billions of mobile consumer devices in use today.

IPO Education Foundation (IPOEF) board of directors has selected Micron President and CEO Sanjay Mehrotra as its 2022 Executive of the Year. The IPOEF Executive of the Year is awarded annually to an executive with strong commitment to the creation, protection and promotion of intellectual property (IP). With his more than 40 years of semiconductor industry experience, Mehrotra has earned over 70 patents, including patents fundamental to flash memory in modern computing.

Commercialisation

Micron, the American semiconductor packaging firm, will invest $825 million in India to set up the assembly and testing facility. The facility in Sanand, Gujarat, will be producing the first 'Make in India' chip, and production is expected to start by December 2024,

Green Steel – Veena Sahazwalla, Australia

Educating from Universities from Mumbai, Canada and Michigan, NRI Veena Sahajwalla became top award-winning scientist and engineer in Australia, invented the "green steel" a process of recycling plastics and rubber tyres.

LinkedIn Profile – https://www.linkedin.com/in/veena-sahajwalla-3a79b420/

Scientia Professor Veena Sahajwalla is the Director of SMaRT Centre (Sustainable Materials Research & Technology) and Associate Dean (Strategic Industry Relations) faculty of Science, UNSW. Her research interests include sustainability of materials and processes with emphasis on environmental benefits. She invented an environmentally friendly process for recycling plastics and rubber tyres in electric arc furnace steelmaking. She is an international award winning engineer. In 2012 she was named Overall Winner of the Australian Innovation Challenge Award. She was awarded the 2012 Banksia Award, the GE Eco Innovation Award and the 2005 Eureka Prize for Scientific Research. She has established excellent working relationships with national and international organisations. She was an ARC – Future Fellow and a long-serving judge on ABC television's The New inventors.

University profile – https://research.unsw.edu.au/people/scientia-professor-veena-sahajwalla

Technology

In conventional EAF steelmaking the injection of coke or anthracite (coal based products) produces a foamy slag, which acts as a blanket over the molten steel during the steelmaking process. Polymer Injection Technology provides benefits to EAF steelmakers by improving the foaming properties of the slag, using a blend of polymer and coke/anthracite. The addition of the polymer to the injecting mix improves the volume and foaminess of the slag. The improved slag foaming results in Superior insulation of molten bath and decreased heat loss through the slag, Improved shrouding of the electrodes and a longer electric arc and improved heat transfer from the arc to the steel.

Innovation

Professor Veena's breakthrough Polymer Injection Technology, or 'Green Steel', is a process that leverages high temperature reactions in electric arc furnace (EAF) steelmaking to transform waste tyres and plastics in the production of high-quality steel. By focussing on the evolution of carbon properties at high-temperature conditions, Veena completely overturned how the properties of carbon-bearing materials are understood, bridging the gap between both pure and applied research, as well as between research and application.

The operating efficiency of EAF-steelmaking (responsible for 40% of global production) is largely dictated by carbon/slag reactions, associated gas evolution and slag forming. In Veena's world-first patented Polymer Injection Technology process, a mixture of coke and recycled polymers have been shown to produce a more stable foamy slag compared to coke only – greatly improving furnace energy efficiency, and yield while reducing raw material cost (without detriment to furnace functioning or the finished product).

Patent

Sahajwalla V, 2020, A method, apparatus and system for processing a composite waste source, Patent No. Japan patent no. 6817314; Germany patent no. 602017030498; France and United Kingdom patent no. 3414507,

https://worldwide.espacenet.com/publicationDetails/biblio?II=0&ND=3&adjacent=true&locale=en_EP&FT=D&date=20190221&CC=JP&NR=2019504762A&KC=A

Commercialisation

The technology has been licensed to steel makers globally, and Sahajwalla and her team are working with Newcastle-based steelmaker MolyCop.

https://molycop.com/innovation/polymer-injection-technology/

Nanocomposite Dental Materials – Sumita Mitra, USA

Dr Sumia Mitra earned her B.S. in chemistry from India's Presidency College, her M.S. in organic chemistry from the University of Calcutta, and her Ph.D. in organic/polymer chemistry from the University of Michigan. She joined Case Western Reserve University as a postdoctoral fellow in polymer chemistry. Mitra retired in 2010 after more than 30 years with 3M, and now runs Mitra Chemical Consulting LLC with her husband.

National Inventors Hall of Fame: https://www.invent.org/inductees/sumita-mitra

https://en.wikipedia.org/wiki/Sumita_Mitra,

https://www.globalindian.com/story/technology/sumita-mitra-the-indian-american-scientist/

Technology

Traditionally dentists performed tooth repairs using a combination of two different materials, microfills and microhybrid composites. Mitra designed the nanomaterials-based filler platform that 3M uses for all state-of-the-art dental restoratives. Nanoparticles ('nanomeric filler particles') within these materials imitate the natural enamel of teeth, which allow them to remain glossy and strong. She showed that these materials could be used to restore teeth in any area of the mouth.

Innovation

In the late 1990s, Sumita Mitra, a chemist at 3M Oral Care, the dental products division of 3M Company, invented the first dental filling material to include nanoparticles. The new composite filling material, called Filtek™ Supreme Universal Restorative, is a versatile material that could be used for restoring teeth in any area of the mouth; mimicked the beauty of natural teeth; had better polish retention; and exhibited superior strength than existing dental composites. Filtek Supreme's improvements over standard composites included versatility of use due to its excellent lasting esthetics, ability to withstand fracture, low shrinkage during curing and extremely good resistance to wear. Tooth-colored composites provide the ability to preserve more of a patient's natural tooth structure and do not pose similar health and environmental concerns as with amalgam fillings containing mercury. Moreover, Filtek Supreme was attractive enough to fill front teeth, and strong enough for all teeth, even molars, which exert heavy chewing pressure.

The first generation Filtek Supreme Restorative was launched in 2002, followed by the second generation in 2005. In 2012, 3M Oral Care launched the third generation, Filtek Supreme Ultra. The Filtek Supreme product line has been highly successful commercially and has been used in over 600 million restorations worldwide since its initial launch.

Patents

U.S. Patent Nos. 6,730,156; 6,572,693; 6,387,981

Mitra holds 98 US patents and their international equivalents. Her inventions have led to a number of breakthrough dental technologies, including nanocomposites, resin-modified glass ionomers and dental adhesives. Other products that have resulted from her innovations include Viteremer™ and Vitrebond™ Resin-modified Glass Ionomers, RelyX™ Luting Cements, Scotchbond Multipurpose™ Adhesive and APC™ Orthodontic Bracket Adhesive.

Winner of the European Inventor Award 2021:

Patent number – EP1225867, EP1227782, EP1229886, EP1771143

https://new.epo.org/en/news-events/european-inventor-award/meet-the-finalists/sumita-mitra

Video – Sumita Mitra – Restoring smiles with nanomaterials: https://youtu.be/ySQqhk7Xrg0

Regrowth of Bones – Nina Tandon, EpiBone, USA

Nina Tandon has a Bachelor's in Electrical Engineering from the Cooper Union, a Master's in Bioelectrical Engineering from MIT, a PhD in Biomedical Engineering, and an MBA from Columbia University. Her PhD research focused on studying electrical signaling in the context of tissue engineering, and has worked with cardiac, skin, bone, and neural tissue. She is Adjunct Professor of Electrical Engineering at the Cooper Union and a former Staff Associate Postdoctoral Researcher in the Laboratory for Stem Cells and Tissue Engineering, Columbia University. She is co-founder of EpiBone. The innovator behind many patents is Sarindr BHUMIRATANA, Chief Scientist.

(https://www.linkedin.com/in/sarindr-bhumiratana-9511b063/)

Nina Tandon is a tissue engineer and entrepreneur working to change the status quo of healthcare by creating the world's first "body shop" of replacement body parts engineered from stem cells.

As the CEO and co-founder of EpiBone, she is successfully bringing a first-in-class pipeline of bone and cartilage tissues through first-in-human clinical trials.

(https://en.wikipedia.org/wiki/Nina_Tandon)

She has published 10 journal articles (cited > 300 times, H = 9) and six book chapters, and she has three patents. She is the co-author of *Super Cells: Building with Biology*, a book that explores the new frontier of biotech. She was named one of the 100 Most Creative People in Business by Fast Company, a Crain's 40 under 40 people who have achieved success in business before turning 40, and a World Economic Forum Tech Pioneer.

LinkedIn Profile: https://www.linkedin.com/in/nina-tandon-phd-mba-03595315/

Technology

Bone regenerative biomaterials are a relatively new class of materials that incorporate a biopolymeric and biodegradable matrix structure with bioactive and easily resorbable fillers that are nano-sized. Tissue-engineered bone uses stem cells. Bone bioreactor technology is considered to provide an ideal environment for the combination of seed cells, growth factors, and scaffolds, and control of the bone bioreactor environment has made it possible to prepare isolated tissue-engineered bone

Innovation

The technology at the heart of EpiBone is the bioreactor. Its task is essential and delicate: to mimic the finely calibrated conditions in the human body that enable bone to grow. Strong, living tissue can only form where the nourishment, temperature, movement, and pressure are just right. The proprietary bioreactor technology is the product of 20 years of fundamental research and experience with orthopedic tissue engineering. Research has shown that cultivating human stem cells in an osteogenic scaffold in a bioreactor supports critical outcomes, including cell survival, differentiation, and maturation and deposition of bone matrix. This approach also restricts the development of unwanted cell lines. Bones that grow in a well-designed bioreactor are ready to continue remodeling and vascularization once they're transplanted into a patient. In the EpiBone bioreactor, we can grow a new, personalized bone in just three weeks.

Patents

https://uspto.report/company/Epibone-Inc/patents

The latest application filed is for *"injectable off-the – shelf cartilage, tendon, and ligament repair compositions and methods of use"*.

Comercialisation

EpiBone uses stem cells from patients in need of new bones to produce skeletal structures based on each individuals DNA profile, which will decrease the likelihood of rejection, simplify surgeries, and possible shorten recovery time for patients. EpiBone uses a three step process which first involves using a CT scan to obtain measurements of the bone to be constructed and stem cells from abdominal fat in adult patients, then a model of the bone is created in a bioreactor to facilitate growth, and finally the stem cells are added to the newly grown bone in the bioreactor to grow a ready-to-use replica bone.

https://www.epibone.com/

Rotimatic – Zimplistic Pte Ltd, Singapore

Pranoti Nagarkar is Founder, Inventor of Rotimatic. A mechanical engineering graduate from National University of Singapore, studied for one year at University of California, Berkeley under exchange program. She as a Mechanical Engineer considers the prototype for an ironing machine she built in her junior year at college as a warm-up to the 8-years-long challenge to launch Rotimatic that she would commence after graduation. Before starting her venture Zimplistic Pte Lte, she worked at Amtek Innovation Design Centre, Singapore designing Robotic Vacuum Cleaner. Rishi Irani, her husband is the Co-Founder. He was founder of tenCube at NUS and joined Zimplistic later.

LinkedIn Profile-https://www.linkedin.com/in/pranoti-nagarkar/

Technology

The task of making rotis is complex and demands labor. It involves mixing the base ingredients – flour, water, and oil – in the correct proportion to knead into a dough of ideal consistency. This dough is then separated into smaller sections and rolled into evenly flattened discs. The last step is to roast these uncooked dough discs on heated pans or directly over a flame. Manually operated Roti makers involves kneading the dough to make extra soft dough balls. These are pressed into thin discs between the heated lid and pan of the appliance where it puffs on reaching the optimum temperature within minutes. Semi-automatic or fully automatic variants of roti makers are popular as well. These semi-automatic or automatic roti makers are huge in size and capacity. They are designed to operate in places where rotis need to be manufactured in large quantities as they dole out 600-900 rotis per hour, and are ideal for restaurants.

Innovation

Pranoti and her husband, Rishi Israni, realized the need for an effective automated flatbread-maker in their initial days in entrepreneurship. Rotimatic-the world's first-ever AI and IOT enabled flatbread making robot. Eight years of R&D and 37 patents later, they created a smart kitchen device that can mimic a very complex human task and give you instant and fresh flatbreads in 90 seconds. This is possible with a 32-bit microprocessor that harmoniously orchestrates 10 motors, 15 sensors and 300 parts in parallel. The 10 motors work together based on the data from 15 different sensors, which measure things like temperature, position and the most complex and important metric, that is, consistency. It manages all processes seamlessly to save every second possible. Rotimatic uses machine learning so each machine takes some time to make good bread; they are also connected to the internet for software upgrades.

Patents

https://patents.google.com/patent/US8820221B2/en

A compact apparatus for automatically making a plurality of flat edibles includes a storage and dispensing unit that makes it unnecessary for a user to pre-measure ingredients. The apparatus also includes a mixing and kneading unit for making dough of optimal consistency. The mixing and kneading unit may be configured to prepare dough. The dough may be prepared by mixing and kneading the ingredients dispensed by the dispensers. The dough prepared may be transferred onto a lower platen from a transfer base by a transfer sweeper. The dough may be flattened in a platen unit. An upper platen and the lower platen of the platen unit may be heated to a pre-programmed temperature for cooking the flat edible. The temperature may also be manually set by the user based on user's preference. The flat may be cooked (e.g., heated, roasted and/or puffed) by the platen unit.

Commercialisation

Rotimatic by Zimplistic is a part of 60,000 homes in 20 countries, the units purchased exclusively through their website. The appliance has been updated to make pizza bases, tortillas, and puris as well to make the product more relevant to broader demography. It is a popular kitchen assistant in the US where the company makes about 60–70% of sales. Other markets where Rotimatic is doing well are in including Australia, the Middle East, Canada, and the United Kingdom. These are the markets that have many Indian expats.

https://rotimatic.com/products/rotimatic

Tiny Robots – Prof Vijay Kumar, USA

Dr VijayKumar got B. Tech., Mechanical Engineering, Indian Institute of Technology, Kanpur, India, May 1983, M.Sc., Mechanical Engineering, Ohio State University, Columbus, Ohio, March 1985 and Ph.D., Mechanical Engineering, Ohio State University, Columbus, Ohio, September 1987. Dr. Kumar is a Fellow of the American Society of Mechanical Engineers (2003), a Fellow of the Institution of Electrical and Electronic Engineers (2005) and a member of the National Academy of Engineering (2013). Dr. Kumar's research interests are in robotics, specifically multi-robot systems, and micro aerial vehicles. His work and teaching have been recognized and highlighted by many institutions and organizations.

Linked In Profile – https://www.linkedin.com/in/vijaykum/

During a scholarly leave in 2012-14, he served in the White House as assistant director for robotics and cyber physical systems in the Office of Science and Technology Policy. He has been named dean of the University of Pennsylvania School of Engineering and Applied Science in 2015.

University profile: https://www.kumarrobotics.org/dr-vijay-kumar/

Technology

Most off-the-shelf consumer drones use GPS drones to orient themselves in three dimensional space and remain stable while in flight. However, GPS-denied environments lack connection to GPS, or the signals are not strong enough, resulting in poor or erratic flying behavior. Autonomous drone processes are different in that an autonomous drone can make some decisions without user input. This is possible through AI systems that gather data from sensors, satellites, cameras, and videos and then use that data to make decisions. Level 4 drones have a high level of autonomy in that they use advanced detect and avoid systems and detect and navigate systems without pilot action. They can freely explore GPS-free and GPS-denied environments, navigate harsh conditions, and identify people in need without needing a pilot on-site, as pilots can monitor level 4 drones remotely.

Innovation

Exyn Technologies is pioneering multi-platform robotic autonomy for complex, GPS-denied environments. The company's full-stack solution enables flexible deployment of single or multi-robots that can intelligently navigate and dynamically adapt to complex environments in real-time. For the first time, industries like mining, logistics, and construction can benefit from a single, integrated solution to capture critical and time-sensitive data in a safer, more affordable, and more efficient way.

Case: https://velodynelidar.com/case-studies/exyn-technologies/

Patents

Vijay Kumar has invented tiny (as small as eight inches!) robots that can outmaneuver human-controlled drones, and even create 3-D maps of what they survey. Kumar is a prolific inventor and entrepreneur led trailblazing research in the area of autonomous robotics that was awarded two patents that are now core intellectual property for Exyn Technologies, one of the many robotics startups emerging out of the GRASP Lab at the Pennovation Center. Exyn is adapting this pioneering autonomous robotic navigation technology for several exciting commercial purposes including navigation and obstacle avoidance in crowded, GPS-denied environments and as a way to bring artificial intelligence and autonomy to the flying robot industry.

Commercialisation

He is the founder of Exyn Technologies, a drone startup that built a mapping aerial robot for GPS-denied environments. Exyn Technologies, Inc. was created in 2014 to commercialize micro aerial vehicle research developed by Dr. Vijay Kumar and the GRASP Lab at Penn. Exyn is also the first collaboration between Penn and IP Group, an investment group which develops new companies based on innovative university research. https://www.exyn.com/

Video: https://youtu.be/UwH9m5rPJlc

Water Technology Visionary – Anil Jha, USA

Anil Jha from Indore is referred to as Water Technology Visionary. In Boston, Massachusetts, he attended Wentworth Institute of Technology, obtained a degree in material science, began working as an R&D technician at Cabot Corporation while attending the University of Massachusetts at night. Soon, he secured a job as a technician at water treatment company Ionics Inc., where he obtained some of his first patents, and later moved to Millipore Corporation. There, along with two of his colleagues (including Gary Ganzi, a member of the IPO Board of Directors), he developed *electrodeionization*—an innovation for which he has been dubbed a "water technology visionary," and which he says has prevented the discharge of hundreds of thousands of chemicals into the environment. Mr. Jha is a named inventor on over 100 international and about 30 U.S. patents, advises companies in the water treatment space, and mentors students at his old college,

Wentworth Institute of Technology, where he received an honorary doctorate for lifetime achievements in 2014.

https://www.ipoef.org/anil-jha-leading-the-world-to-more-eco-friendly-water/

https://www.linkedin.com/in/anil-jha-63883010/

Technology

Traditional methods of water treatment require periodic treatment by chemicals and salts, which regenerate the water purification instruments through which the water flows. Unfortunately, those chemicals and salts are often disposed of or leached into the environment through discharged waste water. This results in toxic effects on agriculture and marine life, as well as the contamination of ground water. Electrodeionization is a method of purifying water using electricity, eliminates the need to use salts and chemicals, and also preserves more water, because its recovery rates are much higher.

Innovation

Electrodeionization uses electricity and an advanced ion-specific membrane to remove dissolved ions from water. In the field use it mostly removes impurities like salts from water. The innovation uses membranes that are made out of certain polymers and when applied an electrical potential across them, the ions are pulled into the membranes and the purified liquid continues on. The technology actually was known in 1950, but attempts to make the process work had failed. It would work for a little while and then cause problems. The secret to Anil Jha success is that they were able to design the equipment such that it would work indefinitely without failing. In residential processes, softeners are used to regenerate polymeric resin in order to soften the water.

Patents

https://patents.google.com/patent/US20050121388

A method and system for providing Water for Injection using reverse osmosis. Water for Injection can be produced by reverse osmosis and the reverse osmosis membrane can be kept in a constantly self-sanitizing condition. One way of obtaining a constantly self-sanitizing condition is to maintain the reverse osmosis membrane at an elevated temperature during production of Water for Injection.

Commercialisation

The technology has proven particularly useful in a number of industries for which the presence of foreign chemicals is undesirable, such as pharmaceuticals and semiconductors. As Director of R&D at Siemens Water Technologies from 2004 to 2009, Mr. Jha also secured patents for inventions geared to the use of electrodeionization in homes, and in 2008 struck an agreement with Siemens to license the technology he had developed. He eventually founded HydroNovation—a California company that offers an environmentally friendly option to the traditional residential water treatment technology, "softener," which dumps 4,000 pounds of salt per household into the ground annually. Mr. Jha sold HydroNovation to a Taiwanese filtration company in 2014.

Now he is co-founder of Aquanovation, a manufacturer of electro-chemical based membrane products for the water treatment, lithium extraction, agricultural/irrigation water and energy storage markets.

https://aquanovation.com/about-aquanovation/

Wearable Sweat Sensor – EnLiSense LLC, USA

Dr Shalini Prasad currently Director of Biomedical Microdevices and Nanotechnology Laboratory at Erik Jonsson School of Engineering and Computer Science, Department of Bioengineering, University of Texas, Dallas had BE from University of Madras, followed by PhD from University of California. She is credited with 174 publications, 18 book chapters, 2026 conference papers, 5 awarded patents and 10 patent applications. She is co-promoter of EnLiSense CCM with Muthukumar.

Relevant publications include: *A new paradigm in sweat based wearable diagnostics biosensors using Room Temperature Ionic Liquids (RTILs)*-Nature Scientific Reports · May 16, 2017. *A wearable biochemical sensor for monitoring alcohol consumption lifestyle through Ethyl glucuronide (EtG) detection in human* Mar 21, 2016

https://www.linkedin.com/in/shalini-prasad-87040aa/

Technology

Wearable sensors for monitoring biomarkers for chronic health conditions is of significant commercial interest. Sweat based biomarker monitoring with multiple measurements within a 24 hour period are particularly attractive as diagnostic devices. Among the various types of wearable sensors, non-faradaic electrochemical sensors are of particular interest as they enable label-free and non-invasive detection of biomarkers. However, to advance these wearable non-faradaic sensors as diagnostics devices, it is essential to address the challenges of stability and reliability of the materials constituting the sensor during prolonged and continuous exposure to body fluids.

Innovations

Medical wearable, an easy-to-use, reliable, and cost-effective sensor technology (No needles, No punctures, No pain, Sensor in contact with the skin) that reports from low volumes (a few microliters) of passively expressed sweat with no external stimulation. The sensor measurements are reported via a proprietary app, which offers guidance towards tracking WELLNESS to ILLNESS and back to WELLNESS in the wearer.

Research student Ambalika Tanak developed a sepsis biosensor by customizing technology developed by her adviser, Shalini Prasad, the head of UTD's department of bioengineering, and Sriram Muthukumar, a UTD adjunct engineering professor. Prasad and Muthukumar cofounded the company EnLiSense specifically to develop biosensors and then partnered with ACESO to determine the greatest need in sepsis care.

(https://www.texasmonthly.com/news-politics/sepsis-ut-dallas-biomedical-sensor/)

Patents

1. Mathew Mathew T. Shalini, Prasad, Markus A. Wimmer; Nadim J Hallab, Joshua Jacobs, United States Patent (11,154,242) Metal-ion electrochemical biosensor and use Thereof.
2. Shalini Prasad and Anjan Panneer Selvam, United States Patent (10,641,721) Tri-electrode apparatus and methods for molecular analysis
3. United States Patent (8,409,411), 2013, Nano-porous membrane based sensors, S. Prasad and R.K.K. Reddy
4. United States Patent (9,222,907), 2015, Nanoporous membrane based sensors, S. Prasad and R.K.K. Reddy
5. United States Patent (10,006,882), 2018, Biosensing system and methods using electron-ionic mechanisms at fluid-sensor interfaces, S. Prasad, S. Muthukumar and A.P. Selvam

Commercialisation

https://enlisense.com/

Corti is a wearable device that monitors and tracks stress in real-time through cortisol levels in passive sweat. Corti is an easy-to-use, reliable, and cost effective way to understand your stress levels relying on skin contact– no needles, pain, or punctures. Whether its post-traumatic stress disorder (PTSD), general anxiety disorder (GAD), or other stress disorders driving your anxiety symptoms, Cortisol monitoring can play a role in your path to wellness and wellbeing. IBD AWARE is a wearable device that monitors and tracks inflammation biomarkers such as Calprotectin, C-reactive protein (CRP), and Interleukins in real-time through passive sweat. IBD AWARE is non-invasive sensor with no needles, no pain, or punctures. Whether its Crohn's disease, Ulcerative colitis (UC), indeterminate colitis, or another Inflammatory Bowel Disease (IBD), IBD AWARE can provide you data on inflammatory biomarkers sensed in real time.

Wearable and Reusable Outpatient Ambulatory ECG Monitoring Products – NimbleHeart, USA

Sonal Tambe co-founder CEO of NimbleHeart has a Bachelors degree in Electronics Engineering from India (Amravati University) and an MBA from UCLA. Worked at Apple as Engineering Lead and founded Nimble Heart in 2012 with Dr Pramod Deshmukh an Electrophysiologist.

LinkedIn Profile-https://www.linkedin.com/in/sonaltambe/

Technology

An ECG sensor harness is a desirable form of a device that can be used by the people for home based cardiac monitoring and that does not require any hook up by medical professionals. The device needs to detect anomalies including, but not limited to, myocardial infarctions (MI), ischemia and arrhythmia. The ECG harnesses that are currently available provide limited information and limited performance. One of the causes for the performance limitation of these systems may be motion artifacts.

Motion artifacts may occur when the subject is in motion during exercise or even moderate movement. Motion artifacts in the ECG signal may be realized in an impedance change seen by the sensor. A distorted signal can result in improper detection of ST segment changes in ECG. In many current solutions to detect ST segment changes, the user must remain relatively still to reduce or eliminate motion artifacts that may interfere with the performance of the system. This makes the detection of exercise-induced Ischemia difficult, if not impossible. The motion artifacts may be divided into two distinct components, those normal to the sensor-body interface and shear those tangential to the sensor-body interface. It is desirable to have a solution that either eliminates or minimizes both of these components so that clinical quality ST changes detection is possible with the obtained ECG signal.

Innovation

Recognizing the limitations of traditional, exercise-based ECG monitoring, NimbleHeart has created a custom hardware design for its ECG Harness with patent-pending motion artifact reduction technology and a biomechanics-based harness design with shape and sensor locations for men and women and for different body types. CEO Sonal Tambe said these can be used for monitoring from home, the office, gym or alternate care settings.

Patents

https://patents.google.com/patent/US20140378848A1/en

Method and Apparatus for Motion Artifact Reduction in ECG Harness

METHOD AND APPARATUS FOR AMBULATORY ECG NOISE MITIGATION DURING SWEATING OF PATIENT, Publication number: 20230165526

Commercialisation

https://nimbleheart.com/products/

NimbleHeart is planning to bring innovative wearable and reusable outpatient ambulatory ECG monitoring products to the market. These products require no sticky electrodes, gel or conductive paste to work and are very light and comfortable for both men and women. These products are targeted for pre-diagnosis patients as well as those living with known risk of cardiovascular events.

Physiotrace Smart is FDA cleared for exercise ECG monitoring in outpatient settings including home, office, gyms and alternate care setting and can be obtained with Physician's prescription or for research. Physiotrace Smart is offered for sale or lease with free iOS enterprise App distribution and streaming to NimbleHeart's secure web portal.

Agriculture

1. 4G NANO" Based Nutritional Agri In-Puts – ICAR & Pratishta Industries, Hyderabad
2. Agri PV-RenCube, Bangalore
3. Anti-Pesticide topical gel – Praveen Kumar Vemula lab at inStem, Sepio Health Private Limited, Bangalore
4. Bio-Stimulants – BioPrime AgriSolutions Pvt Ltd, Pune
5. Digital Moisture Analyzer – A-GRAIN, Ambala
6. DME Tractor – TAFE, IIT Kanpur
7. Food processing plants – Best Engineering Technologies, Hyderabad
8. Fruit bar from prickly pear fruits (opuntia ficus indica) – Dr Chenna Kesava Reddy Sangati, IIPM, Bangalore
9. GroTron autonomous irrigation system – Farmagain Agro Pvt Ltd, Coimbatore
10. Innovative Rhizome Processing-S4 foods, Aurangabad, Maharashtra
11. Kappahycus alvarezii elite seedling production – Dr. M. Ganesan, CSIR-CSMCRI, Gujarat
12. Machine to remove insects from stored grains – Professor (Retd) Mohan Sriramasarma, Tamil Nadu Agriculture University (TNAU), Coimbatore,
13. Multipurpose Processing Machine – Dharamveer Singh Kamboj, Yamuna Nagar, Haryana

14. Non-invasive and non-intrusive honey harvesting device – KLE Technological university, Hubballi
15. Optical fruit sorting system – Zentron Labs pvt ltd, Bangalore
16. Onion warehouse with IOT – Godaam Innovations, Nashik
17. Production of seedlings in agarose yielding red seaweed Gracilaria dura – Dr. Vaibhav A. Mantri, CSIR-CSMCRI
18. Pesticidal water dispersible granule formulation – Parijat Industries (India) Pvt. Ltd, New Delhi
19. Smart soil monitoring system – Proximal Soilsens Technologies Pvt. Ltd, Pune
20. Supply chain management for FPOs Vesatogo Innovations, Nasik
21. Solar Insect Traps – SAFS Ecotech Pvt Ltd, Puducherry

4G NANO" Based Nutritional Agri In-Puts – ICAR & Pratishta Industries, Hyderabad

Dr. Kuchimanchi Venkata Satya Sarveswara Sairam (Dr. KVSS SAIRAM – Dr. RAM) is founder of Partaishta Industries with operations in India, USA and Europe. A Scientist and Entrepreneur graduated in Chemical Technology from College of Technology, Osmania University, Masters in Environmental Engineering & Technology from Rajeev Gandhi Institute of Environmental Engineering & Technology, Delhi, and Ph. D in Agriculture Sciences from Oxford Academic Council, Oxford, UK.. He was awarded honorary Doctorate (PhD) from The University of Chicago, Chicago, US in Project Management along with Scientist of the Year-2016. After serving few Industries, Dr. RAM started closely held Public Limited Company to establish Fermentation (Bio Technology) based process Industry in 1996. Dr. RAM is instrumental in R&D Innovation to launch Innovative formulation BIO-POTASH (both in Water Soluble & Granulated forms), which has received BEST

PRODUCT INNOVATION award from FAPCCI – A.P. Dr. RAM is instrumental in developing "Novel Nutrients" and hence Prathista honored with "Best Novel Nutrients company award for 2019"

https://www.linkedin.com/in/dr-sairam-vss-kuchimanchi-1b60b241/

Technology

1G (First Generation) refers to Cow Manures / Natural farming. "2G" (Second Generation) – Nutritional Chemical Fertilizers to enhance agricultural productivity for growing population, Bio Fertilizers & EM. "3G" (Third Generation) – Proteino-Lacto – gluconates based Nutritional Fertilizers to provide total nutritional requirements for all crops / plants without compromising on productivity while protecting ecology. 4g, Fourth Generation nutritional fertilizers are composed of Nano Fertilizers & Nano Micronutrients, with Proteino – Lacto – Gluconates.

Innovation

ICAR Scientists have developed nano nutrients technology through biological process after extensive research both in lab and fields, involving consortium of ICAR institutions and Agricultural Universities. Prathista is the first company to commercialize the ICAR nano nutrients innovative technology. The research data reveals that, the nano nutrients doses are just in ppm level to meet nutrient requirement for crops, against to 150 to 200 kgs traditional fertilizer dose per acre. In order to have acceptance of ICAR innovation, Prathista incorporated the nano nutrients technology with their present 3G lacto-gluconates technology. The cost of these nutrient fertilizers is at par with subsidised fertilizers and computable to use with all traditional fertilizers. The scalability of technology is commercially and economically feasible and nano nutrients are 100% safe to human / livestock and 100% eco-friendly.

Prathista is a pioneering Bio-Technology company using "state of the art fermentation methodologies" for production of Lacto-Gluconate products with USFDA, GMP, Halal and FSSAI certifications. For Pharmaceutical applications, Prathista has DMF as per U.S. Pharmacopoeia (USP) / European Pharmacopoeia (EP) / British Pharmacopoeia (BP) standards, while for Indian markets, DMF as per Indian Pharmacopeia standards – for individual salts as Lacto – Gluconates are not directed covered under APIs.

Patents

Indian patent, Organic Nano Fertilizers patent and it's process, Patent number 402758, granted in 2022, innovators-Sairam & Vaishnavi.

WIPO-WO/2021/234718, https://patentscope.wipo.int/search/en/detail.jsf?docId=WO2021234718

Commercialisation

Prathista is a leading producer of Natural, Clean Label, NON-GMO, nutraceuticals (Food Ingredients) through the fermentation process & products are licensed by FSSAI – Govt. of India along with other global certifications like " USFDA, Kosher, & Halal. 4G products include Complex & Complete Fertilizers, Potash Fertilizer, Poshphatic Fertilizer, Secondary Nutrient Fertilizer, Zinc Fertilizer, All in One Nutritional Formaula.

https://www.prathista.com/

https://www.prathista.us/

Prathista,an Indian MNC, has presence in USA, Canada, UK, Europe, Philippines, Malaysia and Vietnam.

Agri PV-RenCube, Bangalore

Balaji Lakshmikanth Bangolae is Founder, CEO of RenCube. Balaji has 12 patents approved in the networking area in his previous stint with Cisco Systems. Lead inventor of the MFOT technology. Co-Founder& President, Janardhana did his Ph.D in Birla Institute of Technology, Mesra, in microwave communications. He has been instrumental in developing RADAR solutions for the Indian Army. Lakhmi Sanatham another Co-Founder & COO holds a PhD in Network Security from University of Cincinnati, USA. Deepika Goel, Co-Funder & Researchers has a Masters in Computer Science from UC San Diego.

https://www.linkedin.com/in/bangolae-lakshmikanth-balaji-7733b7103/

Technology

Nonimaging optics (also called anidolic optics) is the branch of optics concerned with the optimal transfer of light radiation between a source and a target. Unlike traditional imaging optics, the techniques involved do not attempt to form an image of the source; instead an optimized optical system for optimal radiative transfer from a source to a target is desired. BDRF (Bi-Directional Reflectance Function) based mirrors is a technology built at Michigan Technology University to boost the illumination on solar cells using mirrors and improve energy generation by up to 20% more.

Innovation

Renkube is bringing to the market an innovative light-harvesting glass that gathers more sunlight and redirects it to the solar cells, thereby increasing the energy yield of the solar panel by 20%. They have applied our expertise in machine learning algorithms to design a glass that can capture more sunlight purely by the nature of its geometric design without any chemical coating or electro-mechanical components. Though this technology is not a retrofit to the existing solar panels, it can work with any underlying solar cell technologies like mono, perc, perovskite etc. The startup also introduced Motion Free Optical Tracking Technology (MFOT). The MFOT panel uses pOrismatic structures that work on the principal of Total Internal Reflection to increase sunlight incident on solar cell. With this new type of geometry with glass that can bend the path of light to make it fall on the solar panel, thereby making the panel generate more units of electricity and become more efficient. Once these light redirectors are fixed on the solar panels, they remain completely stationary. There is no adjusting or tilting needed, and yet it can track the sun throughout the year. Thus, the solution becomes a completely motion-free entity, which functions using only the principles of optics. Hence the name Motion Free Optical Tracking (MFOT). Light redirecting prisms are assembled on the solar panels at the photovoltaic (PV) manufacturing unit, and then gets installed just like any other solar panel.

https://www.slideshare.net/deepap25/renkube

Patents

Publications – Performance Analysis of BDRF based Reflectors, MFOT and Fixed Tilt PV Performance Analysis of BDRF based Reflectors, MFOT and Fixed Tilt PV IEEE PVSC, 2020 · Jun 15, 2020

Patent – A LIGHT REDIRECTING PRISM, A REDIRECTING PRISMATIC WALL AND A SOLAR PANEL INCORPORATING THE SAME, Publication number: 20230144992, Inventors: Balaji Lakshmikanth BANGOLAE, Lakshmi SANTHANAM, Deepika GOPAL, Pradeep Jayaram KATTEMALALAVADI, Sidharth Janardhana KSHIRSAGAR, Bikash MUSIB, 2021

Commercialisation

https://www.renkube.com/s-projects-basic

Telangana Agri PV pilot of 10 KW demonstrates the suitability of our uniquely designed panels for dual usage of land – where solar panel acts as canopy and at the same time 100% of the land can be used for crop cultivations. The Agronomist scientist at PJTSAU are helping with us with the crop study for various seasons. Many agritech startups are supported at PJTSAU – https://ag-hub.co/startups/

Anti-Pesticide Topical Gel – Praveen Kumar Vemula Lab at inStem, Sepio Health Private Limited, Bangalore

Dr Praveen Kumar Vemula is Principal Investigator at the Institute for Stem Cell Science and Regenerative Medicine (inStem), Bangalore. After graduation and post-graduation in Osmania university, had his PhD from IISc in Nano materials and was post doctoral fellow at Harvard Medical School before returning to India. He is currently Principal Investigator and Ramalingaswami Fellow at inStem.

https://www.linkedin.com/in/praveen-kumar-vemula-55717116/

The Institute for Stem Cell Science and Regenerative Medicine (inStem), is a state-of-the-art research institute in Bangalore, India, dedicated to the study of stem cells and regenerative biology with translational emphasis. An autonomous institute funded by the Dept. of Biotechnology (DBT), Govt. of India, inStem's research structure is built on a core of collaborative research with a thematic focus. inStem's mandate to allow this cross-disciplinary, multi-pronged approach to research, straddles the divide between clinical and laboratory research. In trying to answer intractable and challenging questions that face the field, inStem seeks to rewrite the paradigm of the research institute: without barriers and across disciplines.

http://praveenlab.net/

Technology

According to the World Health Organization (WHO) Recommended Classification of Pesticides by Hazard, organophosphate pesticides oxydemeton-methyl and methamedophos belong to class I (extremely/highly hazardous); dimethoate, fenthion, quinalphos, chlorpyrifos, prothiofos, and diazinon belong to class II (moderately hazardous); and malathion and pirimifos-methyl belong to class III (slightly hazardous) (10, 11). It is clear that systemic exposure to pesticides through the dermal route is a health hazard. Although the personal protective equipment (PPE) such as suits, gloves, face masks, headgear, and boots are available, they are scarcely used, mainly because of high cost and discomfort under tropical conditions.

There have been attempts to formulate physical barrier creams in the past to attenuate exposure to pesticides or CWAs (15–17). This design comes with an inherent limitation of expo sure, as the pesticide that is arrested on the surface can still enter the system through the oral or ocular route via hand contact. In addition, each pesticide brand has different additive formulations, and these formulations have variable penetrance through physical barrier creams.

Innovation

Because of the high skin penetration of pesticides, commercial physical barrier creams were not sufficient to prevent pesticide entry into the body. This prompted the researchers to devise a new strategy, which is a chemical deactivation of pesticides on the skin to prevent their entry into the body. They have designed a polymeric super-nucleophile (a-nucleophile)–mediated hydrolysis of pesticides on the skin. Poly-Oxime could be formulated into the dermal gel using excipients. Data suggest that a thin layer of poly-Oxime gel can hydrolyze organophosphates on the skin; therefore, it can prevent AChE inhibition quantitatively in blood and in all internal organs such as brain, lung, liver, and heart.

(https://www.science.org/doi/10.1126/sciadv.aau1780)

Patents

Compositions, materials, and methods for deactivating toxic agents – https://patents.google.com/patent/WO2019180653A1/en

Commercialisation

The anti-pesticide gel is manufactured by Sepio Health Private Limited Promoted by him along with Omprakash Sunnapu, a research scholar at inStem.

Vide: https://youtu.be/VWgOTPWJ4As

Technologies developed at inStem – https://instem.res.in/sites/default/files/inStem_Technologies_31_July_2021.pdf

Bio-Stimulants – Bio Prime Agri Solutions Pvt Ltd, Pune

Dr Renuka Diwan, has completed her PhD in Plant Sciences from University of Pune. She has also done her post doc in genetic engineering in collaboration with Cambia, a Australian company. Bioprime was founded by three researchers, Dr Renuka Diwan, Dr Shekhar Bhosale and Dr Amit Shinde. While Dr Diwan is an expert in genetic engineering, Dr Bhosale is a specialist in mycology and Dr Shinde is an authority in the development of bioactives.

https://www.linkedin.com/in/renukadiwan/

https://www.linkedin.com/in/shekhar-bhosle/

Technology

Indian Government has regulations for Biostimulants – "Biostimulant" means a substance or microorganism or a combination of both whose primary function when applied to plants, seeds or rhizosphere is to stimulate physiological processes in plants and to enhance its nutrient uptake, growth, yield, nutrition efficiency, crop quality and tolerance to stress, regardless of its nutrient content. Live Microbes are not included under Biostimulants, however EU Fertilizing Products Regulation (EU No. 2019/1009) have incorporated the new definition of biostimulants and included microbials as a subcategory of biostimulants. Beneficial microbes can be isolated from prospective environments and characterized, selected, and used to formulate biotechnological applications, widely known as microbial inoculants.

Innovation

BioPrime has taken the drug-discovery approach employed in the pharmaceutical industry to designing agricultural biologicals. Bioprime developed alternative bio organic and sustainable solutions for crop improvement, nutrition and protection that are based on SNIPR. SNIPR Biome is pioneering a novel use of CRISPR/Cas technology for microbial gene therapy. SNIPR (Smart Nanomolecule Induced Physiological Response) (SNIPR) Technology adopted by the firm is based on leads obtained from studying plant environment interaction, plant pest interaction. It makes use of the chemical signaling in the physiological responses manifested by the plants as a mechanism of adaptation in due course of evolution. This makes these signals very unique, target specific. Incorporating these signals in formulation allows Bioprime, rapid & precise manifestation of the results – like building up tolerance to biotic and abiotic stress, activating plants own defense system. This also enables us to tackle the resistance build up in pests, which to the best of our knowledge is a unique feature of our products.

Patents

The firm received Indian Patent for `novel bio-formulation' to manage abiotic stress in plants and to improve the yield.

Commercialisation

The firm offers many products like Prime Chiron, which is Scientifically formulated bioactive consortium containing photosynthetic intermediates and botanical bio-stimulants. These actives are readily absorbable and give instant boost in yield and quality of the crop. The startup received Manage Samunnatti Agri Start up Award 2022. https://bioprimeagri.com/

Digital Moisture Analyzer – AGRAIN, Ambala

Gurvinder Pal Singh is Founder and Managing Director at AGRAIN TECHNOLOGIES PVT LTD. An engineering graduate from SIT, Tumkur, he started A-GRAIN, an agtech company involved in development and manufacturing of moisture measurement solutions for food grains and vision based physical assaying equipments for agriculture produce.

https://www.linkedin.com/in/gurvinder-pal-singh-365b6a13/

Technology

In old days, to check the quantity of moisture in the grain, farmers used to break the grain. If the grain fails quickly, it is considered dry and otherwise not. Now, there are several methods of measuring grain moisture content:

Primary method – The primary method is all about the measurement of the grain. Here farmers do the weight of the grain in the starting phase. Then, with the help of hot air, water is evaporated from the grain. And they keep on sticking to the process until the weight gets changed. On reaching the final weight, the initial weight is subtracted from it in order to check the moisture content for the final weight results. This method is also known as the microwave or oven method.

Secondary Methods – The secondary method measures grain moisture using electrical resistance or electromagnetic properties. In this process, the electrical properties of the grain are being used because grain is a conductor of electricity as it contains water.

Digital Grain Moisture Meter-There are different varieties of moisture meters In Argrain's moisture meter, you need to insert the probe part of the device into a bag of grains.

Innovation

CSIO Offers technology to manufacture Digital Grain Moisture Analyser. It is based on capacitance variation technique. The instrument is based on power efficient, high speed microcontroller (MCU) while sensing system is made up of capacitive transducer that converts moisture contents into an electrical signal. Presence of a very small quantity of water causes considerable change in the dielectric constant of the sensor cell. These moisture variations change capacitance which in turn is measured in terms of frequency variations. These variations are then further linearized and calibrated in terms of percentage moisture. The final result in terms of moisture percentage, temperature of sample, date and time of measurement is displayed on LCD for a given sample under measurement. https://www.csio.res.in/upload/PDF/dgma.pdf

Patent

In 1955 Gerald Gobert built the first moisture meter to assess the moisture level of timber. He called this instrument Protimeter. Initially, Protim built a few meters for use in their own work. There are many patents and publications. Low-Cost Grain Moisture Meter System Networked to Smartphones –

https://docs.lib.purdue.edu/cgi/viewcontent.cgi?article=2648&context=open_access_theses

Commercialisation

https://www.moisturemeterstore.in/about-us-a-grain/

The company manufactures a host of products like Grain Moisture Testers, Seed Dividers, Seed Germinators, Seed Processing plants etc and exports to 25 countries.

DME Tractor – TAFE, IIT Kanpur

Prof. Avinash Kumar Agarwal obtained his Undergraduate Degree in Mechanical Engineering (1994) from Malviya Regional Engineering College, Jaipur and his MTech (Energy, 1996) and PhD (Energy, 1999) from the Indian Institute of Technology (IIT) Delhi. After his Post-Doctoral Fellowship (1999 – 2001) at the ERC, UW, Madison, USA, he returned to India in 2001 and joined IIT Kanpur. PhD research scholar Shanti Mehra carrying out research in the field of DME as an alternative fuel in IC engines at Engine Research Laboratory (ERL), IIT Kanpur

Technology

Dimethyl ether (DME) is a synthetically produced alternative to diesel for use in specially designed compression ignition diesel engines. Under normal atmospheric conditions, DME is a colorless gas. It is used extensively in the chemical industry and as an aerosol propellant. The use of DME in vehicles requires a compression ignition engine with a fuel system specifically developed to operate on DME. A number of DME vehicle demonstrations have been held in Europe and North America. In 2013, Pennsylvania State University, Volvo, and Oak Ridge National Laboratory completed field testing of a prototype DME truck(PDF). The heavy-duty truck performed well under real-world driving conditions, achieving comparable efficiency to a conventional diesel truck. Test results indicated that particulate matter emission standards could be met without the use of a diesel particulate filter. As with conventional diesel vehicles, oxides of nitrogen (NOx) emissions reductions can be handled with standard NOx after-treatment systems. Alternatively, the engine can be calibrated to negate the need for such a system, but this reduces efficiency.

Innovation

India's first 100% Dimethyl Ether (DME) – fuelled tractor/ vehicle for on – and off-road applications has been developed by researchers at IIT Kanpur. The researchers tackled the challenge of a lower calorific value of DME and higher compressibility than baseline diesel by developing a customised high-pressure mechanical fuel pump of higher pressurisation capacity. Besides, customised mechanical injectors of higher nozzle hole diameters than the baseline design were used for DME adaptation and diesel equivalent power generation. Lubricity additives enhanced DME's lubricity. DME-compatible materials were used in the fuel injection equipment (FIE) developed in this study. The fuel supply and return lines were made of DME-compatible materials. Customised DME tanks were developed.

Patents

Relevant patents by Bosch – Injection pump and fuel DME feed device of diesel engine with the injection pump: https://patents.google.com/patent/US6955156B2/en

Comercialisation

The DME-fuelled engine exhibited higher brake thermal efficiency. It produced negligible soot while significantly reducing HC, CO, and CO2 emissions. The results are published in journals such as 'Energy Conversion and Management' and 'Fuel'. The developed engine prototype was installed into the tractor and successfully operated by the industrial partner, TAFE TMTL, Alwar.

Food Processing Plants – Best Engineering Technologies, Hyderabad

Seshasai Mummadi is an engineer with several years experience at APHMEL, Kondapalli started his entrepreneurial journey with Best Engineering Technologies (BET)

Technology

Essential oils are the liquids that are isolated from plants when introduced to solvents, they are liquefied versions of the plants. Popular extraction methods include: Steam Distillation, Solvent Extraction, CO2 Extraction, Maceration, Enfleurage, Cold Press Extraction, and Water Distillation. Steam distillation is utilized for essential oils extraction at temperatures near 100°C, followed by subsequent condensation to form an immiscible liquid from which the essential oil can be separated in a clarifier. Steam distillation is carried out by passing dry steam through the plant material, whereby the steam volatile compounds are volatilized, condensed, and collected in receivers. Solvent extraction employs food grade solvents like hexane and ethanol to isolate essential oils from plant material. It is best suited for plant materials that yield low amounts of essential oil, that are largely resinous, or that are delicate aromatics unable to withstand the pressure and distress of steam distillation.

Innovation

The Extraction process and the plant design of Extraction system is invariably different from Product to product and component to component. The extraction media depends upon the solubility of the components using Aqua (water) or Solvent or mixture of solvents by principle of physical separation. It is very difficult to generalize a process to extract isolate compounds from various herbs, plants are of cGMP standards. Turnkey projects developed are – Herbal Extraction Plant (Aqua / Solvent), Curcumin Extraction Plant, Spices Oleo Resin Extraction Plant, Floral Extraction Plant, Bixin Extraction Plant, Natural Colours Extraction Plant, Gums / Resins Extraction Plant.

The firm developed process and provides plant & machinery for Extraction of Essential oils from various plants materials like Herbs, Grasses, Leaves, Barks, Wood, Roots, Flowers like Distillation Plant for Aromatic Grasses / Leaves Oils. Food processing plants include Fruit juice / pulp processing plant, Fruits and Vegetables dehydration plant, Tomato Sauce / Ketchup / Paste processing plant, Cashew processing plant, Chilly / Masala powder processing plant, Turmeric Powder processing plant, Honey processing plant, Ground Nut processing plant, Moringa leaves powder processing plant

Patents

There were 12-patented inventions pertaining to extraction, isolation, and identification of active substances from Aloe vera. US patent 929051 pertains to extraction, isolation and identification of aloe pectins from gel and rind cell wall fibres of Aloe vera.

Commercialisation

BET journey started in 2005 in a small scale with essential oil distillation plant technology alone but during course of time we are able to develop various process technologies like Aloevera, Amla, Cashew, Bio diesel and Herbal extraction, food processing plants etc., as per the market trends and customer requirement because of our strong based of research and develop team. Today they have to their credit 500 projects of essential oil distillation plants, 50 projects of aloe vera processing plants, 50 projects of amla processing plants, 30 projects of solvent extraction plants and more than 1000 projects of food processing plants across the globe.

https://www.bestengineeringtechnologies.com/

Fruit Bar from Prickly Pear Fruits (Opuntia Ficus Indica) – Dr Chenna Kesava Reddy Sangati, IIPM, Bangalore

Dr Chenna Kesava Reddy Sangati, is Assistant Professor (Nutrition & Technology) at Indian Institute of Plantation Management Bangalore (IIPMB). He had PhD in Food Technology from Venkatesawara University, Tirupath and experience of working in the food production industry. Skilled in Research and Development (R&D), Food & Beverage, Food Processing, Food Science, and Hazard Analysis and Critical Control Points (HACCP).

Technology

Prickly pear (Opuntia-ficus indica L.) grows in arid and semi-arid areas and show good nutritional and medicinal characteristics. Fruit consumption is limited by short harvesting season and shelf life. Drying may resolve such issues. The species produces flowers, cladodes and fruits that are consumed either in raw or in processed products. Recent publications described that consumption of the fruit improves human health, exhibiting antioxidant activity and other relevant pharmacological activities through enzymatic and non-enzymatic mechanisms. Fruit or juice consumption may exert antioxidant activity through non-enzymatic mechanisms or modifying SOD, CAT and GSH enzymatic levels. Polyphenols present in syrup concentrates can display anti-cancer activity in tumorigenic lines of fibroblasts and neuroblastoma, and fermented juice could reduce UV-B damage induced in fibroblasts. Besides its pharmacological importance, fruits have a considerable role contributing to the individual daily intake of minerals and other essential nutrients when are consumed fresh or as food supplements.

Innovation

The present invention discloses a process for preparing dehydrated fruit bar from Prickly Pear Fruits (Opuntia ficus indica) and product thereof. The process involves harvesting Prickly Pear Fruits (Opuntia ficus indica) with predetermined TSS and acidity value followed by deharing and dethorning the fruit to remove glochids and thorn. Then the fruit is blanched in warm water at 60°C for 5 min and pulping of the fruit is carried out by partial cooking of pulp (PCP) method at 65°C for 20 min to obtain a pulp. Subsequently the fruit pulp is pasteurized at 70°C for 15 min for the destruction of microorganism. Then the TSS value, acidity value and consistency is adjusted by adding jagarry, citric acid and papaya pulp extract respectively. After that the pulp was filtered and sheeting is carried out by making the pulp into sheet with predetermined thickness. Finally the sheeted pulp is dried at 60°C for 18 hrs and the dried pulp is cut into small bars to obtain the dehydrated Prickly Pear (Opuntia ficus indica) fruit bar.

Patents

Patent: No.1: A Process for preparing dehydrated fruit bar from prickly pear fruits (opuntia ficus indica) and product thereof. Patent Reg.no:4345/CHE/2012 and filling date 17/10/2012(Granted)

Patent: No.2: A Process for manufacturing of blended fruit squash with prickly pear (opuntia ficus indica & opuntia dillenii) fruit juice and lemon juice.Patent Reg.no: 4485/CHE/2014 and filling date 15/09/2014 (Granted)

Patent :No.3: Production of Alcohol (NATURO-HOL) from Agave albomerginata. Patent Reg.no: 4352/CHE/2015 and filing date 20/08/2015(Granted)

Patent :No.4: A process for Manufacturing of CGP (Conditioned Graded and Packed Sand). Patent Reg.no: 744/CHE/2013 and filing date 21/02/2013. (Final examination and hearing completed)

Commercialisation

Video – The Indian Fig Cactus Pear Fruit! (Opuntia Ficus-Indica) & How to Try it Yourself!

https://youtu.be/QtrrPczXxPU?si=y-sGUWQxq6FdxFGH

For technical consultancy:

Dr.Chenna Kesava Reddy Sangati

Assistant Professor (Nutrition & Technology),

Indian Institute of Plantation Management (IIPM),

(Autonomous Organisation of the Ministry of Commerce & Industry, GOI)

Jnana Bharati Campus, P.O Malathalli,

Bangalore-560056, Karnataka (State), India.

Mobile: 0091-9985663785

Email: chenna2nalas@gmail.com

GroTron Autonomous Irrigation System – Farmagain Agro Pvt Ltd, Coimbatore

Benjamin Raja graduate from University of Madras is Founder & CEO of Farmagain. https://www.linkedin.com/in/benjaminraja/.

Technology

Precision farming technology incorporates – gathering farming data, including historical, predictive modeling and environmental insights to choose suitable crops with higher yields, measure the performance of the site by capturing data in real-time, use digital farming data (soil, crop health, weather, etc.) to provide the exact amount or water, nutrition and optimize pest control, Increase the farm's economic and environmental sustainability, predict weather changes and react to them proactively.

There are many startups active in this field – Aarav Unmanned Systems, Aibono, Aquaconnect, CropIn, Fasal, Gramophone, and

GramworkX are the ones make farming more efficiently; while Agdhi, Intello Labs, and O4S (Original4Sure) concentrate on product quality control. Check the larger list at:

https://tracxn.com/explore/AI-in-Agriculture-Startups-in-India

Innovation

The firm developed IOT devices for micromanagement of farming practices towards precision agriculture. GroTron CROPSENSE senses soil moisture and temperature, operates gate valves automatically and irrigates when required and maintains ideal soil moisture for superior plant productivity. GroTron WATERSENSE automates operation of water pumps based on real-time soil conditions, prevents motor dry run and operates Genset automatically when grid power is not available. GroTron NUTRISENSE manages fertigation of multiple crops in a farm, supplies precise nutrition based on a crop specific fertigation plan and manages automatic operation of fertigation unit, tanks and flushing of pipelines. GroTron CLIMATESENSE monitors protected cultivation environment structures for ideal temperature and humidity and operates fogger automatically to maintain ideal environment.

Patents

Precision ag was initially theorized in the 1980s by Dr. Pierre Robert, the father of modern precision farming. He came up with the concept while in college and spent many years studying and pioneering precision farming principles. He opted to use technology to scan for soil irregularities, germination, drainage, and other key aspects of successful crops.

Check list of Precision agriculture patents:

https://golden.com/query/list-of-precision-agriculture-patents-JGNN5

Commercialisation

The system doesn't have limitations on number of acres, gate valves, motors and fertilization tanks and the tiny GroTron™ device can be placed as per the space availability. Importantly, the user-friendly nature of the device allows anyone with minimum electrical knowledge and internet know-how to operate it without tensions. In addition Farmagain, created marketplace to disseminate information to the stakeholders and enabling them to buy or sell their products or services at the right time at right price with absolute traceability using QR Codes in each transaction.

The firm was awarded "India's Agri Startup 2018" from Dept of Commerce,Govt of India. "India's Best AgriTech Business Model using IoT and Artificial Intelligence in Agriculture" from Dept of Agriculture & Dept of Science and Technology, Govt of India, 2018. And received grant of Rs 25 lakhs from RKVY-RAFTAAR RABI SAIP Cohort II.

https://www.farmagain.in/grotron-marketplace

Innovative Rhizome Processing-S4 Foods, Aurangabad, Maharashtra

Sushil Shelke graduate in Bio_technology from Bangalore University with MBA from Symbiosis promoted S4 Foods and AGRIFOOD TECH PRIVATE LIMITED. https://www.linkedin.com/in/sushilshelke/

He is winner of Agri-Hackathon 2020 – https://blog.mygov.in/winner-announcement-of-agri-india-hackathon/

Technology

Turmeric is a spice derived from the rhizomes of the tropical plant Curcuma longa Linn, which is a member of the ginger family (Zingiberaceae). Rhizomes are horizontal underground stems that send out shoots, as well as roots. The bright yellow-orange color of turmeric comes mainly from fat-soluble, polyphenolic pigments known as curcuminoids. Curcumin, the principal curcuminoid found in turmeric, is generally considered its most active constituent. The extraction method can be categorized as traditional and modern extraction techniques. The most common traditional extraction methods are Soxhlet extraction and maceration. Whereas, ultrasound-assisted extraction (UAE), microwave-assisted extraction (MAE), enzyme-assisted extraction are the most common methods in modern extraction process. Despite many drawbacks such as high temperatures, high operating times, and high organic solvent use, the traditional extraction method is commonly used due to its simple procedures and low operating costs.

Raw turmeric rhizomes are processed to obtain turmeric powder with 6.47 ± 0.01% curcumin percentage. Curcumin is successfully extracted from turmeric powder using the soxhlet extraction method, and the extractability of curcumin is 5.16 ± 0.44%.

(https://pubs.acs.org/doi/10.1021/acsomega.0c06314#)

Innovation

Piloted the Turmeric Processing methodology with Complete In-House Operations that Reduces the Time Of Processing rhyzhomes to powder by eliminating sun drying by use of biotechnology and special engineered equipments such as reactor vessel and cabinet dryers to arrive at the dehydrated rhizome suitable for quality powder products manufacturing. Technology Innovation listed at Office of the Principal Scientific Advisor to the Government of India:

https://www.psa.gov.in/article/rhizone-crop-processing/2185

Rhizome based spices are processed in a tedious, cumbersome, and time-consuming manner. The threat of uncertain climatic conditions makes this process even more cumbersome for farmers. Traditionally rhizome based spices like turmeric and ginger require

15-20 days of sun-drying prior to being sent to market. The inventor has optimized a process where in the same is reduced to one batch of 12 hours and as an added bonus, an improvement of bioactive elements is observed. Also improved the curcumin content in the same crop from 2% in traditional processing to 4.8% in the proprietary process.

This innovative technology was developed in association with Punjab Deshmukh Krishi Vidyapeeth, Akola and IITB in 2015.

Patents

METHOD FOR EXTRACTING HIGH CONTENT OF CURCUMIN FROM TURMERIC USING EMULSIFIER AND ULTRASONICATION –

https://patentscope.wipo.int/search/en/detail.jsf?docId=WO2018056660

Commercialisation

https://s4foods.com/innovation

The firm manufactures and supplies Dried Polished Rhizome which has curcumin content of 2-4% and Flakes with curcumin contact above 4%.

https://youtu.be/I75xyX-fkps

Kappahycus Alvarezii Elite Seedling Production – Dr. M. Ganesan, CSIR-CSMCRI

Dr. M. Ganesan is Ex Senior Principal Scientist at Marine Algal Research Station, Mandpam, Tamil Nadu, an extension centre of CSIR – Central Salt & Marine Chemicals Research Institute. During his long career of 30 years, he developed feasible cultivation techniques for several seaweeds viz. Gracilaria edulis, Gracilaria salicornia, Hypnea musciformis, Gelidiella acerosa and Sarconema filiforme which are of commercial importance. His remarkable contribution is exploration of seaweed diversity of Gulf of Mannar coast an UNESCO identified Marine National Park. Recently, he developed commercial scale production of Kappaphycus alvarzii elite seedlings through micropropagation of tissue cultured plants and also Gracilaria edulis seedling production at commercial scale through spore culture. He published 80 research papers in reputed SCI journals with high impact factor; 1 patent, 1 technology transfer to the industry and guided 2 Ph.D students.

Technology

Kappaphycus alvarezii a red seaweed yields carrageenan and biostiumulant that are having high market value. Therefore, commercial cultivation of K. alvarezii was initiated in 2001 along the southeast coast of Tamil Nadu. Production increased significantly from 021 dry metric tons in 2001 to 1,490 dry tons in 2013. The number of seaweed growers in Tamil Nadu have risen from a mere 6 in 2001 to 950 in 2013. However, the production sharply declined in the subsequent years due to mass mortality. The production achieved till June 2019 was only 181 dry wt. Only few hundred farmers are involving in K. alvarezii cultivation. There is huge demand for seed material for continuing the cultivation. Kappaphycus alvarezii commercial cultivation from isolated spores has been successfully developed in Indonesia to provide seed material to the farmers. However reproductive material of K. alvarezii has not been recorded in India for the last 2 decades. Mass seedling production through micropropagation of shoot initiated plantlets in the lab, outdoor tanks and finally in the sea ensures consistent supply of seed materials to the farmers.

The technology involves the following steps:1) Collection of the parent plant 2) Preparation of the explants 3) Tissue (shoot) initiation in the explants 4) Culture of the tissue culture explants in the laboratory. 5) Hardening of the tissue culture plantlets in the Outdoor tanks 6) Acclimatization of the plantlets in the sea and 7) Commercial seedling production and multiplication 8) Supply of tissue culture seedlings to the seaweed farmers.

Innovation

About 250 – 300 elite seedlings (each seedling @ 50 g fresh wt) were produced from a single mother plant of 100 g fresh wt. in 120 days by adopting this technique. Totally 13,700 seedlings

(@50g fresh wt.) were produced and supplied to the 230 seaweed farmers covering Ramanathapuram District, Pudukkottai District and Tuticorin District of Tamil Nadu. The farmers multiplied these seedlings and produced 30 tonnes of Kappaphycus alvarezii biomass in 2 consecutive cycles.Tissue cultured seedlings produced by this technique have 20 – 30% higher growth as compared to conventional plant. This means farmers earning 20 – 30% higher income.Tissue cultured K.alvarezii has significantly higher carrageenan yield and quality as compared to conventional farmed plants.

Patents

AN IMPROVED PROCESS FOR CULTIVATION OF ALGAE, CSIR – International application number: PCT/IN2000/000084

Commerecialisation

Many seaweed cultivators of Tamil Nadu coast are doing commercial cultivation of Kappaphycus alvarezii using elite germplasm as seed material.

https://www.csmcri.res.in/node/8121

An appraisal on commercial farming of Kappaphycus alvarezii in India: success in diversification of livelihood and prospects – https://pubag.nal.usda.gov/catalog/5756997

https://www.currentscience.ac.in/Volumes/90/05/0619.pdf

Machine to Remove Insects from Stored Grains – Professor (Retd) Mohan Sriramasarma, Tamil Nadu Agriculture University (TNAU), Coimbatore

Professor (Retd) Mohan Sriramasarma from the Tamil Nadu Agriculture University (TNAU), Coimbatore. Mohan has come up with a variety of tools, ranging from simple gadgets to machines produced indigenously to remove not only adult insects but also their life stages (egg, larvae, pupae) and has demonstrated their utility in real life. He has developed seven useful gadgets in this regard and an educational kit containing prototype of these gadgets for teaching and training. This is widely used in Agricultural Institutions in our country for teaching and trainingHis contributions have been recognized by the Tamil Nadu Government and the Government of India through 5 awards, besides 7 Institutional and Agricultural society Awards. . He had guided eleven MSc and 7 Doctoral Students in his area of specialization.

Technology

Once an insect infestation has become established, there are only two treatment options: (1) move the grain and apply a protectant during transfer or (2) fumigation. Both choices have good and bad points. Application of grain protectants during movement will provide some residual protection. But moving grain is costly, time consuming and requires additional bin space. Also, if good control is not achieved, movement will spread the insects throughout the grain mass. On the other hand, fumigation works very well and is relatively cheap. Fumigants are gases that penetrate the grain and kill insects both on and in the grain. They are very toxic to man and animals and should be applied only by trained, experienced operators working in pairs. But because it is very sensitive to poor technique, many failures occur. Also, it is dangerous and provides no residual protection.

Innovation

The insect remover machine can clean grains at a rate of up to 2000kg/hr. As the grains flow through the machine it crushes the eggs to a considerable extent and prevents further insect reproduction. Besides eggs, this machine also effectively removes the adult weevils/beetles (both dead and alive). Free-living larvae of insects are also crushed. The machine works on the principles of impact, smooth brushing, sieving, and blowing.

Patents

He has patented two of his inventions: (i) A device to remove insects and their life stages from stored grains (Indian Patent 198434) and (ii) A stack probe trap for warehouses (Indian Patent284727).

Commercialisation

The entrepreneur manufacturing and marketing this machine Mr. Balaji, Managing Director of Sri Vrintha Traders, Coimbatore, Tamil Nadu. About 60 machines are used in India and 8 machines have been exported to Oman, Dubai, Saudi Arabia, Qatar, and Philippines.

Video demo: Grain Insect cleaning machine (https://www.youtube.com/watch?v=EwhLdUzNyik

Contact: Dr. S. MOHAN, Retired Professor, Dept. of Agricultural Entomology, Tamil Nadu Agricultural University, Coimbatore 641 003. Phone : +91 9488458006, Email: sarmamohan@hotmail.com Web: www.mohantrap.com

Multipurpose Processing Machine – Dharamveer Singh Kamboj, Yamuna Nagar, Haryana

Dharamveer Kamboj, a multifaceted innovator wears many hats. Best known for his multipurpose processing machine that enables farmers to process various farm products on a domestic level, he also sells Aloe vera juice, gel, amla juice and other amla products and a whole range of herbal products. He also grows medicinal plants in his fields in addition to selling safed musli seeds and Aloe vera saplings to other farmers.

https://nif.org.in/upload/innovation/7th/759-dharmveer.pdf

Technology

The gel extraction from Aloe vera leaves, had been carried out by removing of its exudates and its mucilage was scraped out with blunt edged knife. This mucilage was stirred vigorously in a blender to make it uniform. This solution was strained through a muslin cloth and filtered. This uniform solution was extracted for cold – extracted gel (CEG) and hot extracted gel (HEG). The aloe liquid obtained is treated with activated carbon to decolourize the liquid and remove aloin and anthraquinones, which have laxative effects. The resultant liquid is then subjected to various steps of filtration, sterilization and stabilization. The stabilized liquid, thus, obtained could be concentrated to reduce the amount of water or, alternatively, almost all of the water removed to yield a powder. In all these processing techniques, stabilization can be achieved by the addition of preservatives and other additives. Sodium benzoate, potassium sorbate, citric acid, vitamin E are to be used.

Innovation

An innovator at heart, he was the first farmer in the area to cultivate hybrid tomatoes and maintain a record of his produce. In 1990, he developed a battery operated spraying machine using a tape recorder motor. For catching insects, he tried various things including the use of adhesive tape as an insect trap. To maximize returns from his farm, he practiced intercropping by cultivating coriander, bottle gourd and sugarcane. He also developed a special implement to plough the field without disturbing the sugarcane crop.

He started working on the development and by April 2006, was ready with the first prototype of the machine, which he used mainly for juice extraction of Aloe vera. He further modified the machine and used it as an essence extraction unit. With the help of this feature and a few more improvements, he could use the machine for processing of several herbs and farm produce. Multi Purpose Processing machine is a portable machine, which works on a single phase motor and is useful in processing of various fruits, herbs and seeds. It also works as big pressure cooker with temperature control and auto cut-off facility. It also offers condensation mechanism, which helps in extraction of essence and extracts from flowers and medicinal plants.

Patents

Indian Patent Applied for (No: 367/DEL/2008)

A Review of United States Patents (US Patents) on Aloe – https://ijppr.humanjournals.com/wp-content/uploads/2021/01/17.Vishal-P.-Nalamwar-Satish-B.-Kosalge.pdf

Commercialisation

For his innovation of the multipurpose processing machine, NIF gave him the Haryana State award in its Fifth National Biennial Awards function in 2009. Two models of the machine are available, Model 1: Multi-Pro V 60 Price: Rs. 1,10,000, Model 2: Multi-Pro V 120 Price: Rs. 1,80,000/-

https://nif.org.in/innovation/the_multipurpose_processing_machine/759

Non-Invasive and Non-Intrusive Honey Harvesting Device – KLE Technological University, Hubballi

Dr. Guttal Ravi was Director at CIPD – Center for Innovation and Product Development of KLE Technological University, Hubballi. He did MS in Robotics from Carnegie Mellon University after graduation from NIT, Suratkal, ME from IISc. Worked at John Deere India Pvt ltd before joining KLE. https://www.linkedin.com/in/guttalravi/

Farmer's First is a subsidiary company of Green Organic Fresh which is providing services to the farmers to convert chemically fertilized land through organic interventions. Keeping into considerations the need for conservation and sustainability of *apis cerena indica bee*, the company has taken a huge stride and developed a technology focusing on the species mentioned above and designed a beehive which plays a vital role in attracting *Apis cerana indica* and nurture the family within the flow hive box.

Technology

Of all known eight species of honeybees, only Apis Mellifera (western honey bee) and Apis Cerena (eastern honey bee) are domesticated for honey production and crop pollination. Though individually honeybees are cold-blooded flying insects but they maintain constant temperature of 95 OF or 35 OC in their nest. In order to ease the honey harvesting, transport of bees from place to place for crop pollination and better yield of honey. And also, the sizes of these bee boxers are also standardized to develop technical equipment to ease the collection of honey and other products from the bee boxes.

In Karnataka, there are three different models of Bee Boxes available and they are Shimoga Model, Newton Model (famous in Sirisi and Yellapura region) and ISI Model (type A & B). Sagavani, Nandi, Honne, Matti and Devadaru are the woods used in building these bee boxes but Sagavani is best amongst all. Later boxes are painted for better life, dried in sunlight and washed in water to remove any traces of odours before using as presence of any odour may lead to the rejection of bee box by honeybees (They may escape/migrate). These days, instead of wood, plastic foam sheets (mostly PVC foam sheets) are used in making bee boxes. As of now, ventilation in these boxes is very poor and improvements are being implemented.

Innovation

Indian Artificial Beehive follows complete Non-Violence (Ahimsa) method of honey collection. Beehive is accessed from the bottom and only central portion of the beehive moves in vertical direction enabling gravity draining of honey. A simple lever called 'honey collection handle' is used for forced draining of honey from the beehive. Thus, honey is collected without hurting arvae or honey bee or beehive by a single person without using any additional instruments like centrifuge and within lesser time (Approx. 30 min per box). Even Novice or Hobby Beekeepers shall also use the device for beekeeping and collect adulteration-free honey.

Patent

Prior art – Flow hive technology (Patent# US20140370781A1, Year#2012) and Self-extracting honey-box (Patent#, Year# 2015).

Indian Patent granted – Application 202141055978, patent no 431841.

Commercialisation

The technique which our start-up proposed is called the Flow hive method. Currently, this method is practiced in Australia and USA but is only for Italian bee Apis melifera. The Flow Hive design was invented in Australia by Cedar Anderson and his father Stuart Anderson. But for the Indian strain Apis cerana indica, no such flow hive has been developed.

http://cipd.kletech.ac.in/Products/view_product/19

Optical Fruit Sorting System – Zentron Labs Pvt Ltd, Bangalore

Krishnan Ramabhadran is Founder and CEO of Zentron Labs. He did his graduation and post-graduation from IIT Madras, Krishnan was formerly a chip-designer, managing high-tech teams for Texas Instruments. His strong enthusiasm for entrepreneurship drove him to co-found Cosmic Circuits, a successful startup where he honed his business skills; Krishnan turned back into technology with system-design based on Vision and founded Zentron labs.

Technology

Machine vision based fruit grading systems are capable of replacing labour work for inspection of fruit grading. Different researchers used algorithms for image segmentation, feature extraction, training and classification of fruit disease. Out of morphological, colour and texture feature, morphological gave highest accuracy rate. In colour model, HIS (Hue, Saturation, Intensity) colour model is commonly used for grading because it is related to human perception. In machine learning techniques, SVM (Support Vector Machine) gave highest accuracy, but ANFIS (Adaptive Neuro Fuzzy Interference System) showed the best result out of these techniques. Further, Fuzzy gave lowest accuracy rate result, but it is easy to implement.

Innovation

FruiTron is an innovation that automates the task of sorting fruits with higher accuracy and greater throughput. A combination of rigorous image processing algorithms and robust hardware ensures that each fruit is scrutinized comprehensively for all defects before exiting the inspection line. Fruits are also categorized into different grades based on a combination of colour, size, weight, and defect. FruiTron leverages on a machine vision system capable of : Inspecting defects on the surface of fruit, Determining the color of fruit, Determining the shape of fruit, Measuring the size of fruit, Measuring the weight of fruit, Creating farmer wise and bin-wise reports.

Patents

CMERI, CSIR developed a Fruit sorting machine and patented same – https://www.cmeri.res.in/patent/sorting-unit-fruit-sorting-and-grading-machine

Commercialisation

Zentron manufactures hi-speed fruit grading machines that help farmers to be paid based on objective quality assessment. Zentron was awarded the National Innovation award in the year 2021 by

Startup India in the Agriculture – Post Harvest category. Process up to 10 fruits per second per lane– Program is executed on a Real-Time Operating System to give the highest speed. Multiple fruit inspection capability– Perform sorting on fruits such as Apple, Orange, Kinnow and other spherical shaped fruits, Multiple sort options– Sort fruit based on the defect, color, shape, weight, and size of the fruit, Latest machine vision hardware– High-resolution cameras ensure that the system can now detect even the tiniest of defects, Enhanced optical system– Multiple images of the fruit are captured in the visible and near-IR spectrum to improve defect identification, Cutting edge machine learning and image processing algorithms are used to improve the accuracy of the machine and ensure reliable functionality and Advanced Visualization– All results can be overlaid on top of the fruit image for quick verification.

https://zentronlabs.com/systems/fruit-quality-inspection-fruittron/

https://youtu.be/Rs5f8ZJ4_ag

Onion Warehouse with IOT – Godaam Innovations, Nashik

Kalyani Shinde is Founder and CEO of Godaam Innovations. Engineer from Amrutvahini College of Engineering (AVCOE) and mentored at Digital Impact Square.

Technology

Cultivation of onions, from sowing to harvesting, usually takes around 120 days. This is followed by a storage period of eight to six months in the warehouse which becomes the breeding ground for spoilage. When a farmer stores 10 kg of onions, around 40 to 50 percent of it gets spoilt each time.

Tata Steel's Nest-In and Innovent teams have developed Agronest, a smart warehouse solution with a unique structural design that maximises air flow, is spacious thus making it conducive for longer and safer storage of onions, and provides a cost-effective environment control to ensure minimal wastage. The warehouse has sensors installed for monitoring temperature, humidity and gas, thereby enabling early detection of spoilage of the produce. Components from 4 major Tata Steel brands – Tata Structura, Tata Tiscon, Tata Wiron and coated sheets from Tata Steel BSL, have been used in the solution, promising quality and structural longevity to the customers.

The Department of Consumer Affairs (DoCA), Ministry of Consumer Affairs, Food and Public Distribution (MoCAFPD) announces to develop 'Technologies for Primary Processing, Storage and Valorization of Onions' via 'Grand Challenge on Onion Storage'. https://doca.gov.in/goc/

Innovation

The early-stage startup leverages Internet of Things (IoT) technology to detect gases emitted from spoilt onions in warehouses, collect real-time data, and alert the farmers. This has reduced wastage by 20 to 25 percent. The next problem is that most farmers rely on identifying onion spoilage through smell and about 30 percent of the crop is lost under this method. The startup installs IoT devices that can detect early rotting in addition to controlling micro-climate, and alerts the farmers to take action. They can then remove the rotten onion to avoid further rotting and start selling.

Patents

Indian patent application 201821007242 by Sandip Sanjay Gangurde is titled – Iot Based Smart Onion Warehouse.

https://fabacademy.org/2022/labs/vigyanashram/students/ kishor-gaikwad/assignments/finalproject.html

Commercialisation

https://www.godaaminnovations.com/product/

Depending on factors like capacity of storage, the startup's services are packaged into three categories of high, medium, and low. The hardware installations for each are priced between Rs 1 to 1.2 lakh, Rs 70,000 to Rs 90,000, and Rs 30,000 to Rs 40,000 respectively with a monthly charge of Rs 5,000 to Rs 10,000.

https://yourstory.com/herstory/2020/07/woman-entrepreneur-onion-price-agritech-farmer

https://si.puneinternationalcentre.org/mentees/ms-kalyani-shinde/

Agronest fromTata Steel – https://youtu.be/YO2XDCpsHrY

Production of Seedlings in Agarose Yielding Red Seaweed Gracilaria Dura – Dr. Vaibhav A. Mantri, CSIR-CSMCRI

Team from CSMCRI, Dr. Vaibhav A. Mantri, Sr. Principal Scientist, Dr. Mangal S. Rathore, Principal Scientist and Dr. Santlal J. Jaiswar, Sr. Technical Officer have come with this unique innovation on seaweed.

Dr. Vaibhav A. Mantri – Team leader: https://www.csmcri.res.in/node/339

Dr. Mangal Singh Rathore – Member: https://www.csmcri.res.in/node/343

Dr. Santlal Jaiswar – Member: https://www.csmcri.res.in/node/5994

Technology

Gracilaria dura, a source of high-quality agarose, has emerged as the preferred choice for commercial aquaculture in India. The cultivation was carried out at experimental-scale in southeast coast of India by adopting five different techniques namely *floating bamboo raft, polypropylene square net, net bag, net pouch, and single rope floating technique.* On the contrary *tube net method* was adopted for open sea cultivation in the west coast of India.

Innovation

Gracilaria dura is used as principal raw material source of agarose. The biomass availability of this species is poor and scanty distribution and seasonal occurrence hinders utilisation of this alga for industrial production of agarose. The seedling production technology that has been developed would cater need of commercial farming of this species in the country.

Patents

The cost-effective, green processing by surfactant-induced, coagulation of agarose from alkali-treated G. dura was patented by CSMCRI as an alternative to the traditional energy-intensive process of "freeze–thaw" cycles. The Council of Scientific and Industrial Research (CSIR), India has also obtained a trade mark for the agarose produced from G. dura (Sagarose: Number 2123313 dt. 30.03.2011, New Delhi, India).

Commercialisation

The technology has taken care of higher regeneration, survival and growth efficacy of non-apical and non-basal segments. It has demonstrated the use of minimum thallus tissue for utilization of maximum thallus tissue, to increase the number of seedlings per donor tissue. The weight to volume ratio has been standardized to achieve maximum survival and regeneration under controlled laboratory conditions. The various pre-treatments have been developed to get maximum survival and regeneration under controlled laboratory conditions. Besides, outdoor cultivation protocol has been established.

The farming of this species has been adopted in the open sea along the Gujarat coast. The capacity building of 163 fishermen has been accomplished by providing hands on training, under National Fisheries Development Board, Hyderabad sponsored project. The buy-back agreement has been made with our agar-agarose producing industries. The adequate supply of seed material would certainly have bearing in augmenting the efforts to support farmers those are engaged in commercial cultivation of this species to make the livelihood lucrative and sustainable.

Lab scale production @ 50,000 seedlings in a batch has been achieved, and tank cultivation in the field @ 25,000 seedlings in a batch has been achieved. Starting with 2.5 Kg biomass, 1 ton seedling material can be produced in 180-200 days.

Pesticidal Water Dispersible Granule Formulation – Parijat Industries (India) Pvt. Ltd. New Delhi

Keshav Anand is Managing Director and CEO of Parijat industries, an experienced industry professional. Parijat is a three decades old Indian MNC with extensive global presence in 60 countries, 4 International offices, exclusive distribution networks in India, Russia and C.I.S and West Africa.

Technology

Agrochemical, any chemical used in farming, such as fungicides, insecticides, and herbicides. Most are mixture of two or more chemicals; the active ingredients produce the intended effects, while the inert ingredients stabilize, preserve, or facilitate application of the active ingredients in order to get the desired result on the crop and to protect the crop from pests.

Innovation

The product VELEKTIN® is a combination of Insecticides viz., Emamectin Benzoate and Profenofos (IN359450) in water dispersible Granule form. Velektin is a stable and synergistic pesticidal water dispersible granule formulation with an effective quantity of a first ingredient and a liquid active ingredient.Emamectin benzoate is the primary component in use, and Profenofos, an organothiophosphate insecticide, is the liquid active ingredient. The invention's goal is to defend crops against a variety of natural enemies, including coleopteran and lepidopteran species. A low dose of invention does not cause phytotoxic damages to any part of plant. Another product is a combination of herbicides viz., Metamifop and Imidazolines (IN435217), is an excellent combination for controlling undesired vegetation including broad leaf weeds, grasses, and sedges This class of herbicides was used to protect a variety of crops, including beans, soybeans, groundnuts, and pulses.

The two inventions work wonder to control pests, combat resistance with dual mode of killing, cause no damage to crops, and have environmentally benign pesticide formulations that work well at low doses. These pesticide mixtures have a high potential for safeguarding various crops from the activity of weeds and insects while posing no risk to beneficial flora and fauna species.

Patents

Synergistic herbicidal compositions of Metamifop (IN435217), Issued on: 19/06/2023

Synergistic composition of an Auxin and a Triazinone (IN435100), Issued on: 16/06/2023

A Synergistic miticidal composition (IN372550), Issued on: 23/07/2021

A synergistic pesticidal wettable granule formulation comprising an Emamectin benzoate

and Profenofos (IN359450), Issued on: 25/02/2021

A pesticidal Emulsifiable Concentrate formulation (IN316555), Issued on: 22/07/2019

Commercialisation

https://parijatagrochemicals.com/

Velectin is one of the product manufactured by Parijata Chemicals – https://parijatagrochemicals.com/product/velektin/

See the Scientific infrastructure of this Indian MNC – https://parijatagrochemicals.com/wp-content/uploads/2023/07/Parijats-Scientific-Infrastructure-2023.pdf

Smart Soil Monitoring System – Proximal Soilsens Technologies Pvt. Ltd, Pune

Rajul (Maheshwari) Patkar is CEO of Proximal Soilsens Technologies Pvt. Ltd. (https://www.linkedin.com/in/rajulpatkar/) An engineering graduate from Andhra University with M Tech from IITB, she worked as Research Scholar at IITB she worked on developing various sensors and systems for precision agriculture. Prof Marayam S Baghini (https://www.ee.iitb.ac.in/wiki/faculty/mshojaei) and Prof Ramgopal Raos (https://www.linkedin.com/in/ramgopalrao/).are co-founders.

Technology

The invention of the tensiometer for measurement of soil water matric potential is commonly attributed to Willard Gardner, with the first robust design for field applications attributed to Lorenzo A, Richards during the early 1920s. However, evidence shows that the original design was proposed by Burton E. Livingston as early as 1908 (perhaps earlier) with advanced implementation of similar concepts for "measuring the capillary lift of soils" by Lynde and Dupre in 1913. The most common electromagnetic sensors are capacitance sensors or frequency domain reflectometry (FDR) sensors and time domain reflectometry (TDR) sensors. These sensors indirectly measure VWC based on the dielectric and electric properties of the soil medium (soil bulk permittivity or soil dielectric constant).

Innovation

Soilsens product line is developed by Proximal Soilsens Technologies Pvt. Ltd, a startup incubated at Indian Institute of Technology Bombay (IITB), Mumbai with support from the Ministry of Department of Science and Technology (DST) and Ministry of Electronics and Information Technology (Meity) The sensor can be installed at any depth as per the crop requirement and can be installed in any crop and in any soil. Data can be monitored and advisory can be given. When the moisture goes below the pre-set threshold value, it alarms the user about the irrigation. It also collects the data about soil temperature, ambient humidity and ambient temperature which can be used for early prediction of plant diseases. Powered by a battery, the system is charged by solar panel and does not require any external power supply. It is a modular system designed keeping in mind the Indian agricultural community. Height of the system is adjustable and it can be varied from 1m to 3m based on the height of the crop. Data from all the sensors are logged into a cloud using IoT platform.

Data sheet from IITB – Automated, self-sustained and modular apparatus for sensing various soil parameters and ambient parameters, Soil moisture sensor – accuracy of ± 3%, Soil temperature sensor, Ambient humidity sensor and ambient temperature sensor, Equipped with low-power signal conditioning unit and signal processing unit, Solar powered system; can sustain for 8-10 days without solar energy, Can be used with CLOUD using wireless communication/IOT platform; data displayed on mobile.

Patents

Relevant patent – Electrophoretic soil nutrient sensor for agriculture, https://patents.google.com/patent/US10564122B1/en

Commercialisation

Patkar with three other PhD students and another professor formed Proximal Soil Sense. The three other students have different kinds of expertise: one in signal processing, one in system integration, and another in networking. An imported sensor of high quality can cost Rs 10,000. Proximal Soil Sense has a four sensor system with all the other components working at Rs 25,000. One acre needs two such systems. India now has around 7-8 million hectares of fields that use sprinklers.

Nutrisens is a compact, on-site soil testing device which is easy to use, accurate and affordable. Multiple samples are collected and tested in an incredibly short time. This enables instant availability of results, bringing the lab to the field. Nutrisens for soil is comparable to a glucometer for humans. It measures the following soil-health parameters like EC, pH, Nitrate, Phosphate, Potassium, Organic Carbon. Currently, farmers have to send the soil sample to agricultural labs, which is time-consuming and expensive. With NutriSens, trained youth can do soil analysis on the site (farmer's field) and at a very nominal price.

The technology developed at IITB by Prof. Maryam Shojaei Baghini (Electrical Engineering) Licensed to Proximal Soilsens Technologies Pvt. Ltd. Check list of innovations licensed by IITB:

http://rnd.iitb.ac.in/sites/rnd.iitb.ac.in/files/brochures/2019-03/Innovations_licensed_to_industry_web.pdf

Supply Chain Management for FPOs
Vesatogo Innovations, Nasik

Akshay Dixit is Co-founder & CEO at Vesatogo Innovations. He works closely with Farmer Producer Organisations (FPOs) and their associated small holder farmers in optimising their operations and increasing their operating profits. He has a bachelor's degree in computer engineering from Pune University and he graduated in 2018. He has 5.5+ years of working in the social innovation space. He was also the Vice President-HR for the Nashik chapter of AIESEC, world's largest youth run organisation and was part of numerous organisations during college days. Prior to establishing Vesatogo Innovations, he worked for 6 months as the operations head for Preleaf Technologies, a startup working on early detection of high risk pregnancies in India.He was mentored at Digital Impact Square of TCS and had training at Cornell Maha 60, a year-long accelerator program offered by the Cornell University in partnership with the Department of Industries of Maharashtra.

https://www.linkedin.com/in/akshaydixit2010/

Technology

Farmer Producer Organizations (FPOs) emerged as a new form of aggregation model in India. Owing to a hybrid business model (between a private company and a cooperative), the new institutional form of FPOs limits membership to only primary producers who contribute equitably to the working capital and democratically control the FPO, sharing equal voting rights. Thus, being structurally different in membership, governance, and business model from cooperatives, FPOs are viewed as an advantageous alternative to cooperatives, with the key purpose of facilitating smallholder commercialization and increasing farm incomes.

https://tci.cornell.edu/?blog=assessing-indias-fpo-ecosystem

Innovation

The startup developed FMS (FPO Management System) with features such as – A cloud based supply chain management platform for agribusinesses and FPOs to help them better manage their day to day operations. The platform enables them FPOs to better connect with farmers and handle supplies efficiently and more transparent. The platform enables the agri supply chain (including Millets) to become more trustable, traceable and transparent. The platform is cloud based, which can offer any time anywhere any device access and is offered in regional languages

Patents

Guidebook on Buisness planning by FPO: http://nirdpr.org.in/nird_docs/CAS/Practitioners%20Guide%20for%20Business%20Development%20Planning%20in%20FPOs-n.pdf

Commercialisation

https://www.vesatogo.com/products/fpo-management-system-fms

Vesatogo Innovations is a Nashik based agritech startup working on reimagining the agrarian ecosystem by developing seed-to-plate supply chain management solutions for FPOs, agribusinesses and their associated smallholder farmers. Through the products developed, Vesatogo aims at making agriculture more profitable, traceable and transparent for all the stakeholders.

Togo platform is being used by 4000+ farmers across north & west Maharashtra. The platform has enabled movement of more that 1.75 Lakh Metric Tonnes of produce. The platform has also enabled the farmers to have better market realization by at least 10%.

FMS platform is being used by 2 agribusinesses and in the process of being deployed to 5 more. The platform has enabled partner organization to handle more than 2L tonnes of produce. The platform has enabled 3 times optimisation the the procurement processes of these organizations.

Vesatogo Innovations received National Startup Award 2021 for Agriculture sector under the Post Harvest category (Rural Impact) – They have developed a market linkage and aggregated logistics platform through which farmers get information of the current market trends (rates, demand, etc.) and can make intelligent and informed decisions ensuring higher profitability.

https://static.pib.gov.in/WriteReadData/userfiles/file/1MKOP.pdf

Solar Insect Traps – SAFS Ecotech Pvt Ltd, Puducherry

Abdul Kadhar is Chief Operating Officer at SAFS Organic Enterprises. Experienced engineer from Honeywell, he was granted Rs 10 lakhs under RKVY-RAFTAAR-RABI SAIP Cohort I.

Technology

Solar trap includes a light trap unit for attracting the flying insects; a collector unit coupled to the light trap unit for receiving the trapped insects from the light trap. A funnel is fitted to direct lured insects into the insect collecting unit. Funnel supports three baffles which are joined at the top. A hook has been provided at the top portion to install the light trap in the crop fields. Above the light trap unit, a solar panel is fitted for charging a battery which supplies required power to light trap unit. The collection unit is having two chambers separated by a mesh with big size holes to separate the tiny insects (mostly beneficial insects) and in the bottom a cap is provided for opening and closing the chamber. The collector unit further comprises of a vibration assembly, which has a controller; and a sensor coupled to the controller to transmit a first signal to the controller for vibrating the mesh. Once, the mesh will start vibrating, the tiny beneficial insects will fall down and collected in the second chamber. The tiny non-target insects mostly natural enemies trapped so can easily be escaped to the crop environment. The facility of escaping of non-target/natural enemies from the main insect collection unit is a desirable attribute for biointensive approach of pest management. The light trap unit is also provided with sensor which will automatically get lighted during twilight and switched off after three to four hours as per time set by user in the timer. A higher capacity battery has been fitted with the device to store and operate the device even in the cloudy and foggy weather. The battery can store sufficient power on full charged condition to supply required power to the unit to run for four to five days. It is a cost effective as it will run on solar power, besides being portable. The device is easily dismantled and stored when not in use. This automated AELT is an economic and eco-friendly insect trapping device which is easy-to-use and low maintenance, helps in handling insects in large number very efficiently there by reducing the operational cost.

https://icar-nrri.in/patent-granted-for-invention-of-alternate-energy-light-trap/

Innovation

Product developed and marketed by the start-up ishaving the following features and benefits for the customer.

Features: Ultra Violet–A – Lighting technology to capture nymphs and adults of plants damaging Insect and Pests, microcontroller based operation auto Turn ON prior to Sunset and auto Turn OFF by 9.00 – 9.30 PM automatically, fully Solar chargeable and No Power required to operate the device. High power VU-A LED light technology. Modular in design and ease of installation at field. Portable across the crops and plantations.Height Adjustable based on the plant growth stage

Patents

Patent granted for invention of Alternate Energy Light Trap to ICAR-NRRI:

An advanced Solar based Alternate Energy Light trap (AELT) was invented by Dr. Shyamaranjan Das Mohapatra, Principal Scientist (Entomology) and Dr (Mrs) Mayabini Jena, Former Principal Scientist & Head of Crop Protection Division of ICAR-National Rice Research Institute, Cuttack and a patent application No. 341/KOL/2014 was filed by the institute in March 18, 2014. The AELT device traps several flying insects in the crop fields utilizing solar powered system (to lit the lamp at night) which is the first of its kind in India for which the patent has been granted on February 8, 2021 with Patent No. 357993.

Commercialisation

The startup developed crops eco friendly pest management device and traps for Field crops, Horticultural and plantation crops. Models – Solar LED light trap, Timer Insect light trap, Electronic LED Light trap. Other Products include UV treated RE-USABLE STICKY TRAP (Yellow / Blue), Bio fertilizers, Bio pesticide and Plant Growth Promoters.

https://www.safsorganic.in/about.html

Healthcare

1. AI based Breast Cancer detection – NIRAMAI Health Analytix, Bangalore
2. COVIHOME RNA test kit – Prof Shiv Govind Singh, IITH,
3. DNA Clean-up kit – Procyto Labs Pvt. Ltd, Bhubaneswar, Odisha,
4. Dialysis-grade membranes – Prof. Jayesh Bellare, IITB
5. Germicidal fabric technology – Praveen Kumar Vemula Lab, inStem, Bangalore
6. Insect Venom derived Anti-aging Peptide for Dermal Application – Prof. S Ramaswamy Lab, inStem, Bangalore
7. Jaipur Belt – Exoskeleton – Newndra Innovations, Jaipur
8. Lab-on-chip, Microfluidic chips – Prof Anil Prabhakar, IITM
9. Live cell imaging – Fluorescent Bioprobes Pvt Ltd, Goa
10. mRNA Covid-19 vaccine – Gennova Biopharmaceuticals Limited, Pune
11. Magnetic Resonance Imaging (MRI) Scanner – Voxelgrids Innovations Pvt Ltd, Bangalore
12. Microneedles for painless injections – Suman Pahal, inStem, Bangalore
13. Phototherapy device for neonatal Jaundice – Heamc Healthcare, Hyderabad
14. Portable inverted microscope – Prof. Debjani Paul, IIT Bombay

15. Protonated Bio-adhesive Polymer technology (PBT-Axio Biosolutions, Bangalore

16. Poorti, Post-Mastectomy Kit – Aarna Biomedical Products, Faridabad

17. Robotic Surgery – SS Innovations, Gurugram

18. Swasa – Respiratory Healthcare – Salcit Technologies, Hyderabad

19. ToucHb – A Non-invasive Aaemia Screener – Biosense Technologies Pvt. Ltd., Bhiwandi, Maharashtra

20. Video Laryngoscope – Dr. Kumaresh Krishnamoorthy, Bangalore

21. Visual medical data with AI – SigTuple Technologies Pvt. Ltd, Bangalore

22. Voice Prosthesis – inaumation medical devices, Bangalore

23. Wearable EEG device – Neuphony, Noida

AI Based Breast Cancer Detection – NIRAMAI Health Analytix, Bangalore

Dr. Geetha Manjunath is the Founder, CEO and CTO of NIRAMAI Health Analytix, and has led the company to develop a breakthrough artificial-intelligence based test for detecting early stage breast cancer in a non-invasive radiation-free manner. Geetha is a Computer Scientist with a PhD from Indian Institute of Science and management education from Kellogg's Chicago. She has over 25 years of experience in IT innovation and has proposed and led multiple AI projects at Xerox Research and Hewlett Packard Labs. Before starting NIRAMAI, Geetha was the Lab Director for Data Analytics Research at Xerox.

Geetha has received many international and national recognitions for her innovations and entrepreneurial work, including CSI Gold Medal, BIRAC WinER Award 2018 and is also on the Forbes List of

Top 20 Self-Made Women 2020. She was awarded the Accenture Vahini Innovator of the Year Award from Economic Times and Women Entrepreneur of the Year 2020 by BioSpectrum India. Geetha is also a coauthor of book "Moving to the Cloud" and an innovator with 20 US patents and more pending grant.

https://www.linkedin.com/in/geetha-manjunath-82b8058/

Technology

A thermography machine uses an infrared camera to detect temperature differences within the breast tissues. During thermogram screening, the machine never touches the patient's body. On the thermogram image, "hot spots" appear in red compared to surrounding tissues that appear in yellow, green or blue.

Innovation

NIRAMAI breast cancer screening test, Thermalytix, is a computer aided diagnostic engine that is powered by Artificial Intelligence. The solution uses a high resolution thermal sensing device and a cloud hosted analytics solution for analysing the thermal images for reliable, early and accurate breast cancer screening. Results of multiple clinical studies comparing Thermalytix with current standard of care have been published in peer-reviewed conferences/journals. The results from these clinical trials indicate very high accuracy of Thermalytixand that is non-inferior to X-Ray Mammography in general, and 25% better sensitivity than mammography in women with dense breasts.

https://www.thelancet.com/journals/lanonc/article/PIIS1470-2045(22)00419-3/fulltext

Patents

The innovative methods used in NIRMAI test have led to 32 Granted Patents, including 11 Granted US patents, 11 granted Indian patents, and rest granted in Europe, Japan, Singapore, China and Canada.

System and method for adaptive positioning of a subject for capturing a thermal image Patent number: 11534069, 2022, Inventors: Siva Teja Kakileti, Geetha Manjunath, Himanshu J. Madhu

Software interface tool for breast cancer screening, Patent number: 10055542, 2018, Inventors: Krithika Venkataramani, Lalit Keshav Mestha, Michael P. Kehoe, Geetha Manjunath

Commercialization

https://www.niramai.com/home-screening/

Thermalytix cancer screening test has been used by more than 100,000 women in 150+ hospitals/diagnostic center as well as 5000+ screening camps in India. The product is commercially available in India, UAE, Kenya, Philippines, Sweden, Bulgaria and Turkey. Niramai Thermalytix test has obtained CE Mark for all European countries and regulatory clearance in the above countries. Niramai Quality Management Processes are certified to be compliant with ISO 13485 and MDSAP. They follow good clinical practices, comply with information security and data privacy policies, as per EU GDPR and US HIPAA requirements.

COVIHOME RNA Test Kit – Prof Shiv Govind Singh, IITH

Dr. Shiv Govind Singh is a Professor of Department of Electrical Engineering, IIT Hyderabad with PhD from IITB. *Sanni Kumar, Suryasnata Tripathy, Anupam Jyoti, Shiv Govind Singh: Recent advances in biosensors for diagnosis and detection of sepsis: A comprehensive review. Biosensors & Bioelectronics 10/2018; 124, DOI:10.1016/j.bios.2018.10.034* is one of his papers. *A low-cost microfluidic biochip for malaria diagnosis, IoT for Smarter Healthcare* are few of his research projects. Technology for Low temperature Cu-Cu bonding for 3D IC application developed by him was transferred to M/s Solidblocks Semiconductor Solutions Pvt. Ltd.

https://people.iith.ac.in/sgsingh/index.html

Technology

FDA approved Labcorp's combined home collection kit, called The Pixel, is for COVID, flu and RSV only. The FDA authorized the emergency use of the kits for detection of nucleic acid from SARS-CoV-2, influenza A and/or influenza B, and RSV, not for any other viruses or pathogens. The Alinity m Resp-4-Plex assay is a multiplex real-time reverse transcription (RT) polymerase chain reaction (PCR) test intended for the simultaneous qualitative detection and differentiation of RNA from influenza A virus (flu A), influenza B virus (flu B), Respiratory Syncytial Virus (RSV) and SARS-CoV-2 in nasal or nasopharyngeal swab specimens collected by a healthcare provider (HCP).

Opteev Technologies Inc., a pioneering technology company at the forefront of diagnostics, has filed a patent (Patent Application #63/513,007) for a revolutionary multiplex biochip for respiratory infection diagnostics. The groundbreaking polymer-based biochip offers potential to test multiple pathogens responsible for respiratory infections, including SARS-CoV-2, RSV and Influenza, and precisely identifies the specific virus or bacteria in under 1 minute. The tiny biochip can directly detect whole range of viruses in real-time in both processed & unprocessed samples such as saliva or nasal swab and has demonstrated an unprecedented accuracy rate of 99.49% with an impressive limit of detection in its analytical performance evaluation. Furthermore, the biosensor achieves fine-tuned specificity by carefully selecting specific virus-binding peptides, enabling accurate identification of target viruses in complex samples. To ensure precise and reliable virus detection, the biochip utilizes artificial intelligence to optimize the frequency range effectively mitigating the impact of interfering noise signals. Dr Biplab Pal, a product of IIT Kharagpur is Co-Founder of Opteev Technologies.

Innovation

The innovation "Revolutionizing the diagnostic AI Powered low Cost, Point of Care Electronic Testing Kit (X-HOME) Enabling Tele diagnostic and Medicine" was shortlisted by DoT, government of India for G20 delegate demonstration in the year 2023. With end stage configurability this home test kit can be used for Multi-Viral Detections like Dengue, Corona, Malaria, Cancer, Cardiac, Sepsis markers and also Toxic metal, Food spoilage. It is Validated by CCMB Hyderabad. Specificity: 98.2%, Sensitivity: 91.4%, Efficiency: 94.2%.

Patents

Indian Patent granted for A CHEMI-CAPACITIVE NON-INVASIVE SYSTEM FOR DETECTION OF AT LEAST ONE ANALYTE – patent number 432117

Commercialization

https://praanhitabiotronics.com/

Startup Praanhita Biotronics is promoted by the innovator to manufacture and market Biotronics test kit for Covid-19.

DNA Clean-Up Kit – Procyto Labs Pvt. Ltd, Bhubaneswar, Odisha

Dr Neera Singh is Founder & Director of ProCyto Labs Pvt. Ltd. With MSc in Biotechnology from Kurushetra university and PhD from National Institute for Research in Reproductive Health (ICMR) she worked in India and USA before starting her venture.

https://www.linkedin.com/in/neera-singh-phd-mba-2145ba30/

Technology

DNA clean-up, also known as magnetic beads-enabled cleanup, is the targeted at removal of small DNA fragments such as primers, adapters and dimers from a sample mixture for downstream PCR, DNA ligation/cloning, or DNA library etc. Removal of other substances, e.g. salts, proteins and enzymes etc. that are actually involved in the process of DNA extraction is called it pre-clean-up.

In a purification column, the DNA is mixed with a binding buffer. A chaotropic agent in the binding buffer denatures proteins and promotes DNA binding to the silica membrane in the column. Impurities can be removed with a simple wash step. Following the purification of the DNA, the elution buffer is used to elute the purified DNA. Using the recovered DNA, downstream applications can be performed.

https://assets.thermofisher.com/TFSAssets/LSG/manuals/MANO012939_GeneJET_NGS_Cleanup_UG.pdf

Innovation

Procyto Labs Pvt. Ltd.'s DNA clean-up kit is a fast, convenient and economical way to purify DNA fragments (50 bp – 10 Kb). In less than ten minutes, the product allows complete a rapid protocol. A PCR reaction mixture, enzyme mixture, or other reaction mixture that contains primers, dNTPs, and unincorporated labeled nucleotides is removed by this method. Furthermore, it uses a silica-based membrane technology, which facilitates easy resin manipulations and eliminates the need for toxic phenol-chloroform extractions.

Applications include High-quality sequencing, Microassay analysis, Cloning, Gene Silencing, Restriction Digestion, Enzymatic modifications, Library Construction

Patents

Removal of DNA fragments in mRNA production process – US10858647B2

Patents granted in India – https://dbtindia.gov.in/patent-granted-years-2012-2013-2014-2015

- DNA Clean-Up Kit – Procyto Labs Pvt. Ltd, Bhubaneswar, Odisha

Commercialization

https://procyto.com/products.html

This startup manufactures several products – Molecular Biology Products, Molecular Biology Teaching Kits, Bacterial Cell Division Proteins and LAMP Kits. List of products include Plasmid Isolation Kit, DNA Clean Up Kit, Gel Extraction Kit, Red Taq Master Mix (2X), Taq Master Mix (2X), Taq DNA Polymerase, 50 bp DNA Ladder, 100 bp DNA Ladder, 1 kb DNA Ladder. Molecular Biology Teaching kits include PCR, Agarose Gel Electrophoresis, SDS-PAGE, Restriction Digestion, DNA Ligation. Loop Mediated Isothermal Amplification based diagnostic kit for the early detection of neonatal sepsis is under development.

Dialysis-Grade Membranes – Prof. Jayesh Bellare, IITB Mumbai

Dr. Jayesh R. Bellare is a full time Professor at the Department of Chemical Engineering, IIT-Mumbai. He did B.Tech. in Chemical engineering from IIT-Mumbai, earned his Ph.D. in Chemical Engineering and Materials Science from the University of Minnesota, Minneapolis, USA. He was a visiting researcher at the Department of Chemical Engineering, Technion Israel Institute of Technology, Haifa, Israel. He was a post-doctoral fellow in Mathematics and in Polymer Science & Engineering at the University of Massachusetts, Amherst, USA and in Materials Science and Engineering at MIT, Cambridge, USA. He has several international publications, conference presentations and patents.

https://www.che.iitb.ac.in/web/faculty/jb/biodata/biodata.html

Technology

Hemodialysis is an extra-corporeal process in which the blood is cleansed via removal of uremic retention products by a semi-permeable membrane. Traditionally, dialysis membranes have been broadly classified on the basis of their composition (cellulosic or non-cellulosic) and water permeability (low-flux or high-flux). However, advances in materials technology and polymer chemistry have led to the development of membranes with specific characteristics and refined properties that mandate a reconsideration of traditional membrane classification systems.

Innovation

https://youtu.be/dzjsPEiaFeI

Hollow fiber membrane for biomedical application:

End stage renal disease (ESRD) indicates the complete failure of kidney functions, where kidneys can no longer remove wastes, concentrate urine and regulate many other important body functions. Hemodialysis is one the most effective and widely used mode to regulate the kidney functions artificially. The hemodialyzer cartridge (disposable blood filter) is the key component of this treatment technology and is currently imported. At the Department of Chemical Engineering, the team has successfully developed an indigenous and low-cost technology for continuous pilot-scale production of hollow fiber membranes to be used in hemodialysis and built prototype microdialyzer. The formulated special anti-oxidative composite Polysulfone/ vitamin E TPGS membrane material improves the performance in both separation and bio-compatibility front. This will permit faster treatment, lesser side reactions and could spur novel devices like portable/ wearable dialyzers. Along with these the HFM technology was also used in making a step towards bioartificial organs like bioartificial liver and bioartificial pancreas.

Patents

Bio-Artificial PANCREAS, Bellare Jayesh | Teotia Rohit Satvir | Singh Atul Kumar | Verma Surendra Kumar | Kadam Sachin, IIT-BOMBAY | Krishna Institute of Medical Sciences | Department of Biotechnology, Government of India, Patent No. IN201623023433A

Coated Hollow Fiber Membrane Material as a Substrate for Enhanced Liver Cell Attachment and a Process for manufacturing the same, Bellare Jayesh | Verma Surendra Kumar | Singh Atul Kumar | Modi Akshay | Teotia Rohit S. IIT-B | Department of Biotechnology, Government of India, Patent No. IN201721012545A

https://iitb.irins.org/profile/43034

Commercialization

Animal trails are underway for Indigenous membrane cartridges for hemodialysis: composition of dialysis-grade membranes developed at low-cost; excellent compatibility with human blood; high uremic toxins removal efficiency and high permeation flux with minimal side reactions.

First indigenous Hemodialysis Machine in India was developed by Renalyx, a Bangalore based company with whom Dr. Prakash Keshaviah collaborated as a consultant in developing the machine. https://www.renalyx.com/

Germicidal Fabric Technology – Praveen Kumar Vemula Lab, InStem, Bangalore

Dr Praveen Kumar Vemula is Principal Investigator at the Institute for Stem Cell Science and Regenerative Medicine (inStem), Bangalore. After graduation and post-graduation in Osmania university, had his PhD from IISc-Bangalore in Nano materials and was a postdoctoral fellow at the Harvard Medical School before returning to India. He is currently a Principal Investigator and Ramalingaswami Fellow at inStem.

https://www.linkedin.com/in/praveen-kumar-vemula-55717116/

http://praveenlab.net/

Technology

A mask that disinfects itself at the touch of a button has been developed by scientists at Zurich University of Applied Sciences

(ZHAW) and Swiss research and development company Osmotex AG. The Ray® Osmotex Active Sterilising Face Mask® uses Osmotex technology, based on Osmotex's core commercialized technology for electronically controlled moisture migration in fabrics via an electro-osmotic and electro-chemical process. DiOX®, a global producer of textile chemistries and a division of LiquidNano™, has launched an anti-viral finish called D4, a mechanical nano-scale coating that uses silica quaternary salts (QUATS). The chemical kills the virus on contact by piercing the outer cell membrane with millions of microscopic spikes. A nanoscale zinc treatment is the key to the LOG3 anti-viral mask from Claros Technologies, St. Paul, Minnesota, a spinoff from the University of Minnesota. HeiQ Materials AG, a global leader in textile and materials innovation based in Switzerland, uses copper in their HeiQ MetalliQ anti-viral surgical mask.

Innovation

The group of Praveen Vemula (inStem) has developed a proprietary germicidal-molecule that can be covalently attached to the cotton fabric (any type including household cotton). This fabric can be stitched into PPE such as a face mask. It has been demonstrated that this germicidal molecule can be used on clothes and fabric of any kind to deactivate various infectious microbes including Gram positive and Gram negative bacteria and enveloped viruses even.

inStem's Vemula along with colleagues from the National Centre for Biological Sciences, harnessed the antimicrobial powers of quaternary ammonium salts to attack the novel coronavirus. These salts are membrane disruptors, which means they could work against all viruses that feature a lipid membrane envelope, like SARS-CoV-2. The salts contain positively charged nitrogen that can interact with negatively charged ions on virus membranes, as well as greasy hydrocarbon tails that can poke into and disrupt the membranes. Vemula's lab has impregnated cotton fiber with the best performing quaternary ammonium salt.

Patents

https://www.ccamp.res.in/ott-patents

Patents that Describe Antimicrobial Masks: https://www.ncbi.nlm.nih.gov/pmc/articles/PMC7877530/

Commercialization

The fabric retains germicidal property for at-least up to 45 wash cycles and therefore overcomes the drawback of disposable PPEs. It is highly beneficial for hospitals as they require washable and re-usable masks, protective gears, coats, bodysuits, equipment and other surfaces. This G-Fab technology has been licensed to Aditya Birla Pvt. Ltd., which is used for their anti-viral mask and athleisure products. These are manufactured under Van Heusen brand as facemasks with G99 antiviral, ISO 18184 protocols,

https://www.ccamp.res.in/ott-Licenses

https://www.abfrl.com/docs/media/press_release/Van-Heusen-collaborates-with-Color-Threads-Inc-to-launch-inStems-G-Fab-Innovative-Technology-in-India.pdf

Insect Venom Derived Anti-Aging Peptide for Dermal Application – S. Ramaswamy Lab, InStem

Ramaswamy S is an Indian-American structural biologist of Indian origin. He is currently professor of biological sciences, professor at the Weldon School of Biomedical Engineering and director of the Bindley Bioscience Center at Purdue University. Ramaswamy S also held the founding dean's position at inStem, founding CEO of Center for Cellular and molecular platforms (C-CAMP), Bangalore – Biocluster. Ram S obtained his Ph.D. in molecular biophysics from the Indian Institute of Science (IISc) and became a post-doctoral fellow at the Swedish University of Agricultural Sciences (SLU). His research on cockroach protein gain lot of popularity in the scientific community and the media.

https://en.wikipedia.org/wiki/Ramaswamy_S

Technology

Bee venom (BV) is a typical toxin secreted by stingers of honeybee workers. Facial wrinkles are a small crease in the skin, especially the face, which is a natural manifestation of ageing. The skin is the human body's largest organ and is that which is most shown. The reduction in collagen production explains the creation of wrinkles and the reduction of skin flexibility. The need for effective remedies to combat facial wrinkles has contributed to a vast number of products to improve skin appearance. Many cosmeceuticals have been combined with many naturally derived ingredients, and BV is one of them. BV serum has been reported to cease facial wrinkles by clinically decreasing the total area of the wrinkles, count, and size. Electric stimulation is the main method for bee venom collection is by stimulating bees with an electrical current as first described by Markovic and Mollnar (1954) and thereafter by Palmer and others

Innovation

A non-toxic, anti-inflammatory molecule from insect venom was known to have cosmetic benefits for human skin, particularly in improving aging skin. Insect venom products have been isolated and used to formulate a dermal cream. The topical application of the cream reduces wrinkle formation associated with aging by aiding in improving the elasticity of the skin.

Bee Venom helps break down aged cells and molecules and supports blood circulation, which stimulates cell regeneration and collagen formation, resulting in fresher, younger and healthier looking skin. Melectin was the first peptide identified in the solitary bee venom. It is a cationic amphipathic peptide that contains rich hydrophobic and basic amino acid residues and a proline.

Patents

There are many patents worldwide like Cosmetic composition containing bee venom or extracts of the same from Korea – https://patents.google.com/patent/KR20100118629A/en

Technological process of extracting bee venom, China – https://patents.google.com/patent/CN1416827A/en

Dr Nikolai Nikolaev patented a modernized technology of bee venom collection both in Russia and New Zealand (NZ patent #329585).

Commercialization

This technology from inStem is on offer for licensing. There are many commercial products in Indian market based on Beevenom like https://wildfernsindia.com/collections/bee-venom

Jaipur Belt – Ecoskelton – Newndra Innovations, Jaipur

Ganesh Ram Jangir engineering graduate from Jaipur Engineering College and Research Center is CEO & CTO of Newndra Innovations. A serial inventor and a passionate techno-entrepreneur. Dr Anil Jain Head of the dept. at Dr. P.K. Sethi Rehab Centre, Santokba Durlabhji Hospital (Jaipur Foot Centre) is the Chief Medical Adviser.

https://www.linkedin.com/in/ganesh-ram-jangir-a0876324/

Technology

Musculoskeletal disorders (MSD) are common among soldiers and constitute the most common reason for discontinuing military service within different military populations worldwide. The risk of back problem, musculoskeletal injury & fatigue among soldiers in highest to range of demanding tasks. NewndraX is an efficient, unpowered, lightweight, affordable, validated, indigenous and patented exoskeleton. It assists soldiers full body including spine, waist, hands, legs, arms, knees shoulders in Indian defence or for people who are working in musculoskeletal injury prone areas such as soldiers, industrial workers, the people have to work in a back-bent position or have to repeatedly or continuously bend their back or have spine and back problems like Kyposis, Spondylitis, Slip-Disk, due to work load, age life style. NewndraX is to be worn on the shoulders and around the waist. It works on the fundamental of mechanics and energy conservation. It stores the work done by gravity in its propriety hinge mechanism. The same energy used to assist the human body during bend up or continued assistance during bending position.

Innovation

On-body personal lift-assist devices (OBPLAD), via the use of passive elastic elements, are believed to offload the muscles of the spine while performing a lift, thereby delaying their fatigue, minimizing the internal reactionary force, and potentially minimizing the risk of injury. The Jaipur Belt is a newly developed OBPLAD in India. study was to analyse the effect of the Jaipur Belt on trunk muscle activity while performing a single lift task in industrial settings. In a research study a total of 100 subjects involved in manual material handling across various industrial settings were recruited for the study. The electromyography activity of bilateral rectus abdominis, transverse abdominis, quadratus lumborum, and erector spinae were recorded using surface electrodes, while the subjects performed a single lift task under two test conditions: a) wearing the Jaipur Belt, and b) without the OBPLAD. The results had shown a marked reduction in the electrical activity of all the studied muscles (9.5%–49.8%), when the lifting was performed with the Jaipur Belt on. The observed reduction in muscle activation while using the Jaipur Belt could imply a reduction in the internal muscle forces, as well as reactive forces generated at the spine, and could be beneficial in prevention of musculoskeletal disorders of the spine.

Shyam Krishnan K, Nayak MM, Eapen C. et al. The effect of an on-body personal lift-assist device (Jaipur Belt) on spine kinetics during a functional lift task. J Public Health (Berl.) (2023). https://doi.org/10.1007/s10389-023-01948-8

Jaipur Belts, an unpowered and lightweight exoskeleton, which reduces the load on the spine by over 50 percent.

Video – https://youtu.be/eZz7Jqw1yjI

Patents

Ganesh has 11 granted patents in India & internationally including USA, Russia, Europe (EPO), China etc.

Belt system for body support-Patent number: 10376402, granted in 2019

Belt system for spine & waist support – Patent number: D784545, granted in 2017

An Improved Belt System for Body Support – Publication number: 20160317340, granted in 2016

Commercialisation

The product is available in the market at Rs 80,000/ –

https://www.newndra.com/product/jaipurbelt/

Lab-on-Chip, Microfluidic Chips – Prof Anil Prabhakar, IITM

Dr Anil Prabhakar, Professor in IIT Madras, Electrical Engineering, received my PhD in 1997 from Carnegie Mellon University, with a dissertation on the Non-linear Spin-wave Optical Interactions. At IITM he is engaged across multiple laboratories that work on quantum technologies, fibre lasers and opto-fluidics. He is Founder of QuNu Labs, incubated by IITM, an earlier startup, Unilumen Photonics that focused on fibre lasers was acquired by Jiva Sciences. He is also currently the Director of Yali Mobility and Enability Foundation, companies that focus on rehabilitation engineering.

https://publications.iitm.ac.in/researcher/a-prabhakar

Shri Ikram Khan, a scientist from IIT-Madras and founder of ISMO Bio-Photonics developed a low-cost 3D printing system that creates mini brain organoids. https://www.linkedin.com/in/ikram0/

Technology

Spin-based bioreactors grow organoids efficiently but they cannot examine the organoids in detail as it grows. Additionally, it involves physical transferring of organoids to a separate chamber for imaging, causing perturbation and contamination, which can affect the results. The present invention discloses a low-cost 3D printed microfluidic bioreactor was developed which supports simultaneous live organoid imaging and longtime organoid growth with drug delivery support.

Innovation

The primary object of the invention is to provide a novel, compact and simple system for providing a live cell growth culture platform and simultaneously imaging the non-perturbed live cells growing in the microfluidic chip by using an optically transparent glass disk window. Another objective of the present invention is to provide a cost-effective 3D printed or moulded microfluidic chip for imaging each single cell growing in the chip without physical transferring of cells to prevent perturbation and contamination. Advantages are: low cost, live organoid imaging, tracking of neuron/cells on-chip

Patents

https://sites.google.com/ee.iitm.ac.in/anilprabhakar/research/patents

Commercialisation

https://ismobiophotonics.com/

The technology was transferred to ISMO Bio-Photonics Private Limited, a startup incubated at IIT Madras, Bio-Incubator working on developing products like microfluidic bio-reactors, microfluidic accessories, fiber laser, sensing.

The startup announced *groundbreaking 3D organ on a chip technology at ISMO Bio-Photonics, revolutionizing biomedical research.* The cutting-edge technology offers a more accurate and ethical alternative to animal trials, with significant benefits for both the scientific community and pharmaceutical industry. Approximately 90% of drugs fail during human trials, resulting in billions of dollars in losses and the sacrifice of countless animal lives. The 3D organ on a chip technology aims to address this challenge, providing a reliable solution and cost-effective.

To learn more about how the technology revolutionized pre-clinical trials and personalized drug screening, a mail may be sent to: ikram@ismobiophotonics.com .

https://www.thebetterindia.com/252994/iit-madras-scientist-research-growing-tiny-brain-research-organoid-tissue-development-mit-ros174/

Live Cell Imaging – Fluorescent Bioprobes Pvt Ltd, Goa

Nivedita Sarkar is Co-Founder-Director, Fluorescent Bioprobes Pvt. Ltd. She did her doctoral research from Chittaranjan National Cancer Institute, Kolkata, as a DST Women Scientist A. The startup is supported by BITS Pilani and currently incubated at BGIIES, BITS Goa. Subhadeep Banerjee, Chemistry Associate Professor at BITS-Pilani Goa is co-founder director. He is a mentor to researchers in the field of organic chemistry of fluorescent molecules.

Technology

Fluorescent Boprobes are compounds that absorb light at a given wavelength and emit light at a higher wavelength, producing fluorescence in various colors. Their use in biological labeling and staining began as early as the 1930s, and the research community has come a long way since then. Biologists now have at their disposal a plethora of fluorescent bioprobes with different colors, structural properties and functions. They are employed in a wide range of research applications. These include: Antibody labels to indicate the presence of a target antigen in a sample via immunofluorescence, reporter molecules when introducing a gene construct into a cell, stains for the quantitative measurement of nucleic acids, and indicators of cell health. Biological fluorophores are large molecules, typically fluorescent proteins, the most famous of all being GFP (Green Fluorescent Protein). DNA, which falls into this category, does not display intrinsic fluorescence but can be used as a biotag once coupled to a fluorophore.

Innovation

Fluorescent molecular probes are very powerful tools that have been generally applied in cell imaging in the research fields of biology, pathology, pharmacology, biochemistry, and medical science. In the last couple of decades, numerous molecular probes endowed with high specificity to particular organelles have been designed to illustrate intracellular images in more detail at the subcellular level. Nowadays, the development of cell biology has enabled the investigation process to go deeply into cells, even at the molecular level. Therefore, probes that can sketch a particular organelle's location while responding to certain parameters to evaluate intracellular bioprocesses are under urgent demand.

The stratup is developing green biochemical probes for in vitro cell imaging. 3D imaging of live HeLa cells multiplexed with our Mandovi Green 306 and commercial TMRE.

Patents

BACKGROUND-FREE FLUORESCENT PROBES FOR LIVE CELL IMAGING, Singapore – https://patents.google.com/patent/WO2017078623A1/en

Papers of Nivedita Sarkar – https://www.researchgate.net/profile/Nivedita-Sarkar-2

Papers of Dr Sandeep – https://bits-pilani.irins.org/profile/229994

Commercialisation

https://www.linkedin.com/company/fluoresight/people/

A Chemtech based startup is creating the next generation bioimaging probes

mRNA Covid-19 Vaccine – Dr. Sanjay Singh, Gennova Biopharmaceuticals Limited, Pune

Dr. Sanjay Singh holds a PhD degree in Biochemistry from Central Drug Research Institute (CDRI), Lucknow, India. Before joining Gennova, he headed the Antigen Research Section at the Malaria Vaccine Development Unit of the National Institutes of Allergy and Infectious Diseases (NIAID), NIH, USA. His scientific research work earned him many international awards: In 1996, Dr. Singh received the much-coveted Research Fellowship award from WHO TDR, World Health Organization Tropical Disease Research. While he was working at the National Institutes of Health (NIH), in the USA, he received awards from the United States Department of Health and Human Services, HHS, for

FIVE consecutive years for scientific excellence in recognition of his work

Technology

mRNA can be used to create practically any protein in the body: antigen against which antibodies can be developed, growth factors, enzymes for rare diseases, host-specific proteins, etc. The establishment of the 'mRNA-based platform technology' could be an important tool for developing variant-proof, safe and effective vaccines. mRNA vaccines do not contain live virus and carry no risk of causing disease in the vaccinated person thus making it suitable for people with compromised immune systems. mRNA-based vaccines are the ideal choice because of their rapid development and production timeline. mRNA vaccines are considered safe as mRNA is noninfectious, non-integrating in nature, and is degraded by standard cellular mechanisms. They are highly efficacious because of their inherent capability of being translated into proteins. Additionally, mRNA vaccines are fully synthetic and do not require a host for growth, e.g., eggs or bacteria. Therefore, they can be quickly manufactured in a cost effective manner under cGMP conditions to ensure their "availability" and "accessibility" for mass vaccination on a sustainable basis. These vaccines are safe as mRNA is non-infectious, non – integrating in nature, and degraded by normal cellular mechanisms.

Innovation

Gennova has developed two mRNA-based vaccines against COVID-19, GEMCOVAC®-19 and GEMCOVAC®-OM. GEMCOVAC®-OM has recently received Emergency Use Authorization (EUA) as a single dose booster specifically targeting the Omicron strain. Notably, individuals who have previously received primary immunization with either COVISHIELD™ or COVAXIN® can safely receive GEMCOVAC®-OM as a booster after a four-month interval. The GEMCOVAC® vaccines overcome the limitations associated with the currently approved mRNA vaccines. The currently approved mRNA vaccines have certain inherent limitations like: Ultra-low temperature logistics, Ease of Manufacturing, Supply of raw materials, Scalability, Technology transfer

GEMCOVAC® is stable at 2 – 8 °C and can be considered superior in terms of deployability in developing nations (especially LMICs) compared to other approved mRNA vaccines. In GEMCOVAC®, the mRNA is adsorbed on the surface of the nano-lipid emulsion (as opposed to it being entrapped in other mRNA vaccines using NLPs), thereby easing manufacturability and minimizing losses.

Patents

The product patent: Pharmaceutical compositions of Tenecteplase is granted in the US, India, Japan, Australia, New Zealand, Mexico, Indonesia, 8 countries of Eurasia, and 18 countries of Europe. Lyophilized composition of Pegaspargase is granted in India. It is under examination in other countries.

The process patent: A novel purification process for isolation and commercial production of recombinant Tenecteplase is granted in the USA, Columbia, and 18 countries of Europe. It is under examination in other countries. The process patent – A novel process for purification of recombinant human filgrastim is granted in the USA, India, New Zealand, Australia, and Indonesia. It is under examination in other countries.

Commercialisation

https://gennova.bio/gemcovac-19-2/

COVID-19 Vaccines Authorized for Emergency Use or FDA-Approved: Pfizer-BioNTech COVID-19 Vaccine, Bivalent, Moderna COVID-19 Vaccine, Bivalent, Novavax COVID-19 Vaccine, Adjuvanted.

Magnetic Resonance Imaging (MRI) Scanner – Voxelgrids Innovations Pvt Ltd, Bangalore

Arjun Arunachalam is the Founder and CEO of the company, studied at the University of Wisconsin-Madison from where he received his MS and PhD degrees. From 2006-2008, he worked at the GE Global Research Center, Niskayuna, NY. Joined IIT-B as a faculty in EE and continued to work in the field of MRI. While in Singapore, Arjun received a Grant from Spring Singapore for developing MRI related intellectual property. A small test scanner platform for MRI was built from this grant for initial proof of concept tests

https://www.linkedin.com/in/arjun-arunachalam-6524029/

Technology

MRI is usually traced back to the discovery, in the 1930s and 1940s, of the underlying physical phenomenon known as nuclear magnetic resonance (NMR). Lauterbur's technique (which involved varying the magnetic field applied to the subject) proved more feasible and in 2003, Lauterbur shared a Nobel Prize with Peter Mansfield.

Ministry of Electronics and Information Technology (MeitY), Government of India launched SCAN ERA (SWADESHI CHUMBAKIYA ANUNAD CHITRAN – EK RASHTRIYA ABHIYAN) – a National Mission program for indigenous development of MRI as a part of the Make in India initiative. (https://www.indianradiologist.com/index.php/review/made-in-india-mri). Scientists at New Delhi's Inter-University Accelerator Centre (IUAC), led by its director and Allahabad University's adjunct professor, Prof Avinash Chandra Pandey, have successfully developed India's first superconducting magnet system used in MRI machines for whole-body clinical scanner.

Innovation

The first MRI product Voxelgrids has developed and deployed is a compact, lightweight, full body 1.5 Tesla MRI scanner that is capable of being used in both stationary and mobile configurations. First, the team invented an imaging software technology that enables the use of next generation compact, inexpensive, lightweight and completely liquid helium-free MRI magnets. Then they combined these next-generation magnets with smaller, faster gradient coils to exceed the performance of current state-of-the-art scanners. Lastly, they invented novel imaging techniques that enhance the MRI scan speeds with potential applications in cardiac and real-time imaging. The results are evident for all to see. Compared to standard MRI scanners, the 1.5 Tesla whole-body scanner with the sensible structured imaging protocols, weighs 2.3 tons (as opposed to the regular 4-6 ton scanner), making it lightweight and portable. It costs approximately Rs. 3.5 crore, as opposed to the usual Rs. 5 to Rs. 8.5 crore, and cuts the cost per scan by 60%. It also scans three to four times faster, consumes less power and reduces the cost of switching 'on' and 'off'.

Patents

https://patents.justia.com/inventor/arjun-arunachalam

Method for constructing image from MRI data, Patent number: 10663551,2020, Construction of diagnostic images from MRI data acquired in an inhomogeneous polarizing magnetic field, Patent number: 10295642,2019, Method for Constructing Image from MRI Data, Publication number: 20180038932,2018, CONSTRUCTION OF DIAGNOSTIC IMAGES FROM MRI DATA ACQUIRED IN AN INHOMOGENEOUS POLARIZING MAGNETIC FIELD, Publication number: 20170363703, 2017, Method and system for rapid MRI acquisition using tailored signal excitation modules ()Patent number: 9684047, 2017, Method and System for Rapid MRI Acquisition Using Tailored Signal Excitation Modules (RATE), Publication number: 20140091798, 2014

Commercialisation

https://www.voxelgrids.com/products/

The Voxelgrids journey eventually started under FISE (Foundation for Innovation and Social Entrepreneurship) of Tata Trust. Voxelgrids team worked as FISE employees and developed a proto-MRI scanner. This prototype was deployed in mid-2017 at The Sathya Sai Institute of Higher Medical Sciences, Bengaluru, under an MoU signed between the two parties. In mid-2019, Voxelgrids received a significant grant from BIRAC for development of indigenous cryogenic magnet and MRI technologies. The company was previously awarded a grant by the United States-India Science & Technology Endowment Fund as well.

Microneedles for Painless Injections – Suman Pahal, Vemula Lab at InStem

Dr Suman Pahal is young Scientist at inStem (https://www.linkedin.com/in/suman-pahal-a7b99524/). After MTech from Guru Jambheshwar University, She earned PhD from IISc, Bangalore in Nano Engineering.

She worked on Microneedles projects:

Single Step Fabrication of Hollow Microneedles and an Experimental Package for Controlled Drug Delivery,

Methotrexate delivering microneedle patches for improved therapeutic efficacy in treatment of rheumatoid arthritis and holds relevant patents.

Technology

Microneedles (MNs) have been explored as a medium of physical enhancement of transdermal drug delivery for several years. Originally, the purpose of this technique was to facilitate drugs in overcoming the stratum corneum layer of skin, which is a formidable barrier that is almost impermeable for large and hydrophilic molecules. In the last 10 years, due to advancements in design engineering and silicon microfabrication technology, several new MNs designs have been developed for a variety of applications

Dissolvable microneedles (DMNs) consist of microscopic polymeric needles confining the drug formulations within their matrix. Once these DMNs are inserted into the skin, the matrix degradation is facilitated by the aqueous environment inside the skin and leading to release of the drug cargo. On-demand microneedle devices with drug release by external trigger – these active trigger mechanisms make development of wearable devices with drug reservoirs and closed loop feedback control systems possible.

Innovation

Drug delivery using hollow microneedles is the most preferred method for delivering generic transdermal drugs in the clinical setup. The needle tip must be extremely short as the drug is administered to sub-millimeter depths. Also, they need to be sharp enough to pierce through the skin with minimal skin flexing. There are multiple challenges in engineering a tip profile that is short and sharp at the same time. Stainless steel (SS) hypodermic needles with the lancet tip profile are ubiquitous in subcutaneous and intramuscular injections. They have long bevel lengths that make them inappropriate as microneedles. Thus, designing a unique tip profile and developing the manufacturing technology for microneedle applications are necessary.

Patents

Single-step molding process for fabrication of hollow microneedle array Single-step molding process for fabrication of hollow microneedle array IPP 202241006792 · Filed Feb 8, 2022IPP 202241006792 · Filed Feb 8, 2022

Hollow microneedle device Hollow microneedle device IPP 201941050005 · Filed Dec 4, 2019IPP 201941050005 · Filed Dec 4, 2019

Master mold assembly for fabrication of microneedles Master mold assembly for fabrication of microneedles IN 201941019470 · Filed May 1, 2019

Commercialisation

Technology available for transfer. Manufacturing is described in the paper – Single step fabrication of hollow microneedles and an experimental package for controlled drug delivery:

https://www.sciencedirect.com/science/article/abs/pii/S0378517322011012?via%3Dihub

Scientists at Hyderabad campus of Birla Institute of Technology and Science (BITS) Pilani have developed a microneedle patch for drug delivery using a biopolymer – zein. The research team included Dr. Venkata Vamsi Krishna Venuganti, Shubhmita Bhatnagar, Sumeet Rajesh Chawla, Onkar Prakash Kulkari, Pooja Kumari and Srijanaki Paravastu Pattarabhiran.

Phototherapy Device for Neonatal Jaundice – Heamac Healthcare Pvt. Ltd., Hyderabad

Prasad Muddam is Founder, CEO and Chief Designer at HeaMac, a startup incubated at IITH. He is an industrial Designer from MIT Institute of Design, Pune, India, worked with various big Companies of the medical device industry for over a decade designing and developing biomedical products and medical devices. Started entrepreneurial journey with the bio design fellowship at CfHE, IIT Hyderabad. CfHE was established since 2016 andwe have graduated 3 cohorts of entrepreneurs and the fourth batch is currently running. Seven start-ups are incubated out of the program into CfHE at IIT-H: NemoCare, BeAble, Kvayat, Haemac, AeroBiosys, ChemiOptic pct ltd, Jivika Solutions Pvt Ltd. All the start-ups have completed their product prototype and have won BIRAC start up grants for their product development. Prof Renu John heads the team at IITH. Akitha kolloju is co-founder and Chief Technology

Officer. She had Master's degree focused in Biomedical/Medical Engineering from Osmania University.

https://www.linkedin.com/in/prasadmuddam/

https://cfhe.org.in/

Technology

Most neonates, term and preterm, will have elevated levels of unconjugated bilirubin and some amount of jaundice during the first one to two weeks of life due to increased levels of unconjugated bilirubin with transient impaired excretion, which is normal in this age group. This condition is particularly prevalent in preterm babies and, if the levels of unconjugated bilirubin are very high and left untreated, may lead to irreversible neurologic damage known as kernicterus. Phototherapy treats unconjugated hyperbilirubinemia that exceeds safe levels. These levels are based on day of life and risk factors and typically occur within the first one to two weeks of life. Treatment with blue light phototherapy is necessary to prevent morbidity and mortality from dangerous levels of neonatal jaundice. The blue light is absorbed by bilirubin, which is then broken down in the blood, allowing the infant to excrete the excess bilirubin before it can accumulate and cause permanent brain damage (kernicterus) or death. Jaundice is preventable and treatable; however, kernicterus is permanent and /*irreversible, resulting in life-long disability.

Innovation

Present phototherapy apparatuses for infant phototherapy are crude apparatuses, typically comprising a light bar or light generating surface suspended directly above the infant, or above the infant but not directly above, with the light generating surface angled towards the infant, disposed beneath a glass surface on which the infant has been placed and being angled in an upward direction ˙˙ so that emitted radiations from the light generating surface is directed towards the infant. Such apparatuses are bulky, immoveable and unwieldy, and do not offer solutions that allow incorporation into incubators (which are typically small in size), or which allow the phototherapy apparatus to be operated simultaneously with other clinical apparatuses – such as radiant warmers etc.

The startup developed a compact, phototherapy device that is capable of illuminating phototherapy light from multiple angles on infant, and which angles can be altered or configured dynamically. Additionally this device can regulate and control various phototherapy parameters including positioning of the phototherapy illumination sources and intensity of the illumination in response to feedback regarding the neonatal bilirubin concentration, and to provide optimum irradiance required for that specific condition of a neonate.

Patents

NEONATAL PHOTOTHERAPY DEVICE – Design Patent 370353-001, 2023

Phototherapy system, apparatus and kitPhototherapy system, apparatus and kit 425250, 2023

An automated system and non-invasive method for assistive neonatal diagnostic monitoring. WO2021186418A1, 2021-

https://patents.google.com/patent/WO2021186418A1/en?inventor=Prasad+MUDDAM

Phototherapy system, apparatus, and kit – https://patents.google.com/patent/CA3105550A1/en?inventor=Prasad+MUDDAM

Commercialisation

The product is commercialized and has received several awards.

https://heamac.com/

Portable Inverted Microscope – Prof. Debjani Paul, IIT Bombay

Dr. Debjani Paul is Professor in-charge, Wadhwani Research Centre for Bioengineering, IIT Bombay with PhD in integrated Physics from IISc.

https://www.bio.iitb.ac.in/people/faculty/paul-d/

Technology

Microscope is an essential tool in research allowing for observation of micro-sized objects and life forms. Contemporary commercial high-resolution microscopes have long optical paths involving series of lenses and filters. Although this configuration precisely corrects for optical distortions and produces clear images, it makes modern microscopes very costly and bulky, restricting their usage to low-funded research laboratories and at remote places.

Inverted microscopes are useful for observing living cells or organisms at the bottom of a large container (e.g. a tissue culture flask) under more natural conditions than on a glass slide, as is the case with a conventional microscope. An inverted microscope is a microscope with its light source and condenser on the top, above the stage pointing down, while the objects and turret are below the stage pointing up. It was invented in 1850 by J. Lawrence Smith, a faculty member of Tulane University

Innovation

The IIT Bombay team has developed two lines of portable and battery-operated brightfield microscopes (single and variable magnification), fitted with digital displays that are capable of capturing, storing, and transmitting high-resolution colour images and videos. Both are inverted microscopes, and therefore capable of imaging slides as well as liquid samples. Their internal optical and mechanical designs have been optimised for image quality and stability. They are compact and ergonomic, making them easy to use. They can be easily carried into the field, making microscopy-based diagnostics more accessible to remote locations.

Video – https://youtu.be/Y97Il9Q6fPI

Patents

Digital inverted bright field microscopes with single and variable magnifications, Debjani Paul, Samrat, Dipendra Bhadauriya, Sathya Murthy, Indian patent application 202221003972 (filed on Jan 24, 2022).

Commercialisation

Technology is available for transfer from IITB.

Ambala has over 5,000 micro, small and medium units which are engaged in manufacturing scientific instruments. The size of the industry is around Rs 1,800 crore. Out of this, the exports are to the tune of Rs.800 crore. The cluster exports instruments to the Gulf nations, European countries. There are several manufacturers in Ambala cluster like Banbros Engineering Pvt. Ltd, Kwality Micro Scientific.

CSIO, Chandigarh also has developed Portable Multi-view Smart Microscope – (PMSM). (https://www.csio.res.in/upload/PDF/PMSM.pdf)

Protonated Bio-Adhesive Polymer Technology (PBT) – Axio Biosolutions, Bangalore

Leo Mavely is Founder & CEO of Axio Biosolutions. A graduate in Applied Bioengineering from MDH, Rohtak and mentored at Nirma Lbs. In the college he worked on developing Microfluidic devices like Micropumps, Microcentrifuges from biopolymers Poly Di-Methyl Siloxane. These devices were developed on a lab scale without using costly techniques such as Photolithography. The working model was developed with the help of Dr. Amit Astana (Mentor) as part of 5 member team. The project won awards at IIT-Roorkee Techfest 2006. Leo was featured in the list of 40 under 40 emerging business leaders by Fortune Magazine consecutively in 2016, 2017, 2018 and 2019 and in the list of 35 under 35 entrepreneurs by Entrepreneur magazine in 2020. Leo was honored as a Champion of Change by Prime minister, Shri Narendra Modi in 2017. He was the recipient of Silicon valley challenge 2014, Anjani Mashelkar Inclusive Innovation

Award 2013, CNBC Samsung Social Innovation Award 2012 and was invited speaker at Indian Science congress 2010.

https://www.linkedin.com/in/leomavely/

Technology

The concept of clamping a bleeding vessel with an instrument before tying it off is generally attributed to Galen (second century AD). This method of hemostasis was largely forgotten until it was rediscovered by the French barber-surgeon Ambroise Paré in the 16th century. QuikClot is a proprietary hemostatic technology consisting of a nonwoven material impregnated with kaolin, an inorganic mineral that activates Factor XII1 which in turn accelerates the body's natural clotting ability. This bleeding control solution creates a robust clot6,7 to control bleeding fast.

Innovation

Axio Biosolutions employs the proprietary Protonated Bio-adhesive Polymer technology (PBT) to make its biopolymer-based hemostats, drug delivery systems and scaffolds with tailorable bio-adhesive properties. The essence of PBT technology lies in maximizing the bio-adhesive properties of native chitosan without chemical modifications in its backbone. Axiostat is the first commercial product based on the PBT. Its uniform microscopic porous structure provides a unique molecular chemistry of chitosan within the matrix, which helps in retaining its positive charge for prolonged duration and even under physiological conditions. This method of bleeding control is robust enough that it works irrespective of the natural clotting factors, hence PBT is successful even in patients taking the blood thinning medications. Lastly the enhanced cationic charge provided by the PBT biopolymer also provides strong anti-microbial properties to the material and restricts entry of external bacteria into the wound site.

Patents

Mucoadhesive preparations, methods and applications thereof, Patent number: 11491107, granted 2022.

COMPOSITE DRESSINGS, MANUFACTURING METHODS AND APPLICATIONS THEREOF, Publication number: 20210252182, Granted 2021

Co-Inventor Kiran Sonaje was Head of R&D: https://www.linkedin.com/in/kiransonaje/

Commercialisation

https://axiobio.com/

Axio developed Axiostat – India's First and only USFDA approved trauma hemostat that stops life threatening bleeding instantly. Axiostat is is being used by soldiers in over 350 battallions across India to manage bleeding from injuries in battlefield. It is approved in over 40 countries and used by major armed forces globally. Axiostat is a bioactive haemostatic dressing that works on a unique charge-based mechanism to stop the bleeding quickly.

The startup announced another USFDA 510K thousands clearance for Axiostat Patch for control of moderate to severe bleeding in vascular procedures, surgical debridement sites, puncture sites and more. This clearance opens the door to enter markets such as Vascular closure, Hemodialysis, EMS and Military segments in the US soon. Axiostat had also received CE mark in Europe earlier and is also approved in over 40 countries worldwide. Over half a million units have been deployed since inception globally especially in battlefields to control bleeding from trauma injuries and in hospitals to control for vascular closure bleeding.

Poorti, Post Mastectomy Kit – Aarna Biomedical Products, Faridabad

Dr. Pawan Mehrotra, a PhD in Cancer Science, promoted this social healthcare enterprise Aarna Biomedical Products to develop a device that can help breast cancer patients. Received Padmashri Suri Innovation Award-IIT Delhi. Translational Health Science and Technology Institute, Faridabad is a networked organization linking many centers of excellence, THSTI is envisioned as a collective of scientists, engineers and physicians that will effectively enhance the quality of human life through integrating a culture of shared excellence in research, education and translational knowledge with the entrepreneurial spirit to take technologies into the public sphere. Many technologies transferred and available for licensing:

https://thsti.res.in/en/Info/technologie-develope-an-transferred

https://thsti.res.in/en/patents-and-licensing

P.V. Madhusudhan Rao, professor in the departments of mechanical engineering and Design at IIT Delhi helped Dr. Mehrotra learn the art of manufacturing and product development. https://web.iitd.ac.in/~pvmrao/

Technology

A breast prosthesis is an artificial breast form that replaces the shape of all or part of the breast that has been removed. 'Prostheses' is the word for more than one prosthesis. After breast surgery nurse will usually give a fabric-covered temporary prosthesis, often called a 'softie' or 'comfie', to wear during this time. Once wound is healed and any swelling has gone down (usually within six to eight weeks) one can be fitted for a permanent prosthesis. A permanent breast prosthesis fits in a bra cup with or without a bra pocket. Most breast prostheses are made from soft silicone gel (which is anti-allergenic), encased in a thin film. They're moulded to resemble the natural shape of a woman's breast, or part of a breast. The outer surface feels soft and smooth and may include a nipple outline. In 1961 American plastic surgeons Thomas Cronin and Frank Gerow, and the Dow Corning Corporation, developed the first silicone breast prosthesis, filled with silicone gel.

Innovation

"Poorti" – a user-centric post mastectomy kit has been designed utilising a product co-evolution strategy where each component of the kit has been developed with iterative feedback as per the aspirations of the end user leading to both technical and anthropometric betterment than the available alternatives together with a one-minute product self-use video thereby dispensing the need of any external help. The kit comprises of a superlative design based light-weight pre-made silicone gel breast prosthesis (available in ten different sizes & two shapes as per the needs of the user), two pocketed brassieres (available in eight different sizes & two colours as per the needs of the user), two prosthesis covers, one prosthesis holder, information & usage manual & an outer waterproof kit which accommodates all the aforementioned components discreetly. CE certified silicone gel imported from Germany is used in this prosthesis.

Patents

There are many patents, this one is about Gel filled silicone rubber breast prosthesis adapted to be worn inside of a brassiere by a woman who has had her own breast removed.

https://patents.google.com/patent/US3911503A/en

Commercialisation

The Sampoorti-Poorti system evolved with support from Biotechnology Industry Research Assistance Council (BIRAC), Foundation for Innovation and Technology Transfer (FITT-IIT Delhi), Translational Health Science and Technology Institute (THSTI), Tata Trusts – Foundation for Innovation and Social Entrepreneurship (FISE) – Social Alpha, Venture Center – National Chemical Laboratories (VC-NCL), SIIC Startup Incubation & Innovation Centre – IIT Kanpur (SIIC-IITK), Pune International Centre (PIC), numerous hospitals and NGOs spread across India. This kit has been validated across 30 cities in 14 states in India.

https://www.aarnabiomed.in/how-to-buy

Robotic Surgery – SS Innovations, Gurugram

Dr Sudhir Srivastava, MD is Founder, Chairman & CEO at SS Innovations International Inc. Graduated from JLN Medical College in Jaipur, Rajasthan, founded Alliance Hospital with 10 other doctors in Texas. He got involved with robotic cardiac surgeries and was also a part of the trials for FDA approval of the Da Vinci system for coronary bypass surgery. During this period, he performed the world's first single vessel beating heart TECAB in the US, and proceeded to perform the world's first double and triple vessel TECAB on a beating heart. With a American Board Certification of Thoracic surgery he focused in Cardiovascular and Thoracic Surgery from The University of British Columbia, is now leading innovations to create the new generation Robotic Surgery System along with several other Surgical equipment & devices. He is CEO of International Centre for Robotic Surgery, Delhi.

https://www.linkedin.com/in/sudhir-srivastava-md-65ba9911/

Technology

After the US FDA approval of the da Vinci system in 2000, India got its first urologic robotic installation at the All India Institute of Medical Sciences, New Delhi, in 2006. The following decade saw an unprecedented growth of robotic surgery in India. There are currently 66 centers and 71 robotic installations as on July 2019, with more than 500 trained robotic surgeons in our country. More than 12,800 surgeries have been performed with robotic assistance in these 12 years. The imported robot currently costs around US $1,500,000 as an initial investment with a yearly maintenance cost of US $100,000. Besides the cost of the machine, the expenditure incurred in setting up a facility dedicated to robotic surgery is also huge.

Innovation

After performing 1,400 cardiac surgeries using the Da Vinci system and putting a team of young engineers together, the average age was 26-27, Dr Sudhir created a system that is better than the Da Vinci one as it costs less. Currently installed in four hospitals, the SSI Mantra costs Rs 5 crore while the Da Vinci surgical robot's price tag is Rs 15 crore. The Indian surgical robot is a modular design with over 5 detachable arms, which can be helpful even in heart surgery. The surgeon sits at the console station, which has a 32-inch monitor and 3D vision. 3D vision reduces mistakes and accidents. The instruments used in the surgery are 8 mm in size.

Patents

An Overview of the Robotic Surgery Patent Landscape: https://www.mddionline.com/business/overview-robotic-surgery-patent-landscape

Commercialisation

https://ssinnovations.com/ssi-mantra/

Mantra is a modular, robotic surgical system that has been designed specifically for the Indian healthcare market. The system consists of several components, including a surgeon's console, an operating table, and robotic arms that are equipped with surgical instruments. The surgeon's console is the control center of the system, allowing the surgeon to control the robotic arms and instruments. The console has a high-resolution display that provides a 3D view of the surgical site, allowing the surgeon to see the procedure in real-time. The console is also equipped with hand controls that allow the surgeon to manipulate the robotic arms and instruments with precision and ease. The operating table is an integral part of the system, providing a stable platform for the patient during the procedure. The table is designed to accommodate patients of different sizes and shapes, and can be adjusted to different positions as required. The robotic arms are the most important component of the system, as they are responsible for performing the actual surgery. The arms are equipped with surgical instruments, including scissors, scalpels, and graspers, which are controlled by the surgeon through the console. The arms are designed to move in a smooth and precise manner, allowing the surgeon to perform complex procedures with ease.

Swasa-Respiratory Healthcare-Salcit Technologies, Hyderabad

Narayana Rao Sripada is Founder / Director at Salcit Technologies. Engineering graduate from Andhra University, with MTech from Kurushetra university, he worked in Industry for several years before starting Salcit Technologies a startup focusing on building Digital Health Solutions for Respiratory Diseases based on respiratory sounds. Dr Padma Sai, Professor in VNRVJIET is the Director. The startup was initially incubated at VJ Hub of VNRVJIET, Hyderabad

https://www.linkedin.com/in/narayanaraosripada/

Technology

Patients with primary or secondary active TB have characteristic symptoms: Lymph nodes in the neck or other areas may be swollen or tender. Lung sounds (crackles) Chest fullness due to fluid around the lungs (pleural effusion). For lung TB, the doctor cannot always hear enough to make a diagnosis by just using a stethoscope. If the physician suspects there is something wrong and that it is not just a cold, he may refer to an outpatient department for people with lung diseases or to an X-ray department. Culture of Mtb in a suitable medium remains the gold standard diagnostic test. The specimen can be cultured in solid (e.g. Löwenstein–Jensen or Middlebrook 7H11) or liquid media (e.g. for use with the BACTEC Mycobacterium Growth Indicator Tube (MGIT) 960 system).

Innovation

Swaasa® uses machine learning models to analyse the cough sounds in combination with other information like temperature, oxygen saturation, symptoms to assess the performance of lungs. Swaasa® aims to substitute spirometry and make the pulmonary healthcare accessible and affordable.

Validation report: https://www.nature.com/articles/s41598-023-31772-9

The main objective of this cross-sectional validation study was to develop and validate the Swaasa AI platform to screen and prioritize at risk patients for PTB based on the signature cough sound as well as symptomatic information provided by the subjects. The pilot testing of model was conducted at a peripheral health care centre, RHC Simhachalam (India) on 65 presumptive PTB cases. Out of which, 15 subjects truly turned out to be PTB positive with a positive predictive value of 75%. The validation results obtained from the model are quite encouraging. This platform has the potential to fulfil the unmet need of a cost-effective PTB screening method.

Patents

Method and system for analyzing risk associated with respiratory sounds – WO2019116381A1. The system comprises of a respiratory monitoring device to assign risk category to a plurality of respiratory sound signals captured by at least one acoustic sensor.

Commercialisation

https://swaasa.ai/

App – https://apps.apple.com/in/app/swaasa/id1529923164 Swaasa is for doctors and health workers to capture the symptoms and record cough samples of patients. The app sends this data to Swaasa AI platform for analysis. Using Swaasa doctors and health workers can screen users for respiratory health issues.

ToucHb, a Non-Invasive Anaemia Screener – Biosense Technologies Private Limited, Bhiwandi, Maharashtra

Dr Yogesh Pail, MBBS from Maharashra University of Health Services was co-founder and Director of Biosense Technologies till 2022. Dr Abhishek Sen, MBBS from TN Medical College was the co-founder.

Technology

Anaemia is a blood disorder which results from a decrease in the number of red blood cells or abnormally low haemoglobin in the blood. Haemoglobin is a protein in red blood cell responsible for transporting oxygen to vital organs. Often, the first test used to diagnose anemia is a complete blood count (CBC). The CBC measures many parts of your blood. This test checks your hemoglobin and hematocrit (hee-MAT-oh-crit) levels. Hemoglobin is an iron-rich protein in red blood cells that carries oxygen to the body. Electrical engineers and computer scientists from the University of Washington have developed HemaApp, which uses a smartphone camera to estimate hemoglobin concentrations and screen for anemia.

Innovation

ToucHb is a non-invasive anaemia screener which mean it detects anaemia without a needle poke by identifying the presence of pallor in conjunctiva. ToucHb not only focus on the easy functionality factor but also on the affordability factor. Haemoglobin test result displayed in about one minute. Hand held device weighing less than 300g

Patents

Method and system for haemoglobin measurement – WO2016013023A3

https://patents.google.com/patent/WO2016013023A3/un

Inventors-Abhishek Sen, Aman Midha, Sreyas V. Pariyath

Commercialisation

https://www.biosense.in/touchb.php

Other products of the firm are:

SYNC Glucometer – Biosense SYNC is a Smart & All-in-one compact sized Glucometer designed for personal use.

Uchek – UChek is a smart phone based portable diagnostic system which measures micro albumin to creatine ratio.

The startup was mentored by Villgro and Menterra. Later, the firm is acquired by Tulip Diagnostics (P) Ltd, Goa. The individual companies Tulip Diagnostics (P) Ltd, Microxpress, Orchid Biomedical Systems, Qualpro Diagnostics, Zephyr Biomedicals, Viola Diagnostic Systems, Coral Clinical Systems, BioShields and Biosense Technologies specialize in research, development and design of specific systems & platforms within the assigned technological areas. PerkinElmer, Inc. a global leader with reported revenue of approximately $2.3 billion in 2015 acquired Tulip Diagnostics in 2017.

Video Laryngoscope – Dr. Kumaresh Krishnamoorthy, Bangalore

Dr. Kumaresh Krishnamoorthy is a Practicing Surgeon and Healthcare Entrepreneur with MBBS from PSG Institute of Medical Sciences and Research followed by Fellow Neurotology, University of Cincinnati College of Medicine. First collaborative fellow from AIMS to Roswell Park Cancer Institute and Distinguished as the first Fellow and first Indian for the Otology & Neurotology Fellowship, University of Cincinnati. Skilled in advanced specialized surgeries such as Laser, Coblator, Implantation Otology, Sleep Apnea Procedures and Minimally Invasive Head & Neck Procedures. Owner of Dr Kumaresh ENT Clinic and Founder of AUM Medtech.

https://www.linkedin.com/in/drkumaresh/

Technology

Video laryngoscopy (VL) utilizes video camera technology to visualize airway structures and facilitate endotracheal intubation (ETI). Video laryngoscopes can be broadly categorized as follows: Standard blade style, angulated blade style, and anatomically shaped, channeled design. Designed by Dr. John Pacey, the GlideScope (Verathon; Bothell, Washington) was introduced as the first commercially available video laryngoscope in 2001. With this innovation, Dr. Pacey was actually introducing two new technologies simultaneously: the video laryngoscope, and the hyper-angulated laryngoscope.

Innovation

Video Laryngoscopes are standard of care in developed countries, in developing countries its use was limited due to financial limitations, AUM Video Laryngoscopes (VLS) are affordable to all including trainees. Wi-Fi enabled VLS is an advanced version of our video laryngoscope which transmits high-definition video image to a stand-alone large display like tablet or android TV. The Wi-Fi version comes with a rechargeable battery and in addition to viewing on the tablet inside the OR it also allows for real time remote viewing and monitoring of images and videos, a feature not available or not affordable until now. It has two parts: 1) Handheld unit with the blade 2) Display device. Special Features: Video and still image documentation in real time. HD camera with White Light LED for true colour rendering. Special camera lens coated with anti-fog. No batteries are required. Sterilization of handle, blade and mobile through patent pending mobile box sterilizer. Ergonomically designed. The handles are of medical grade | Sterilization unit.

Video – https://youtu.be/BCnfc2h6Af4

Patents

UVC Disinfection Bot for Hospital/Hospitality/Airlines – (Design Patent Received)

UVC Handy – (Utility Patent Published, awaiting final patent certificate)

Real-time remote viewing Adult/Natal/Neo-Natal Video Laryngoscope – (Design and Utility Patent Published, awaiting final patent certificate)

US Patent for UVC Bot – (Published, awaiting final patent certificate)

Commercialisation

https://www.aummedtech.com/

VIDEO LARYNGOSCOPE WITH Wi-Fi – https://www.aummedtech.com/video-laryngoscope-wi-fi/

UVC DISINFECTANT BOT – https://www.aummedtech.com/uvc-disinfectant-bot1/

Visual Medical Data with AI – SigTuple Technologies Pvt. Ltd, Bangalore

Tathagato Rai Dastidar Founder & CEO at SigTuple Technoloies is tech industry veteran with a B.Tech and Ph.D. in Computer Science from Indian Institute of Technology, Kharagpur. He started his career back in the year 2000 at National Semiconductor, building software for semiconductor design automation, over the years, held technical leadership positions in premier technology companies like Yahoo! American Express and GraceNote. Rohit Kumar Pandey from IIIT Bangalore and Apporv Anand from IITD are co-founders. The three worked at American Express Big Data Labs Bangalore.

https://www.linkedin.com/in/trdastidar/

Technology

Digital pathology refers to the environment that includes tools & systems for digitizing pathology slides and associated metadata, in addition their storage, evaluation, and analysis, as well as supporting infrastructure. AI approaches aided by deep learning results are frequently used to combine information from digitized pathology images with their associated metadata. Using AI approaches that computationally evaluate the entire slide image, researchers can detect features that are difficult to detect by eye alone, which is now the state-of-the-art in digital pathology.

Innovation

Manthana is home grown data and AI platform of the startup that enables five major capabilities, data management, annotations, model training, continuous learning, and analysis/reporting.

AI 100 is an in-vitro diagnostic device designed to automate manual microscopy in a diagnostic laboratory. It uses robotics and AI to digitize any biological sample on a glass slide to enable AI aided remote review. Can digitize and analyse both blood and urine.

Shonit An AI application to analyse blood cell morphology Identifies and pre-classifies WBCs, RBCs and platelets in a peripheral blood smear.

Shrava An AI application to analyse urine sediment identifies and pre-classifies multiple elements present in urine sediment.

Patents

Method and system for auto focusing a microscopic imaging system, Patent number: 11340439, 2022, Inventor: Tathagato Rai Dastidar.

Method and system for Reconstructing a field of view, Patent number: 11269172,2022, Inventors: Harshit Pande, Abdul Aziz, Bharath Cheluvaraju, Tathagato Rai Dastidar, Apurv Anand, Rohit Kumar Pandey.

Method and system for Auto Focusing a Microscopic Imaging System, Publication number: 20210405339, 2021, Inventor: Tathagato Rai Dastidar and 7 more.

Commercialisation

https://sigtuple.com/products

In 2015, Tatha co-founded SigTuple with the goal of applying artificial intelligence and computer vision to the healthcare domain. The aim is to assist pathologists in the microscopy work, thereby making their lives easier, and ultimately improving patient outcome. SigTuple has remained true to this vision throughout its journey, and today it is en route to putting India on the global map of deep tech startups. The typical pricing of SigTuple's device is ₹14 lakh for corporates, followed by a monthly cost of ₹15,000 which includes cloud, AI, and maintenance costs. The SigTuple group has three companies under its umbrella which include SigTuple Technologies Pvt. Ltd, Mirable Health Services Pvt. Ltd and Truelyser BioSystems Pvt. Ltd.

Voice Prosthesis – Inaumation Medical Devices, Bangalore

Dr. Vishal Rao is presently the Chief of Head & Neck Surgical oncology & Robotic surgery at HCG Cancer Centre, Bangalore. He completed his post-graduation in otorhinolaryngology from a reputed institute in Karnataka & fellowship in Head & Neck oncology surgery from a well-known institute in Mumbai. His area of expertise is head & neck surgery, which includes surgery for benign and malignant tumours of the thyroid, parotid and salivary gland surgeries, complex neck surgeries, such as radical and modified neck dissections, carotid body, other vascular tumours, and parapharyngeal space tumours. Dr.Vishal is the inventor of 'Aum Voice Prosthesis' a $1 speaking device for throat cancer patients. As a recognition to his contributions, he has been conferred the Honorary FRCS from Royal College of Surgeons in Glasgow. He has also received Judy Wilkenfield award for Global Excellence in tobacco control and has been a recipient of multiple state level awards including the Kempegowda award. The Infosys Foundation recognised Dr. Rao and Shashank's efforts in the previous edition of the Aarohan Social Innovation Award, 2019.

Shashank Mahesh is the Co-Founder of inaumation medical devices and Madhukar is the CEO.

https://drvishalrao.in/

Technology

Prosthesis is an artificial device that replaces a missing body part lost through trauma, disease, or congenital conditions. Voice prosthesis is an artificial device, made of silicone that is used to help laryngectomized patients to speak. During laryngectomy, the entire voice box is removed and the trachea and esophagus are separated from each other. During laryngectomy an opening between the food pipe and the windpipe can be created. This opening can also be created at a later time. This opening is called a tracheo-esophageal puncture (TEP). Most patients of throat cancer who undergo laryngectomy are unable to speak due to removal of voice box. The patients eat through their mouths but they cannot speak as there is no voice box. Accordingly there remains a need for an improved device with one way valve that enables laryngectomy patients to speak.

Innovation

Aum voice prosthesis is a device for patients with throat cancer,helps patients whose voice box is removed to speak again. On an average the lifespan of a prosthesis is 6-12 months, the reason being the regular wear and tear due to the use and biological colonization of the device. Also, food particles accelerate the wear and tear process. Innaumation hvae created a kit that has a few essential products that for laryngectomy patients. These products help in the protection and cleaning of the stoma. The products are available in the form of an accessories kit which can be purchased by the patients and contains three cloth bibs, three cleaning brushes and one bathing bib.

Video – https://youtu.be/9kwyvcEJqCs?si=DdXyRBADFURxO8yj

Patents

In 1869 the first artificial voice box (larynx) was built by Czermak. In 1873 Theodor Billroth made a total laryngectomy (in steps) and implanted an artificial voice box.

Vishal Rao has more than 18 patents filed for his innovations on medical devices, drugs, techniques and theories.

Commercialisation

Innaumation Medical Devices Private Limited is a Bangalore based medical device start up working on area of voice restoration for throat cancer patients and has invented the Aum voice prosthesis as its core product. The present invention created by Innaumation Medical Devices Pvt Ltd comprises of a voice prosthesis device, which is implanted in patients undergoing laryngectomy enabling the patient to speak after surgery. We are also working on a similar such innovations for tracheostomy tubes, which helps patients breathe and could assist patients with low cost maintenance without suctioning.

Patient's Kit – A Voice Prosthesis, A Cleaning Brush, A Capsule, An inserter, Two Scarves, A guide Wire & Instruction Manual

Surgeon's Kit – A Voice Prosthesis, Sushruth Inserter, Guide Wire, J Probe, TEP Brush, Scarf, Canvas Pouch, VR Fish eyed curved Trochar with Cannula (Patent Filed)

https://innaumation.com/products-services/

Wearable EEG device – Neuphony, Noida (UP)

Ria Rustagi an engineering graduate from Jaypee Institute of Information Technology followed by MSc in IC Design from Nanyang Technology University, Singapore and Technical University, Munich is Co-founder & CEO at Neuphony. Featured in & as Forbes 30 Under 30 – Consumer Tech (Special Mention), YourStory Tech 50, YourStory Women on a Mission Award, INC42 Top 30 Startups to Watch, Top 10 Female-led startups by Google. Bhavya Madan also an engineering graduate from Jaypee is Co-founder and CTO.

https://www.linkedin.com/in/ria-rustagi/

https://www.linkedin.com/in/bhavya-madan-07/

Technology

Though it was discovered in the 1950s, neurofeedback therapy was used by NASA to treat and train astronauts. The method of neurofeedback therapy teaches self-control of brain functions, treating various disorders of brain and central nervous system like anxiety, depression, insomnia cognitive deficits, focus and concentration deficits, emotional deficits, headaches, pain, etc. There are four lobes in the brain – namely the Frontal lobes, the Temporal lobes, the Parietal lobes, and the Occipital lobes. These lobes are collectively referred to as the cortex. Also, there are two specialized areas that are referred to as the prefrontal cortex; and the motor strip and sensory motor strip.

The QEEG and neurofeedback training first involves brain mapping, which includes reviewing this whole structure. Neurotherapy works by teaching a person to produce more optimal EEG patterns using positive reinforcement. The client is wired up to EEG sensors that track their brain activity throughout a neurofeedback session. The sensors are linked to a computer, and a straightforward video game is controlled by the EEG signals. The real-time feedback on brain activity is measured by sensors on the scalp and typically in the form of audio and visual rewards. A positive reward, such as a more brightened and clear video is given as a reward, when the brain activity changes in the positive direction, and when the brain produces less harmonious brain wave patterns, there is a formation of dull video (dim screen).

Innovation

Neuphony is a neurofeedback-based wearable brain device (EEG Headband) that captures key mind parameters and allows users to know their stress and external focus scores. The device has 8 sensors distributed in the brain's parietal, frontal & temporal lobes. These are polymer sensors that are conducive in nature. Cognitive

States to Measure: Stress vs. Calm, Mood Analysis, External Focus vs. Distractions, PDR (Posterior Dominant Rhythm).

https://tyke-startup-bucket.s3.ap-south-1.amazonaws.com/Neuphony/pdfPitch/pankhtech_india_pvt_ltd-pitch.pdf

Patents

There are many patents on this. One example is – https://patents.google.com/patent/US20180103917A1/en,

Commercialisation

https://neuphony.com/prod/headband/

The products are sold online at Amazon:

Neuphony – Mental Health Monitor (as seen on Shark Tank India) | Wearable EEG Headband | Wireless Interaction-Rs 49,000/-

Neuphony – The Best Research Grade 8 Channel EEG Cap with Movable electrodes (as seen on Shark Tank India) Wearable EEG Flex Cap – Rs 75,000/-

Water & Sanitation

1. Artistic Air purification Tower – Verto-Studio Symbiosis, New Delhi
2. Electrolytic De-fluoridation (EDF) Technique – NEERI Nagpur
3. e-Waste recycling – Ecoreco, Mumbai
4. HeliborneTEM technology for aquifer mapping – CSIR-NGRI, Hyderabad
5. Hot water dissolvable sanitary napkins, Cresa Greentech, Pune
6. Hydrogen Electrolyzer – Newtrace Pvt. Ltd.
7. Hydrogen Fuel Cell bus – Sentient labs/ KIIT, Pune,
8. Intelligently Stirred Thermophilic Anaerobic Reactor – Sankar Ganesh Palani, BITS Pilani, Hyderabad campus
9. Marine Oil Spill Remediation – NIOT, Chennai
10. Moving Bed Biofilm Reactor (MBBR) – NIT Warangal
11. Muffler and Particulate Separator for Internal Combustion Engine Exhaust – RnA Vortech Innovations, Chandigarh
12. Plastic Waste into Green Fuel and Energy – DBT-ICT Centre for Energy Biosciences
13. Sanitary pad waste recycling – Pad Care Labs, Pune
14. Water Management Platform (MIDAS) – Ekatvam Innovations, Thane
15. Waterless urinal – Ekam Eco Solutions, New Delhi

Artistic Air Purification Tower – Verto-Studio Symbiosis, New Delhi

Britta Knobel Gupta, Amit Gupta are founding partners of Studio Symbiosis an architectural practice based out of Stuttgart and New Delhi. Amit Born in Delhi, moved to London in 2004 to pursue his Masters in Architecture & Urbanism from Architectural Association. Amit has won the prestigious `40 under 40 award' by Perceive Global, Hong Kong; was awarded for Hotel Architect of the year by IDE and was also was featured by CNN Style & Forbes India. Born in Stuttgart Germany, Britta Knobel Gupta pursued her Architectural studies in Konstanz Germany and Lyon France. She has also received the Estrade International Award, Iconic Award, German Design award and Golden A Design Award for her notable contributions to the fields of architecture, design and landscape.

https://studio-symbiosis.com/studio/

Technology

Smog towers are structures designed as large-scale air purifiers to reduce air pollution particles (smog). The world's first smog free tower was built by Dutch artist Daan Roosegaarde. It was unveiled in September 2015 in Rotterdam. In Delhi, India Kurin Systems is developing a 12-metre (40 ft) tall smog tower, called the "Kurin City Cleaner". It is different from Daan Roosegaarde's Smog Tower in that it won't depend on the ionization technique to clean the air. The H14 grade HEPA filter, known for being able to clean up to 99.99% of the particulate matter, will be used instead, together with a pre-filter and activated carbon.

Innovation

VERTO can clean 600,000 CuM of air per day, equivalent to an area twice the size of a cricket field with a height of 2 meters. The triangular perforations are designed as a performance driven system, with bigger openings at inlet and outlets. The air is sucked in from energy efficient fans and then get filtered using fine dust filters to remove the pollutants from the ambient air. An IOT control system enables the operation according to the demand. VERTO has been designed using the principals of aerodynamics, to create a form that propagates maximum surface area, increased wind speed and 360 degree air purification.

Patents

Red Dot Award 2023 – Product Design Category, WA (World Architecture) Award 43rd cycle by the World Architecture Community.

https://worldarchitecture.org/architecture-projects/hmmgz/verto---360-air-purification-tower-project

https://www.red-dot.org/project/verto-63271

Commercialisation

The first VERTO was inaugurated on the 26th of August 2022 in Sunder Nursery Park, New Delhi, by Dr Philip Ackermann (German Ambassador to India & Bhutan). Design & Execution by Studio Symbiosis Architects, Filtration from Mann+Hummel, Contractor: VARE – Varunodya Prefab LLP, Structure Consultant: Acecon.

This is acclaimed as India's first Artistic Air purification tower.

https://vertoair.com/

Electrolytic De-Fluoridation (EDF) Technique – NEERI

Subhash Parashram Andey, is Indian environmental engineer, researcher at NEERI. Achievements include patents pending for potable water filter for emergency water supply. Recipient Nina Saxena Excellence Technical award, 2008.

Technology

A research study was carried to evaluate the performance of the Nalgonda technique and seek ways to enhance the fluoride uptake capacities. Further, pilot testing of the EDF system was conducted in the Rift Valley of Ethiopia to evaluate its effectiveness at fluoride removal using natural groundwater in this setting. This study has shown that the performance of the Nalgonda system was significantly enhanced by adding aluminum hydro(oxide) (AO) and cow bone char powder into the existing Nalgonda systems; the initial fluoride concentration of 9.3 mg/L was lowered to 2.5 mg/L on average. In addition to the increased effectiveness at fluoride removal, the addition of AO and cow bone char powder produced significantly less sludge compared to the existing Nalgonda system. The EDF system proved to be effective at removing the excess fluoride concentration in drinking water in the Rift Valley of Ethiopia; the initial fluoride concentration of 7.9 mg/L was lowered to 2.8 mg/L meeting the USEPA standard fluoride level of 4 mg/L. The pilot study showed Aluminum leaching into the treated water. Thus, further optimization of the electrode size, electrolysis time, and voltage/current used during the electrolysis process is needed to meet the WHO target treatment goal of 1.5 mg/L fluoride level and eliminate aluminum leaching as well.

https://academicjournals.org/journal/AJEST/article-full-text-pdf/ADO895858797

Innovation

National Environmental Engineering research Institute (CSIR-NEERI), India has developed Electrolytic De-fluoridation (EDF) technique for the treatment of excessive fluoride in water sources. The process is based on the principle of electrolysis by passing Direct Current (DC) obtained from solar photovoltaic cells through aluminum plate electrodes placed in fluoride containing water. During the process aluminum plate connected to anode dissolves and forms polyhydroxy aluminum species which remove fluoride in water by complex formation followed by adsorption and removal by settling. EDF technology provides a technically sound, cost-effective and reliable community drinking water de-fluoridation system for supplying safe drinking water, which meets the guideline value (1 mg/L) of the World Health. It is ideal for treating raw water with fluoride concentration up to 10mg/L. It produces portable water with a palatable taste. Compared to conventional methods, the sludge regenerated is 60-70% less. It can reduce fluoride to as low as 0.25 mg/L while also lowering the bacterial count (total coliform and E-Coli).

https://www.psipw.org/attachments/article/341/IJWRAE_2(3) 139-145.pdf

Patents

IITM has a patent – US 10, 035, 131 B2

An overview – https://www.un-igrac.org/sites/default/files/ resources/files/IGRAC-SP2007-1_Fluoride-removal.pdf

Commercialisation

Know-how transferred to 9 firms for installation of EDF plants in the fluoride affected areas in the country CSIR-NEERI has installed EDF demonstration plants in MP and CG states with the financial support from MDWS, GOI and UNICEF Nearly 200 EDF plants have been installed and more plants will be installed in fluoride affected areas of various states by State Water Supply Departments.

HES Water Engineers India Pvt. Ltd. –

https://hesweindia.com/product/csir-neeri-oximax-electrolytic-defluoridation-edf-system/

NEERI – https://www.neeri.res.in/abouts/technology_detail/ electrolytic-defluoridation-edf-technique/5b1f95ae232a3#googtr ans(en|en)

e-Waste Recycling – Ecoreco, Mumbai

B.K. Soni a Charted Accountant by qualification is the Chairman and Managing Director of Eco Recycling Ltd (Ecoreco) and the chief promoter of the group. Recognized as a visionary and expert in e-waste management, Soni saw the opportunity of the Indian e-waste management industry way back in 2005 much ahead of other players.

https://www.linkedin.com/in/bksoni/

Technology

The growing problem of e-waste required greater emphasis on recycling of the e-waste and better e-waste management. In the light of above, the Ministry of Environment, Forest & Climate Change (MOEFCC) on 2 November 2022, has notified E-waste (Management) Rules, 2022 (2022 Rules) which has replaced the E-waste (Management) Rules, 2016 (2016 Rules). EPR mechanism under the 2016 Rules focused more on the producer's responsibility to collect back the e-waste introduced in the market and provided collection targets, whereas the EPR regime under 2022 Rules provide an annual e-waste recycling targets to the producers.

Some see it as an opportunity. The potential value of the rare elements contained e-waste is vast. According to a 2019 report by the World Economic Forum, the world's e-waste has a material value of $62.5 billion (£46 billion) – more than the GDP of most countries. The director of UN's Sustainable Cycles (S CYCLE) programme points out that a ton of discarded mobile phones is richer in gold than a ton of gold ore.

Innovation

BookMyJunk: A mobile App available on both Android & iOS to facilitate on line booking of Ecoreco services for collection of electrical & electronic waste at no cost to the end consumers. Reverse Logistics Pvt., Ltd. a registered start-up and an Ecoreco Group company, innovated and placed this solution for the environment conscious e-waste generators The firm has deployed 5 Maruti Vehicles and 2 Mahindra Vehicles on the roads of Mumbai & surrounding to serve such environment conscious generators of e-waste.

Recycling on Wheels – SmartER is another innovation. The vehicle is equipped with a very robust shredder. The Shredder meets two very important requirement, one on the spot shredding of data devices like Mobile Phones, Hard disks, Pen drives and other data devices, secondly the shredder is used to shred all the proprietary devices, scientific equipment, military devices, home appliances etc. with an object to give complete comfort & confidence that their e-waste is no longer useful and no one can misuse.

Patents

Patent Landscape Report on E-Waste Recycling Technologies – https://www.wipo.int/publications/en/details.jsp?id=388

E-waste Recycling Technology Patents filed in India – http://docs.manupatra.in/newsline/articles/Upload/521E50FE-05CB-4347-BA6B-80636AA574DB.pdf

Commercialisation

https://ecoreco.com/services-weee-recycling.aspx

Thw state-of-the-art de-manufacturing line combines high-tech automation and manual processing methods to sort, dismantle and shred e-waste. A member of the ISRI and Electronic Recyclers Association (ERA), Ecoreco deploys WEEE Recycling processes that are ISO 9001, 14001 & OHSAS 18001 certified.

Startups in e-waste recycling –

https://enterprise-services.siliconindia.com/ranking/ewaste-management-companies-2018-rid-398.html

Heliborne TEM Technology for Aquifer Mapping – CSIR-NGRI, Hyderabad

Dr. Virendra M. Tiwari obtained his post-graduate degree in Geophysics from Banaras Hindu University (BHU), Varanasi. He took up a scientific career at CSIR-National Geophysical Research Institute (CSIR-NGRI), after receiving a Ph.D. in Geophysics from NGRI-BHU. He has worked as a Post-Doctoral Researcher at the IPGP, Paris, France, and LAGOS-CNES, Toulouse, France, and as Visiting Scientist at the GEOMAR/CU Kiel, Germany, and CU, Boulder, USA. Dr. Subash Chandra works as Sr. Scientist at CSIR-NGRI and Assistant professor in AcSIR. He has been working in the field of Hydro-physics since 2000. He added a new chapter in the Indian Hydrogeology by employing Heliborne Geophysics for aquifer mapping to develop effective aquifer based groundwater management.   (https://www.researchgate.net/profile/Subash-Chandra-2)

https://www.ngri.res.in/researcher/dr-v-m-tiwari.php

Technology

The helicopter borne geophysical investigation comprises two components viz., electromagnetic and magnetic methods. A system developed by Danish technologists and deployed in South Africa, SkyTEM, picks up variations in electrical resistivity to map the Earth's subsurface. The system consists of a transmitter loop, about twice the area of a tennis court, suspended below a helicopter. The system flies over the study area at a height of 30 metres and emits an electromagnetic field into the ground and the receiver coil measures the response. Various rocks and soil types have different electrical characteristics and each responds differently to the transmitted signal, giving indications about geologic structure. Interpretations of the subsurface material are used to produce a 3D geologic model of the earth to depths of up to 350 metres. It allows for detailed analysis of the subsurface geology and can contribute to the development of a groundwater model for the area. In addition, the subsurface mapping provides an insight into where to locate and drill wells, and to identify potential recharge areas. It's quick too: The helicopter can potentially cover 300 kilometers in a day.

Innovation

The HeliborneTEM technology for aquifer mapping was first time adopted and deployed by CSIR-NGRI in India with high resolution subsurface scanning up to about 500M depth for mapping the groundwater resources in different geological terrains. The electromagnetic field is generated by a large hexagonal loop carrying current known as transmitter. It is towed below the helicopter by a rope and is kept about 30 m above the ground. The electromagnetic field is induced in the ground by transient pulses i.e. turned off and on at repetition certain frequency. The transient pulse induces the ground, generating eddy current in the subsurface conductor that further generates secondary EM fields, which are recorded in the receiver loop and converted into subsurface resistivity distributions. The presence of groundwater and variation in the groundwater quality within the aquifer result in variation in electrical conductivity within the ground. The electromagnetic induction in the ground is dependent on these conductivity variations and hence the secondary field generated and measured at different time scale varying from micro second to millisecond gives an idea of conductivity distribution with depth and thus the aquifers are delineated. For a resistive earth, the information can be obtained up to depths of 500 m or more (1500 to 2000 ft). These two data sets (low and high moments) are combined to get seamless information on the subsurface right from very shallow to deeper regions. Its advantages in comparison with other geophysical methods are (1) rapid scanning (~2000 measurements/hour), (2) highly data dense data (makes measurements at 2-3 m along the flight lines at flying speed of 60-80 km/h), (3) high-resolution, (4) cost-economic provided measured at considerably larger scale i.e. ~1000 sq.km area or more, and (5) can be conducted in remote and inaccessible areas and (6) Once an area is surveyed with Helibrone TEM, there is no need of further measurement and it is equally useful for other geotechnical purposes such as geological mapping, mineral exploration, engineering applications, etc.

Patents

Similar patent – MEASURING EQUIPMENT AND METHOD FOR MAPPING THE GEOLOGY IN AN UNDERGROUND FORMATION, CA 2514609

Commercialisation

The technology was initially employed at pilot scale in six representative major hydrogeological terrains located in Rajasthan,

Bihar, Maharashtra, Karnataka and Tamilnadu. Subsequently it was extended to Surat smart city, Gujarat; Paleo-channel mapping at Prayagraj, UP; CGWB`s Arid Project and major infrastructure projects carried out by Konkan Railways and Rail Vikas Nigam Ltd. It has established guidelines for aquifer mapping with varying resolution in different geological terrains of the country.

Hot Water Dissolvable Sanitary Napkins, Cresa Greentech, Pune

Sarika Kulkarni Pathak is a mechanical engineer and industrial designer from Philadelphia University (currently known as Thomas Jefferson University), collaborated with Johnson & Johnson for a university project, and learned a lot about feminine hygiene. She worked on product initially called SANECO. She is the Founder & CEO of Cresa GreenTech which won 'Prabhaav Innovation Grand Challenge' by TECHIN of IIT Palakkad, Kerala.

https://www.linkedin.com/in/sarika-kulkarni-pathak-02014b16/

(https://www3.wipo.int/wipogreen/en/news/2020/news_0007.html)

Technology

Disposal of used sanitary napkins is a major issue. Many innovations abound on biodegradability. Kristin Kagetsu co-founded Saathi, a sanitary pad company based in India and built on nine of those sustainable development goals, including gender equality and sanitation for all. Saathi uses biodegradable and compostable banana and bamboo fiber to make its pads. Scientists at the International Islamic University Malaysia have fabricated a durable, absorbent, biodegradable sanitary pad using sago, a starch extracted from the spongy centre of tropical palm stems.

Innovation

Fluss pads are designed to breakdown through flushing, and so a bin may not provide the right conditions for them to fully biodegrade. By flushing them, you know they will break down into clean water, renewable energy and fertilizer at your local water treatment centre. Planera has created a flushable and biodegradable sanitary pad a move expected to positively impact the level of waste the industry produces and fails to dispose of each year. Planera's pads have been successfully and independently tested in accordance with WIS 4-02-06, the water industry specification for flushability testing. The pad breaks down in two parts. First, with the hydraulic action of the toilet flush pulls the layers of the pad apart allowing it to start making its way down the drain line. Then, the 3mm cellulose fibres loosen and break apart. These steps ensure that the sanitary pad disintegrates by the time it reaches the wastewater treatment plant and can be treated along with toilet paper and sewage.

The startup introduced Hot water soluble sanitary Pads. The water needs to be very hot around 75 – 80 degrees Celsius! At this temperature, the outer layers dissolve, and the internal absorbent core gets dispersed. Cresa's sanitary pads are the only sanitary products that can dissolve in hot water to flush away its slurry.

Video – https://youtu.be/ulArLJansyg

Patents

A Disposable Absorbent Product and a Process for its preparation, 202121026878 · Filed Jun 15, 2021

Flushable sanitary napkin, US3913579A, Johnson and Johnson Consumer Inc

Commercialisation

https://cresagreentech.com/pages/why-cresa

Cresa Greentech is a brand of eco-friendly sanitary pads that focuses on sustainable menstruation. Kick out the old and unhygienic way of disposing of the pads. Instead, use sanitary napkins that get easily dissolved in hot water in just a few minutes.

Hydrogen (H2) Electrolyzers – Newtrace Pvt Ltd Bangalore

Prasanta Sarkar, Co-founder & CEO, received PhD from Université Grenoble Alpes, 2x Marie-curie fellowship from EC and graduated with a Master's degree in Aerospace engineering from University of Manchester. Previously worked for Leonardo helicopters on helicopter design, Convergent science on software development, Kwest research on market research and analytics. Was a Founder-in-residence with Entrepreneur First India for 2 cohorts. Rochan Sinha is the Co-founder &CTO, with a PhD from Eindhoven University of Technology and a research scholar at Dutch Institute for Fundamental Energy Research (DIFFER).

https://www.linkedin.com/in/prasantasarkarin/

Technology

Catalysts are the heart of electrolyzers, driving the electrochemical reactions that produce hydrogen. Scientific research has focused on finding alternative materials to expensive and scarce elements like platinum, which is commonly used as a catalyst in traditional electrolyzers. Recent innovations have introduced earth-abundant and cost-effective catalysts, such as nickel-based materials, transition metal oxides, and metal-organic frameworks. Electrode designs are pivotal to optimizing the efficiency of electrolyzer. Innovations in electrode architecture have focused on increasing the surface area, improving electron and ion transport, and enhancing catalytic activity.

Innovation

In the conventional electrolyzer, the membrane serves to keep the hydrogen and oxygen separate as they can be an explosive mix. The startup decided to remove the membrane altogether and use the flow of water to separate the gases. The ingenious electrode architecture paved a pathway for developing a dual-electrode electrolyzer system that requires 9-10% lower voltage to drive industrially relevant current densities.

Patents

Similar patents – Methods for hydrogen gas production through water electrolysis https://www.osti.gov/biblio/1860164

Patent trends – https://www.irena.org/-/media/Files/IRENA/Agency/Publication/2022/May/IRENA_EPO_Electrolysers_H2_production_2022.pdf?

Commercialisation

https://www.newtrace.io/product

The startup uses an abundant earth metal-based electrocatalyst which allows it to achieve performance close to that of PEM electrolyzer at or below the cost of an alkaline electrolyzer system.

Top seven Hydrogen producing companies in India – https://www.blackridgeresearch.com/blog/list-of-top-green-hydrogen-producing-manufacturing-companies-in-india#

MNRE scheme to promote Electrolysers manufacture in India – https://mnre.gov.in/img/documents/uploads/file_f-1687964057675.pdf

Hydrogen Fuel Cell Bus – Sentient Labs/ KPIT, Pune

Ravi Pandit is the Co-founder and Chairman of KPIT Technologies Ltd. Ravi is a gold medalist and a fellow member of the Institute of Chartered Accountants of India, an associate member of the Institute of Cost and Works Accountants of India, holds masters from Sloan School of Management, MIT, Cambridge, USA. Sentient Labs, an R&D innovation lab, building on technologies incubated by KPIT Technologies Ltd.

Technology

Various research groups in India are engaged in R&D projects on Hydrogen production – read the report: (https://dst.gov.in/sites/default/files/Country%20status%20report%20final%20Hydrogen.pdf)

PEMFC technology has been developed to the commercialization stage in many countries like Canada, USA, Japan, Germany etc. Parallel with Pratt & Whitney Aircraft, General Electric developed the first Proton Exchange Membrane Fuel cell (PEMFC) for Gemini space missions in the early 1960s. The first mission to use PEMFCs was Gemini-V. As per Industry Review, the shipment of PEMFC units dominated in 2011 for the stationary and transport applications. In India, a large number of groups are engaged in the research, development and demonstration activities of PEMFC but it has not reached the stage of commercialization. A few projects/ organizations like CFCT-ARCI, CSIR-Network Labs, NMRL, VSSC and BHEL are engaged in complete development of PEMFC system. Engineering input and infrastructure for producing such system in large numbers for trials / demonstration are lacking.

Innovation

Sentient Labs announced hydrogen fuel cell bus that runs on indigenously developed electric powertrain and hydrogen fuel cell. Fuel cell technology is the result of extensive collaboration between Sentient Labs, CSIR and NCL. In addition to the hydrogen fuel cell technology, Sentient Labs also indigenously designed and developed other key components like balance of plant, powertrain and battery-pack. All of these components have been deployed on a 9-meter, 32-seater, air-conditioned bus. This is designed to provide a range of 450 kms while utilizing 30 kgs of Hydrogen. A modular architecture allows for changes in the design to suit requirements of range and operating conditions.

Initially, CSIR and KPIT have successfully developed a 10 kWe automotive grade LT-PEMFC fuel cell stack based on CSIR's know-how. The heart of the PEM fuel cell technology includes the membrane electrode assembly, which is wholly a CSIR knowhow. KPIT brought in their expertise in stack engineering which included light-weight metal bipolar plate and gasket design, development of the balance of plant (BoP), system integration, control software and electric powertrain that enabled running the fuel cell vehicle. The fuel cell stack uses extremely thin metal bipolar plates, thus reducing the stack weight by about two-thirds.

Patents

Patent analysis –

https://www.energy.gov/sites/prod/files/2014/03/f12/pathways_2013.pdf

Commercialisation

http://www.sentientlabs.in/

Hydrogen powered trains – Hyderabad-based railway technology company Medha Servo Drives is currently working on retrofitting two of IR's diesel-electric locomotives with hydrogen fuel cells, made by Canada's Ballard Power Systems.

Intelligently Stirred Thermophilic Anaerobic Reactor – Sankar Ganesh Palani, BITS Pilani, Hyderabad

Prof. Sankar Ganesh is an Associate Professor of Environmental Biotechnology and the Coordinator of Graduate School in Global Sanitation at BITS Pilani, Hyderabad Campus. He did his PhD in Environmental Science and Engineering from Pondicherry (Central) University, India and had his post-doctoral training at Institut National des Sciences Appliquees, Toulouse, France.

https://universe.bits-pilani.ac.in/hyderabad/psankarganesh/profile

Technology

In anaerobic digestion process, temperature is not only important for microbial metabolic activities but also for the overall digestion rate, specifically the rates of hydrolysis and methane formation. In general, anaerobic digestion process can occur within a wide range of temperatures. This temperature range has been broadly divided into two groups: mesophilic – 30 to 42 degree centigrade and thermophilic – 43 to 55 degree centigrade. In practice, most of the digesters are designed to operate at mesophilic range between 30 to 38 degree centigrade while some of them are designed for thermophilic temperature range of 50 to 57 degree centigrade (Metcalf and Eddy, 2003). In general, thermophilic digestion processes potentially allow higher loadings with reduced hydraulic retention times, higher conversion efficiencies and pathogen disinfection while mesophilic digestion is more stable, less at risk from ammonia nitrogen toxicity and requires less process heat. Solar Thermophilic Anaerobic Reactors for cow dung are reported from Egypt.

Innovation

iSTAR® is an anaerobic reactor technology developed for efficient bio-methanation of organic waste. Key Features & Benefits: single-stage anaerobic digestion, maintains homogeneous substrate concentration in the reactor, maintains uniform temperature throughout the reactor, continuously monitors critical parameters of the reactor, Reduces overall energy consumption of the system.

Thermophilic anaerobic digestion can offer higher biogas production, more complete volatile organic destruction and pathogen destruction. Some researchers have reported that they have been able to reduce the hydraulic retention time (HRT) from a necessary 15 to 20 days in mesophilic digestion down to as little as 3 days at a thermophilic temperature in the region of (55°C) with stable fermentation & methanogenic activity. That is an illustration of just how much of effect the temperature of an AD plant reactor can have but for reliance on the lowest possible hydraulic retention time any AD facility developer would need to be very confident in their ability to keep the system stable in operation as there would be very little time to react if the reactor started to experience problems. Loss of reactor up-time while high rate reactors can be teased back into full health, can be very costly and all decisions on optimizing throughput need to balance economy of initial capital spend, and robustness in plant operation throughout its life.

Publications: https://www.researchgate.net/scientific-contributions/P-Sankar-Ganesh-2158032975

Patents

Indian Patent No.202111051662

Commercialisation

Ready to launch at industry-scale. Ideal for urban & rural local bodies, restaurants, institutions and gated communities. As part of the CoRE project, a 12,000 Lt thermophilic biogas digester was commissioned in 2014 at the students' hostel dining hall to treat food waste. The biogas produced is used as a supplement for cooking gas and the spent slurry is used as a soil amendment/biofertilizer for horticulture.

Video:

Other technologies available from BITs:

https://www.bits-pilani.ac.in/university/research/AvailableTechnologies

Marine Oil Spill Remediation – NIOT, Chennai

A Ganesh Kumar is Scientist-E at NIOT. He along with N NivedhaRajan and R Kirubagaran of NIOT worked on Marine Oil Spill Remediation.

https://www.researchgate.net/profile/A-Ganesh-Kumar

Technology

Bioremediation can be defined as any process that uses microorganisms or their enzymes to remove and or neutralize contaminants within the environment (i.e. within soil and water) to their original condition. In marine ecosystem, hydrocarbonoclastic deep sea microbial consortium (two or more group of bacteria) plays an important role in breaking down oil in the event of a spill. The microbial community serves as energetic primary degraders of complex mixture of petroleum hydrocarbons into various aldehydes, ketones and acidic metabolites.

Innovation

The National Institute of Ocean Technology (NIOT) has developed an eco-friendly crude oil bio-remediation mechanism technology using consortia of marine microbes wheat bran (WB) immobilized on agro-residue bacterial cells. During the study, nine different hydrocarbon-degrading bacteria extracted from the ocean sediment and collected from a depth of 2,100 metres, were used. These hydrocarbon degrading bacteria don't depend on hydrocarbon for survival, but have a metabolic mechanism where they use petroleum products as carbon and energy source and thus, help cleaning up oil spills. It was found that complete breakdown and degradation of crude oil was achievable using wheat bran marine bacterial consortia (which are low-cost non-toxic agro residues) immobilised on low-cost nontoxic agro-residues bacterial cells in an environmentally sustainable manner. It was also found that they were more effective in their immobilised state than the free bacteria cells in degrading the oil spills, in addition to being more versatile and resistant to adverse conditions. The NIOT study found that immobilised bacterial cells had better oil degrading capacity than the free bacterial cells. They could remove 84 per cent of the oils within 10 days. The free bacterial cells degraded a maximum of 60 per cent of the crude oil at optimised conditions.

https://www.niot.res.in/media/Technology%20Transfer/Bioremediation%20of%20crude%20oil%20PTN_07_09_2021%20(GKF)20230206110207.pdf

Patents

Publications – https://www.nature.com/articles/s41598-019-55115-9

N. exalbescens COD22 is a novel deep sea strain and degraded 87.5 and 92% of toluene at ambient and high pressure growth conditions within a short incubation period of 72h. Toluene degradation pathway has been elucidated for the first time in deep sea strain under high pressure conditions.

Commercialisation

National Research Development Corporation (NRDC) has transferred and signed technology licensing agreement for innovative technologies "Marine oil spill bioremediation technology" developed by National Institute of Ocean Technology (NIOT), Chennai to M/s Eco Buildcorp Pvt. Ltd. (EBPL), Bengaluru, Karnataka.

http://ecobuildcorp.com/

Technologies available for transfer from NIOT – https://www.niot.res.in/niot_tech_transfer.php

Moving Bed Biofilm Reactor (MBBR) – NIT Warangal

Prof. Sonawane Shirish Hari, Department of Chemical Engineering, NIT, Warangal with a PhD in Chemical Technology, North Maharashtra University, India is a researcher with 8873 citations and H-Index: 54. He along with Dr. Murali Mohan Seepana, NIT Warangal, Dr. Ajey Kumar Patel, NIT Warangal and Dr. Mousumi Debnath, Manipal University Jaipur (MUJ) developed individual systems at the laboratories and the process parameters were optimized. The biosurfactant to be used in Moving Bed Biofilm Reactor (MBBR) was extracted from microorganisms isolated from textile effluent and textile effluent contaminated soil by MUJ.

https://www.researchgate.net/profile/Shirish-Sonawane

https://jaipur.manipal.edu/fos/schools-faculty/faculty-list/Mousumi-Debnath.html

Technology

The MBBR is a biological process that uses bacteria to decompose waste. This technology consists of a tank that features a bio-media (inert object facilitating the treatment of the influent) that allows bacteria to grow freely. The bacteria growing in the media in multiple layers allows the organic elements and nutrients to be removed from the waste stream and "convert the soluble material into biomass" that will be removed further along the stream. The MBBR process is carried out in a tank. These "MBBR aeration tanks are open at the top, exposing the water to open air, which makes this an aerobic filtration process." It is a municipal and wastewater treatment process created in 1980s.

Innovation

NIT Warangal along with Prime Textiles, Rampur located in Kakatiya Mega Textile Park (KMTP), with support from IMPRINT, a joint effort of MoE and SERB, developed a pilot-scale textile effluent treatment plant using biosurfactants (BS), cavitation (a process in which pressure variations in a liquid can in a short period of time cause countless small cavities to form and then implode-C), and membrane (M) technology. The use of BS in MBBR helped in dye removal and was effective in reducing operational time and cost (with respect to other biological treatment methods). Cavitation (C), an advanced oxidation process (AOP), aided in reducing installation cost as well as reducing carbon footprint. The ability of the technology to generate oxidizing radicals in-situ, significantly reduced the reliance on external oxidizing agents. On the other hand, modifying the membrane (M) surface using boehmite sol synthesized using sol-gel process, decreased the pore size from micro-scale to nano-scale and led to a significant improvement in its performance. After optimizing individual systems, a pilot-scale setup has been set up at the Prime Textiles premises.

The sequence of events that takes place in the pilot plant plays an important role in the treatment process of the effluent. The coagulation removes turbidity caused by suspended solids by destabilizing the charges of the particles using a chemical coagulant. The biofilm grown on MBBR reduces the heavy metal content, degrades the biodegradable pollutants while the cavitation phenomenon destroys all types of pollutants, resulting in the in situ generation of radicals, and energy which are responsible for the pollutant degradation. Finally, surface modified membrane separates all the pollutants present in the wastewater. With this sequence, the pilot plant of 200L per day capacity removes pollutants and the treated water can be utilized for agricultural activities, and cleaning purposes.

https://serb.gov.in/page/nit_warangal

Patents

Filed – Development and demonstration of Pilot-scale hybrid Wastewater Treatment system with Hydrodynamic Caitation and Biosurfactant for Recycling of Textile effluent – https://oldweb.nitw.ac.in/media/uploads/2022/03/10/patent-v1.pdf

Other patents – https://www.allindianpatents.com/patents/230949-a-process-for-the-treatment-of-textile-industries-effluent

Commercialisation

IMPacting Research, INnovation and Technology (IMPRINT) is a unique technology development initiative of the Government of India through the Ministry of Human resource Development (MHRD) for translation of research knowledge into viable technology (products and processes).

https://www.serbonline.in/SERB/IMPRINT2C

Muffler and Particulate Separator for Internal Combustion Engine Exhaust – RnA Vortech Innovations, Chandigarh

Adess Singh, physicist & inventor with accomplishments in developing and patenting technologies in energy, security, environment, automotive and health sectors among others is the Promoter Director & Chief Technology officer of RnA Vortech Innovations Private Limited. Rajandeep Singh (Rajan) Tiwana is co-Director and co-innovator along with Adess Singh. RnA Vortech Innovations Private Limited is a DPIIT recognized clean-tech startup for commercialization of one of their patented technologies under the tradename 'CentriAirFlow'. Received National Award for Commercializable Patents in 2014 by TIFAC.

https://www.linkedin.com/in/adess-singh-2a84242a/

https://www.linkedin.com/in/rajandeep-singh-tiwana-03200a12b/

Technology

Reeves designed and patented his unique silencing instrument in 1897, now known as muffler. Dr. Christopher Dean of Palm Coast, FL has created a replaceable muffler exhaust filtration system to catch and properly dispose a significant portion of toxic products and carbon emissions, so they no longer pose a threat to the environment or people who live in it.

Innovation

CentriAirFlow uses the kinetic energy of the exhaust gases to cause separation of fine particulates (unlike the present technology which neutralizes it to reduce noise). This objective is achieved by utilizing the high speed of exhaust gases to create a vortex, which in turn, causes centrifugal separation of particulates without creating back pressure on the engine due to which fuel efficiency improves significantly. CentriAirflow is configured for particulates to undergo multiple passes of spin resulting in efficient removal of particulates from engine exhaust. Without increasing back pressure the devise entraps the finest of particulate matter from exhaust of internal combustion engine, while it also achieves the following objectives at the same time: Reduces emissions of NOx, CO and CO2, Improves engine efficiency giving a saving of fuel by 15%.

Tet results – https://centriairflow.com/industries#test_result

Patents

Devise for Removing Particulate Matter from Exhaust gases of Internal Combustion Engine, US US 9,885,270 · Issued Feb 6, 2018

Devise for Removing Particulate Matter from Exhaust Gases of internal combustion, GB EP3058189 · Issued Aug 24, 2016

A Muffler and Particulate Separator for Internal Combustion Engine, IN 254858 · Issued Dec 27, 2012

Commercialisation

https://centriairflow.com/product

https://www.linkedin.com/company/rna-vortech-innovations-private-limited/

CentriAirFlow is an improved exhaust device for trapping and removing Particulate Matter from the exhaust gases of any internal combustion engine without increasing the resistance to the flow of exhaust gases (Engine Exhaust Backpressure).CentriAirFlow, when fitted to the exhaust system of a vehicle replacing its muffler,

1. Improves emission compliance of the vehicle by capture and trapping particulate matter to the extent of 70% or more,
2. Improves the fuel efficiency of the vehicle by minimum 20%,
3. Reduces the exhaust noise better than the vehicle's muffler, and
4. Provides better driving experience.

Plastic Waste into Green Fuel and Energy – DBT-ICT Centre for Energy Biosciences

Dr Hitesh S Pawar is Assistant Professor, Center of Energy Biosciences. This patented technology is developed by his team along with Dr. Vishwanath H Dalvi, Assistant Professor under the guidance of Prof. Anniruddha B Pandit, Vice Chancellor.

https://www.ictmumbai.edu.in/EMPBiodata.aspx

Technology

Converting waste polymers into fuel has been also reported using methods such as thermal cracking, flow cracking, catalytic cracking, and pyrolysis. A wide range of catalysts have been employed in plastic pyrolysis processes, but the most extensively used catalysts are ZSM-5, zeolite, Y-zeolite, FCC, and MCM-41.

Innovation

Poly-Urja process: Plastic waste has been identified as a potent feedstock for liquefaction to produce hydrocarbon liquid oil (HC-Oil) by employing Catalytic Thermo Liquefaction (CTL). The resulting process for liquefaction of plastic was termed as Poly-Urja process and produced hydrocarbon oil was termed as HC-Oil. The CTL explores copper doped TiO_2 (Cu@TiO_2) catalyst as a selective, robust, non-toxic, inexpensive and promising material for liquefaction of poly-olefinic plastic waste with minimum char and gas formation. The use of simple, non-expensive and non-complex co-precipitation method has provided a series of Cu@TiO_2 catalysts with variable composition of the metal. Of the synthesized catalysts, Cu@TiO_2 with 5% metal loading gave maximum conversion and yield of HC-Oil in laboratory batch reactor. The physicochemical and surface morphological properties of the catalyst were studied by using ATR-FTIR, XRD, SEM-EDX, BET and ICP-MS. Process intensification study was conducted to obtain maximum conversion and yield. The intensified CTL process gave >85% conversion and >80% yield of HC-Oil at less stringent conditions. HC-Oil is a carbon rich substrate comprises of 75–85% carbon, 5–15% hydrogen, 5–10% other elements and have a calorific value of ~42 MJ/kg thus it can be used for multiple applications of energy, fuels and chemicals etc. Physicochemical characterization of HC-Oil showed the presence of long and short; straight and branched chains of hydrocarbons (C8-C28). Moreover, CTL can convert any combination of plastic waste into HC-Oil with minimum carbon loss and >80% yield. Thus, the CTL process for poly-olefinic waste provides an efficient, sustainable and environmentally friendly alternative to convert plastic waste into energy.

Patents

Patent-PROCESS FOR CATALYTIC THERMO LIQUEFACTION OF PLASTIC WASTE INTO LIQUID HYDROCARBON OIL AND CATALYST

THEREOF. Indian Application Number: 202121007438, Indian Grant Number: 428938

A catalytic liquefaction (CTL) method for production of bio-crude oil using ionic liquid catalyst and preparation thereof, WO2018020511A1, published in 2018

Paper – A Cu doped TiO2 catalyst mediated Catalytic Thermo Liquefaction (CTL) of polyolefinic plastic waste into hydrocarbon oil. Fuel Volume 285, 1 February 2021, 119155, https://www.sciencedirect.com/science/article/abs/pii/S0016236120321517

Other patents of Dr Hitesh Pawar – https://www.ictmumbai.edu.in/PatentDetails.aspx?nEmpId=caesg

Commercialisation

Many patents available for exploitation by industry. Check:

https://www.ictmumbai.edu.in/res_innovation.aspx?sCatid=7

For incubation:

https://www.linkedin.com/in/ict-nice-venture-incubator-and-foundation-s-m-mokashi-incubation-centre-59ba07239/

MIT founded – https://renewone.co/about/

See other technologies funded by DST: https://dst.gov.in/dst-supported-technologies-brings-solutions-plastic-pollution-environment

Sanitary Pad Waste Recycling – Pad Care Labs, Pune

Ajinkya Dhariya is Founder and CEO at PadCare Labs is a Mechanical Engineer from Shri Guru Gobind Singhji Institute of Engineering and Technology, Vishnupuri, Nanded. Awards – Forbes 30 Under 30 Asia, FICCI – BEST SANITATION STARTUP 2020, Most Innovative Startup Award 2019, Infosys Aarohan award, ASME ISHOW 2020

Technology

Most developments in west are focused in collection of used sanitary pads and aesthetic design of bins often place in personal bathrooms. In India, https://www.envmart.com/, offers Napkin incinerator in various sizes. PSU, ITI, Bangalore developed incinerator – https://www.itiltd.in/mkp_sanitary_fauna_l

Innovation

The pads are collected in 'PadCare Bins' which are placed in women's washrooms along with Sanitary napkins vending machine. Each bin is equipped with an inner liner in which the used pads are placed; these liners curb microbial activity and also eliminate odours. They can be stored upto 30 days. Waste collectors benefit because handling the liners helps prevent direct exposure to and contact with the used pads. Once a bin is full, a cloud-connected volume tracking mechanism indicates the need for waste pickup. The waste is collected and brought to a central processing unit where a machine shreds the pads and then deactivates the absorbent chemicals used in them. The pads undergo a multistep process including disinfection, decolorization, deodorization, and deactivation to transform them into cellulose and plastic pellets. In turn, these pellets are used to make various products like packaging material, tabletops, and plant pots. Body fluids (menstrual waste) which are a by-product of the process are directed towards a sewage outlet. Their patent pending 5D technology is instant, odourless, and colourless in operation unlike traditional incinerators.

Video – https://youtu.be/Vb19LscAQeQ

Patents

A SMART PORTABLE DEVICE AND SYSTEM FOR DISPOSAL OF SANITARY WASTEA SMART PORTABLE DEVICE AND SYSTEM FOR DISPOSAL OF SANITARY WASTE, IN 201921023476 · Filed Jun 13, 2019

Commercialisation

https://www.padcarelabs.com/CSR

As a trailblazing startup in menstrual hygiene management, PadCare offers a unique opportunity for companies to partner in implementing impactful CSR initiatives. At PadCare, an impactful initiative has reached over 11,000 females and is still counting. It also tackles the challenges of awareness, accessibility, segregation and recycling in menstrual hygiene management. The PadCare Vending Machine, PadCare Bin and end-to-end recycling solution, ensures that females have the utmost comfort, privacy and easy access to essential products and services. CSR projects in schools, communities and housing societies eliminate the need for manual collection of used sanitary pads by safai karamcharis. With strategically placed bins, females can dispose of their used pads at the source, ensuring no manual handling for the workers. This fosters a healthier, more dignified and hygienic environment for all.

Water Management Platform (MIDAS) – Ekatvam Innovations, Thane

Rishabh Ravichandran is Founder at Ekatvam Innovations, an engineer from VIT, mentored at Digital Impact Square, Villgro. Rishabh heads the business and innovation at Ekatvam Innovation. Piyush heads management at Ekatvam innovations. He holds a bachelor's in Production Engineering at K.K. Wagh Institute of Technology.

Technology

Frequent attempts are made to find technical solutions to the groundwater crisis. Aquifers can be refilled with treated wastewater or water from storm surges, for instance, or water-saving and wastewater-treatment technologies can be employed to reduce consumption. Satellite monitoring of land-use change can help to identify sources of pollution and overexploitation or aid with the collection of usage-based water charges. Institutional reforms to protect and maintain groundwater resources are also being initiated in many places. Vulnerable drinking water catchment areas are being closed to use, and licences are being required for the construction and utilisation of wells. Two local institutions are mainly involved in groundwater management in India: Water User Associations (WUA) and groundwater management committees (GWMC).

Legal framework in India does not explicitly define groundwater ownership and rights. These rights tied to land ownership rights. CGWA is also authorized to declare certain zones as 'notified areas' with stringent regulations such as issuing No Objection Certificates (NOCs) and restricting energy use to extract water. The top-down approach of groundwater management failed to establish a behavioral transition among its users. People are crucial in maintaining the common pool resource nature of groundwater and to protect it against climate change impacts.

Innovation

Ekatvam is working in the agri-water tech space aiming at providing data-centric water management solutions to village communities and key decision-makers. Unregulated groundwater extraction and lack of participatory water resource management are prime factors for this crisis. This has resulted in more than 10,000 Indian villages going into groundwater over-exploitation stage and affecting millions of farmers. Ekatvam aims to equip the village community with digital and non-digital tools that can provide them with visibility on the water condition of their villages and simulate multiple corrective scenarios that could improve it.

MIDAS – Web Dashboard is a planning tool that can provide decision makers with monthly visibility on the villages water condition along with seasonal water budgets on a click of a button. Automatic data triangulation from satellite, primary and secondary sources; Village level access to historical and near real-time water data. Provision for decision-makers to visualize the impact of intervention through simulations.

A mobile app for the village community that showcases their water budget on a monthly basis. Through this mobile platform they are creating a paradigm shift from tabular water accounting to one which is more interactive with simulations and scenarios thus enabling behavioral change in the village community.

Patents

A system developed in Australia – https://www.csiro.au/en/work-with-us/industries/mining-resources/social-and-enviromental-performance/vesi

From USA – https://www.osti.gov/doepatents/biblio/866266-groundwater-monitoring-system

Commercialisation

Groundwater is a shared resource thus it is highly important that water management is community-led activity. This requires a considerable amount of behavioral change to be brought about in the community. Ekatvam's platform solves for this by showcasing various simulations and scenarios aimed at aiding its NGO partners to bring about 'Jan Andolan' in the villages. Currently, Ekatvam is aiding four such NGOs in 50 villages across Maharashtra, Gujarat and Andhra Pradesh. At the village level, and has provided visibility to almost 800+ farmers on the water condition of their villages. More than 40 farmers have now started to monitor their wells on a weekly basis. 40 seasonal water meetings have been conducted in the village which has led to improvement in the irrigation practices like drip and mulching. Approximately 216 farmers have adopted these practices in Gujarat alone.

https://ekatvaminnovations.com/

Waterless urinal – Ekam Eco Solutions, New Delhi

Uttam Banerjee graduate from Oriental Institute of Science & Technology and PG from IITD in Industrial Design founded Ekam Eco Solutions. Prior to Ekam Eco, he had a few stints with design teams in large organizations. Honors & awards – Millennium Alliance Award issued by USAID, TDB, FICCI, UKAID, ICICI Foundation, India Innovation Growth Programme India issued by Lockheed Martin Corporation, DST. Banerjee in partnership with his IIT professor V.M. Chariar, has designed a urinal which, instead of consuming water, prevents it being wasted and – amazingly – remains stink free.

https://www.linkedin.com/in/banerjeeuttam/

https://web.iitd.ac.in/~chariarv/design-sustainibility.php

Technology

A Waterless Urinal is an innovative plumbing fixture designed to conserve water by eliminating the need for flushing. This ecofriendly retrofit to conventional urinals is increasingly embraced in both commercial and institutional settings for its efficiency and environmental benefits. Waterless urinals are designed to save water and reduce maintenance costs by eliminating the need for flushing with water. They are useful in public restrooms or other facilities where a large number of people use the restrooms on a daily basis. There are different types of waterless urinals available in the market working on different principles. Some have chemical sealant cartridge which uses chemicals as a sealant to allow passage of liquid urine. Another technology which is used frequently is Membrane based cartridge which has a membrane flap that opens for passage of urine.

Innovation

Zerodor Waterless Urinal is a frugally designed plumbing kit which can be retrofitted to any conventional urinal pan with a waste coupling. It is a patented mechanical device that does not use any consumables or power supply for its functioning. It does not have any recurring cost and makes the restroom odor free and water free. This kit have a mechanical one way ball valve which allows the urine to flow into the drain line but does not allow the odor causing gases to come back into the restroom. This allows the urinals to operate without flushing.

Chemistry behind odor and Zerodor waterless urinals – Hydrolysis of urea present in human urine generates odor in urinals. The enzyme urease hydrolyses urea into ammonia and carbamate. The latter compound decomposes spontaneously to carbonic acid and a second molecule of ammonia. Ammonia (NH_3) is a colorless gas with a pungent odor. Ammonia exists naturally in the air at levels between one part and five parts per billion (ppb) of air. The normal human detection level of ammonia is approximately 50 ppm. Once the urine passes through the drain and the odour evolves the float valve will have enough weight to block the odour from refluxing back in the water closet. As the float is hand moulded out of polymeric material it does not have aging.

Patents

Patent entitled "Novel Toilet Design for separation of urine from faeces" V M Chariar and S Ramesh Sakthivel (2012), (Indian Patent Application under process).

Patent entitled "An odour prevention device" V M Chariar and S Ramesh Sakthivel (2010), Indian Patent Application No. 60/Del/2010.

Patent entitled "Synergistic removal of ammonium and nitrate ions from aqueous solutions" V M Chariar, Uttam Banerjee and Azizur Rahman (Under Process)

Patent entitled "Inline combined removal and recovery of ammonium and phosphate from sewage and urinal pipelines" V M Chariar, Uttam Banerjee and Azizur Rahman (Under Process)

Commercialisation

www.ekameco.com

www.noflush.in

Ekam Eco Solutions, founded in 2013, is a research spin-off of IIT Delhi's works on Sanitation. Over five thousand man hours of research on Sanitation forms the backbone of this organization. Ekam is a Sanskrit word meaning Oneness and Interconnectedness.

Ekam's approach is based on the fundamental principles of Happiness, Simplicity and Positivity. Ekam focuses on developing sustainable technologies and solutions to conserves water and convert waste into resource using natural means.

Defence & Aerospace

1. Aero Structure Components – LMW Advanced Technology Centre (ATC), Coimbatore
2. Air Independent Propulsion system – Naval Materials Research Laboratory (NMRL) and L&T
3. AI-based Aircraft Engine Inspection Tool – Awiros, Gurugram
4. BeagleZ-explosive detector – Prof Anil Kumar, IITB/ NewTec Lab, Bangalore
5. Long Range Surveillance-Optimized Electrotech, Ahmedabad
6. Smallest short range VTOL quadcopter – Idea Forge, Mumabi
7. Satellite systems – Ananth Technologies, Hyderabad
8. Satellite Bus Technology, ISRO/ Alpha Design Technologies, Bangalore
9. Solar Ultraviolet Imaging Telescope (SUIT) – IUCAA,Pune
10. Smart policing – Staqu Technologies, Gurugram
11. Unmanned autonomous vessel – Sagar Defence Engineering, Pune

Aero Structure Components – LMW Advanced Technology Centre (ATC)

Vijayasekaran Veluchamy, Senior Vice President, Built the brown field integrated aerospace setup focussing structure, engine, sheet metal,special process and structural assembly. Integrated the facility with AGV's to minimise the human in material and finished part handling. Built a CoE for bleed valves for Pratt engine series GP7000, NGPF engine for MRJ, Bombardier engines. Developed 27 special process with Nadcap approval and received customer approval like Boeing, Pratt, Honeywell, Magellan, UTCAS including All HAL divisions in 3 years time. Received a single order for 6 M USD from DRDO for building the antenna Dome structure. Indigenously designed and fabricated the assembly jigs for assembling the entire structure. Established a structural assembly cell for helicopter tail boom, SU30 structural assembly, Dome structural assembly.Built a 250 engineers team to specialise the machining, sheet metal, Spl process and Engine & structural assembly. Made the breakeven in 5 yrs of operation.

https://www.lmwatc.com

A graduate from Thiagarajar College of Engineering followed by double masters from Defense Institute of Advanced Technology (DIAT), DU, DRDO he worked in DRDO for 18 years on aero engines & Accessories.

https://www.linkedin.com/in/vijayasekaran-1103455/

Technology

Indian Government policy encouraged legacy companies to develop capabilities and venture into Defence & Aerospace manufacturing. To diversify operations, LMW collaborated with Japan's Mori Seiki Co. Ltd to establish the Machine Tools Division in 1988, which is the first-of-its-kind plant in India that manufactures CNC lathes, machining centres, and other machine tools. A state-of-the-art Foundry Division was established in 1993. The foundry that covers more than 16,000 sq. m. built-up area manufactures ductile iron and grey iron castings according to customer demands using the unique 'No Bake' Process. LMW LTE was established in 2004, to focus on high precision manufacturing, assemblies and sub-assemblies for Aerospace and Defence applications. LMW established Advanced Technology Centre (ATC) in 2010 to cater to the growing requirements of the global Aerospace industry.

Innovation

Establishing manufacturing facility with unique capabilities viz a viz Structural machining of up to 10m length with 5 axis capability, Multi axis capable machining centre, Sheet metal capability with fabrication and welding technology and Special process including

MPI, FPI, Anodizing, Painting, and phosphating along with Solitionzing furnaces.

Patents

Technology is in production processes, employees skills and certified facilities.

Commercialisation

https://www.lmwatc.com/

In the year 2010, Lakshmi Machine Works (LMW) added to their formidable manufacturing resources, a new plant to produce critical components and sub-assemblies for Aerospace industry. Product portfolio:

Space And Defence Components – Pay load fairings, Composite interstage structures, Radomes for space, airborne and ground applications, Antenna reflectors, Solar panel substrates, Pressure vessels, Motor cases, Missile launcher tubes.

Fixed-Wing Aircraft Components – Fuselage components, Fin and Rudder, Interior components, Floor beams and panels, Fixed wing structures, Flaps, Ailerons and Spoilers, Engine nacelles.

Rotary-Wing Aircraft Components – Main rotor blade and Hub plate, Tail rotor blade and Hub plate, Door assembly and interiors, Engine cowlings, Landing skids, Empennage components

Air Independent Propulsion System – Naval Materials Research Laboratory (NMRL) and L&T

French firm Naval Group signed a pact with India's DRDO to fit indigenous Air Independent Propulsion (AIP) system on Kalvari class submarines. The indigenous fuel cell-based AIP system will be fitted on INS Kalvari soon.The AIP has been developed by DRDO's Naval Materials Research Laboratory (NMRL), and the land-based prototype has been tested. The technology has been successfully developed with the support of industry partners L&T and Thermax.

KEYNOTE SPEECH: "Air Independent Propulsion (AIP)"-Dr. Suman Roy Choudhury//RSD 2021//IIT MADRAS, Video: https://youtu.be/SOEVJCKxfBA

Technology

Air-independent propulsion (AIP), or air-independent power, is any marine propulsion technology that allows a non-nuclear submarine to operate without ac cess to atmospheric oxygen. Air Independent Propulsion (AIP) allows diesel electric submarines to remain underwater for longer periods besides making them quieter. In April 2006, a German Navy submarine U-32, equipped with a Siemens proton exchange membrane (PEM) compressed hydrogen f uel cell AIP, made a 2800 km uninterrupted underwater journey without surfacing/snorkeling! This is in stark contrast to non-AIP equipped submarines which can cover only 500-800 km before they have to surface and recharge their batteries by running noisy diesel generators.

Innovation

AIP enhances the submerged endurance of the boat. Fuel cell-based AIP has merits in performance compared to other technologies. While there are different types of AIP systems being pursued internationally, fuel cell based AIP of NMRL is unique as the hydrogen is generated onboard. Larsen & Toubro and DRDO signed a contract for realisation of two Air Independent Propulsion (AIP) System Modules for Kalvari Class of Submarines of the Indian Navy. These Modules constitute the core of the fuel cell based AIP System, indigenously developed by Naval Materials Research Laboratory (NMRL) of DRDO with L&T as prime industry partner, an association spanning more than a decade. The Energy Modules (EMs) comprising Fuel Cells produce the required power, along with on-board Hydrogen generation. The Fuel cells are based on PAFC technology with max power of 300W. The technology of this indigenous AIP system is a unique one that generates hydrogen on demand thereby obviating the need for carrying hydrogen onboard which is a major safety concern for a submarine. The manufacturing, integration and factory acceptance trials of the EMs will be undertaken in L&T's AM Naik Heavy Engineering Complex at Surat. The EMs will be supplied for integration into the AIP Plug that will be retrofitted into the submarine.

http://trishul-trident.blogspot.com/2019/12/explained-mareem-aip-plug-in-module-for.html

Patents

Air independent propulsion system for submarines based on phosphoric acid fuel cell with onboard hydrogen generator, WO2017145068A1 WIPO (PCT), Priority claimed from IN201611006254, Inventors – Suman ROY CHOUDHURY, Janardhan Narayanadas PILLAI, Boddu SOMAIAH, Mahendra PARETA, Prasad SATVILKAR, Amit Kumar, Prem Kant NEGI, Nitin Nana MAHTRE, Suhasini ROY CHOUDHURY, Vaibhav Verma, Vishal DALVI, Parvin Kumar SINGH, Shivaji Eknath,SURYAWANSHI, Shambhu Kumar MANDAL

Publications – https://www.researchgate.net/profile/Suman-Roy-9

Commercialisation

The DRDO handed over Licensing Agreements for ToT (LAToT) for 14 DRDO developed technologies to 20 industries. The technologies transferred are from the area of electronics, laser technology, armaments, life sciences, materials science, combat vehicles, naval systems, aeronautics, sensors, etc. The product technologies transferred are Low Level Transportable Radar (LLTR), Inertial Navigation System for Ship Application (INS-SA), Long Range Optical Target Locator (OTL 1500), Hand Held Through Wall Imaging Radar (HH-TWIR) and Commander TI (Thermal Imager) Sight for T-72 Tank are the sensor technologies transferred to various industries. NMRL-Fuel Cell based Air Independent Propulsion Technology for Naval Submarines named NMFCAIP is a unique capability developed by DRDO and now transferred to the industry. Multi Agent Robotic System (MARS) will be produced by Indian industry based on DRDO design.

https://www.makeinindiadefence.gov.in/

AI-based Aircraft Engine Inspection Tool – Awiros, Gurugram

Vikram Gupta and Yatin Kavishwar, Co-founders of Awiros. Awiros is an open platform for computer vision and AI developers, providing them with all of the necessary resources for transforming AI algorithms into end-to-end solutions. Vikram Gupta is graduate from Visvesvaraya National Institute of Technology and dual-PhD Student Researcher from Carnegie Mellon University & CISTER. Yatin had commerce degree from Devi Ahilya Vishwavidyalaya and MBA from SIDTM,Pune.

https://www.linkedin.com/in/vkrmgpta/

https://www.linkedin.com/in/yatinkavishwar/

Technology

Aircraft leasing is a popular option for airlines and operators who want to access modern and efficient aircraft without the high costs of ownership. However, leasing also comes with certain obligations and responsibilities, especially when the lease term is about to end. A lease return inspection is a critical process that determines whether the aircraft meets the contractual conditions and standards of the lessor. If not, the lessee may face hefty penalties and charges for any discrepancies or damages.

Innovation

Percept is a computer vision product that operates on top of the Awiros Video Intelligence Operating System (OS). Its cloud-based interface allows users to capture images and videos of aircraft engines on their mobile devices and receive real-time responses on parts availability. This helps enable faster and cost-efficient turnaround of leased engine assets. Instead of an inspector having to examine an engine and check part-by-part, Percept automates this inspection, and reduces time taken by nearly 90%. Percept's high-fidelity scanning of Pratt & Whitney engines with handheld mobiles phones, without any specialized hardware, is being commercially deployed in the aerospace industry. Pratt & Whitney debuted a new artificial intelligence inspection tool at the Paris Air Show this week aimed at simplifying pre – and post-lease analysis of aircraft engines. According to Pratt & Whitney (P&W), Percept automates inspections so inspectors do not need to check leased engines part-by-part, reducing inspection time by around 90%. It adds that this functionality enables faster, more cost-efficient turnaround of leased engine assets. "The Percept tool empowers our customers to scan engines on their own, so they know what needs to be done to properly return an engine before it's redelivered. Our customers can then determine what is the quickest and most cost-effective solution for missing parts identified by Percept before an engine is lease returned," says a spokesperson for P&W.

Patents

MANUFACTURING INTELLIGENCE SERVICE SYSTEM CONNECTED TO MES IN SMART FACTORY, Patent Publication number: 20230152781, S Korea

Commercialisation

Awiros was selected as the winner of the RTX Innovation Challenge. The Innovation Challenge was launched in September 2019 with over 60 Indian and global startups in Computer Vision, AI, and Machine learning (ML)domains. The teams proposed solutions to optimize and automate aircraft engine inspections with reduced human interventions. Awiros Software Platform can be easily deployed and accessed over any public or private cloud. Awiros utilizes the orchestration capabilities of the cloud and provides unmatched flexibility to cater to your Video Intelligence needs. Ideally suited for enterprises, SME's and Smart Homes. Tailored to work with any cloud service provider. Easy to setup and use. Easy access to data & alerts. Cost-effective. Scales on demand. Platform as a service (PaaS).On-Demand compute and storage availability. Awiros is building the world's first community of Video AI developers. In the form of Awiros Spira, we are stitching together an ecosystem of talent, resources, products and business opportunities for the entire community to benefit mutually. It is a comprehensive program for onboarding apps from Computer Vision and AI developers onto the Awiros AppStack where they can productize, market as well as monetize their Video AI algorithms.

https://awiros.com/awiros-os

BeagleZ-Explosive Detector – Prof Anil Kumar, IITB/ BIGTEC LABS, Bangalore

Prof Anil Kumar from IITB had his masters from IITD and PhD from IISc, with several papers to his credit –

https://www.researchgate.net/profile/Anil-Kumar-50, https://iitb.irins.org/profile/12001

The product is developed in partnership with Bigtec Labs. Chandrasekhar Nair is a co-founder of bigtec Labs and Molbio Diagnostics. His interests are in the development of rapid, low cost, high quality affordable diagnostic platforms. He holds several Indian and International patents. Chandrasekhar Nair is a co-founder of bigtec Labs and Molbio Diagnostics. Gopalkrishna Kini is another Co-founder.

National Center of Excellence in Technology for Internal Security (NCETIS) at Indian Institute of Technology Bombay developed many technologies including Beagle. See lsi of projects – http://www.ee.iitb.ac.in/~ncetis/category/project-list/page/2/

Technology

DRDO lab HEMRL has designed and developed OPX Revilator – an optronic trace Explosives Detector for detection and identification of pure explosives as well as trace explosives in mixtures/ IEDs/ contaminants like mud, sand, sugar, salt, diesel oil etc based on the principle of optical image processing. It is a portable, miniaturized, electronic detector capable of identifying almost all the explosives like CL-20, FOX-7, NTO, RDX, HMX, CE, PETN, TNT, NC ; inorganic compounds of class nitrates like ammonium nitrate (AN) and combinations thereof ANFO, Composition A, Composition B, Composition C-4, Octol, Cyclotol, PEK-I, LTPE, Amatol, Ammonal, Single base propellant, Pentolite, Dentex, Torpex and Tritonal.

Innovation

Amplifying Fluorescent Polymers (AFP) are conjugate polymers that exhibit solid state fluorescence when excited by light of particular wavelength. These AFP materials exhibit a quenching of fluorescence in the presence of explosive molecules. Conventional fluorescence sensors quench one polymer unit when interacted with one explosive molecule. But, in the case of AFPs the interaction of one explosives molecule with the polymer quenches the fluorescence of many polymer repeat units thereby amplifying the response to explosives and exhibiting high sensitivity in ppb-ppm. This amplifying quenching response of AFP to explosives molecules specifically is the key factor contributing to its exceptional sensitivity. Beaglez uses this technology of amplifying fluorescent polymers (AFP) in effectively detecting explosives such as TNT, RDX, HMX, PETN, PEK, Sheet explosives etc in trace quantities in both vapor and particle mode. BEAGLEZ is based on Amplifying

Fluorescent Polymer (AFP) technology to detect almost all military, commercial and country made explosives existing to date

Patents

Amplified fluorescence polymers and sensor thereof, WO2010049797A1, InventorAnil KumarJasmine SinhaPhani Kumar Pullela, Priority claimed from IN2319MU2008

Commercialisation

Bigtec is an ISO 9001:2015 company based in Bangalore, India. Our State of the Art facility is recognised by the Department of Scientific & Industrial Research (DSIR). In line with our vision of productising innovation, we associated with an excellent team of IIT Bombay to develop BEAGLEZ – a Hand-held Explosive Detector. BEAGLEZ is the smallest & lightest in its class and has no attachments/accessories. BEAGLEZ was launched by the Ministry of Electronics & Information Technology (MEITY) in Delhi on 14th February 2019, in the presence of senior officials from various arms of the Government of India. BEAGLEZ is CE certified, NTH certified (NABL accredited Lab in India.) & ASTM (American Society for Testing & Materials) certified.

https://beaglez.co.in/about-us.php

Long Range Surveillance-Optimized Electrotech, Ahmedabad

Kuldeep Saxena is Co-Founder & COO at Optimized Electrotech Solutions. After M Tech in from IITD, he worked for 16 years at ISRO on space borne optical modules for imaging and non-imaging applications, moved to Singapore where he worked with MNCs and founded C-Infinite Optical engineering consultants in Singapore. Optimized Electrotech Solutions was founded by by Sandeep Shah along with Anil Yekkala, Dharin Shah, Kuldeep Saxena, and Purvi Shah

(https://yourstory.com/2020/08/electro-optics-startup-optimized-electrotech-defence-security)

https://www.linkedin.com/in/kuldeepsaxena1/

https://www.linkedin.com/in/anilyekkala/

https://www.linkedin.com/in/shah-dharin-9836558/

Technology

Long-Range Reconnaissance and Observation System or LORROS is a sensor system developed by Elbit Systems to provide long-range daytime and night-time surveillance. Range for vehicle a) Detection – 40 Km (Min) b) Recognition-15 Km (min) Place a vehicle having size 4.3x1. 8x1. 5m target or better, in moving and stationary conditions, at side angle (for maximum surface area facing towards the camera) at a distance of 40 Kms & 15 Kms.

Indian Secifications – https://www.mha.gov.in/sites/default/files/LongRangeReconnaissance_17112021.pdf

Innovation

InfiVISION is a ruggedized Electro-Optic Surveillance System for Long Range Surveillance and other mission-critical situations.The system provides high-contrast images for interpretation and analysis from daybreak to nightfall. It adapts and adjusts to varying light conditions to offer crisp images even in Low Light conditions. The InfiVISION product comes with Near Infra-Red Manipulation Detectors. The Friend or Foe detection functionality facilitates military and civilian homeland security systems to cue InfiVISION – 1 from the command system. The system further identifies people and vehicles, determining their bearing. Long-range identification and narrow field of view make InfiVISION – 1 a precise tool for observing cross-border traffic and enabling critical infrastructure surveillance. The product automatically detects and alerts based on the detection of motion of any person from 5 km or vehicles from a farther distance.

Patents

Patents of Kuldeep include Integrated optical moduleIntegrated optical module, US 8428450, Optical input device, and methods of detecting input to an electronic deviceOptical input device, and methods of detecting input to an electronic device US 20070221828.

Patents of Anil Kumar include Content detection of a part of an imageContent detection of a part of an image, US US20100073393-A1. Content detection of an image comprising pixelsContent detection of an image comprising pixels,US US20100027878 A1

Commercialisation

https://optimizedelectrotech.com/products/vision-series/infi-vision/

Optimized Electrotech Private Limited is an imaging surveillance technology company with focus on Electro Optics. We are excited about fusion of AI into surveillance and have Indigeneously Designed Developed and Manufactured surveillance platforms. Applications – Access Control, Perimeter Surveillance, Anti-Drone, People & Vehicle Monitoring, Border Surveillance, Space & Aerial Surveillance, Weapon Sights, Vehicle Mounted Surveillance.

Smallest Short Range VTOL Quadcopter – Idea Forge

Ankit Mehta is CEO of idea Forge Technogy ltd, the first startup to move and scale up from IITB incubator SINE to an public issue of shares.He had a duel degree Btech and MTech from IITB.

Technology

Bayraktar VTOL is a vertical take-off and landing (VTOL) unmanned aerial vehicle system developed by Baykar Defense, and announced for the first time in 2019 .A new British-made Vertical Takeoff and Landing (VTOL) drone called JACKAL has just successfully fired a Thales Lightweight Multirole Missile (LMM). The test, which the Royal Air Force's Rapid Capabilities Office (RCO) sponsored, has reportedly marked a significant advancement in uncrewed air combat.

Innovation

SWITCH UAV is a fixed wing and VTOL hybrid UAV. SWITCH UAV features advanced flight time, higher safety and simple operation with additional fail-safe redundancies. It is used for long range, high endurance, high altitude last mile surveillance and security operations. The SWITCH UAV has been tested for the internationally recognized military quality standard of JSS 55555* and MIL Standard 461E for EMI EMC. It is built to cater to the demanding surveillance operations in all terrains. This lightweight VTOL and fixed wing hybrid UAV have the large time-on-target compared to any other UAV in its class. The biggest global Mini VTOL UAV contract was awarded to ideaForge's SWITCH UAV by the Indian Army, beating competitors from Russia, Israel, France, Ukraine, and other countries. This marks the third major order for the SWITCH UAV, as there were two previous contracts awarded to SWITCH UAV's high-altitude variant in 2020 & 2021.

Patents

https://www.patentguru.com/assignee/ideaforge-technology-pvt-ltd

UNMANNED AERIAL VEHICLE WITH CO-AXIAL REVERSIBLE ROTORS Patent Number: EP3684686B1, Publication Date: 2023-03-01

Single arm failure redundancy in a multi-rotor aerial vehicle with least rotors/propellers Patent Number: US11608187B2 Publication Date: 2023-03-21

Fixed-wing vertical take-off and landing hybrid UAV, Patent Number: US11655023B2, Publication Date: 2023-05-23

Unmanned aerial vehicle with co-axial reversible rotors Patent Number: US11565809B2, Publication Date: 2023-01-31

Commercialisation

Index Drone is India's largest satellite and drone-focused marketplace for goods and services including drones, parts, pilot training, crop spraying, satellite mapping, etc.

https://indexdrone.com/product/ideaforge-q-series-drone/

Q Series is ideaForge's smallest short range VTOL Unmanned Aerial Vehicle (UAV) based on our best-in-class drone technology. It is ideaForge's most economical and efficient drone built with tried-and-tested military design philosophies. Q Series UAV can ideally be used for Surveying, Mapping, Security & Surveillance, Inspection, Photogrammetry, Traffic Management, Crowd Management & Disaster Relief.

ideaForge is the pioneer and the pre-eminent market leader in the Indian unmanned aircraft systems ("UAS") market. We had the largest operational deployment of indigenous UAVs across India, with an ideaForge manufactured drone taking off every five minutes for surveillance and mapping on an average. Our customers have completed over 300,000 flights using our UAVs. We ranked 7th globally in the dual-use category (civil and defense) drone manufacturers as per the report published by Drone Industry Insights in December 2022.

https://ideaforgetech.com/

Satellite Systems – Ananth Technologies, Hyderabad

Dr. Subba Rao Pavuluri is Founder, Chairman and Managing Director of Ananth Technologies. A graduate from REC, Calicut with PhD from IISc, he founded Ananth Technologies and IN-RIMT in 1992 after working for a decade with the Indian Space Program. These founded organizations were at the forefront of the private-public sector colloboration, manufacturing electronics and embedded systems that had enabled the Indian Space program and the Civial Aviation industry. Also a pioneer in the GIS space, Ananth pushed the envelope of the GIS technologies. Ananth is an internationally certified aerospace Master Systems Integrator (MSI).

Technology

Satellite development has historically been slow and extremely costly because of proprietary hardware and software, excessive vertical integration and outdated interfaces, APIs and protocols. Antaris has changed all that. Antaris co-founders Tom Barton and Karthik Govindhasamy, who previously worked together in executive leadership roles at Planet Labs, created Antaris in 2021 as a response to their frustration with the exorbitant cost and timelines typically associated with satellite development. Antharis cloud-based platform has enabled constellation sponsors, satellite designers, component providers and manufacturers from across the globe to come together seamlessly and collaborate to get a satellite ready for launch in just months, not years, from start to finish. Antaris recently open sourced its SatOS Payload Software Development Kit (SDK), which enables users of the platform to effectively integrate payloads into SatOS-powered satellites. Additionally, Antaris released the go-satcom library to help the broader space community work with open space communications protocols.

JANUS-1, involved eight organizations spanning seven countries collaborating virtually through the Antaris cloud-based platform, which features open APIs and core open source elements. JANUS-1 is a 6U satellite conceived as a technical demonstration to showcase the unprecedented efficiency and cost-effectiveness of the Antaris platform and will feature five different payloads running on its SatOS™ satellite software once in orbit. XDLINX Labs and Ananth Technologies served as the primary manufacturing partners for the JANUS-1 satellite with ATLAS Space Operations providing ground station services. JANUS-1 satellite was launched aboard ISRO's Small Satellite Launch Vehicle (SSLV-D2) on February 10, 2023. The complete Assembly, Integration, and Test process was carried out successfully at Ananth Technologies' new facility in Bangalore's Aerospace Park, where the high-efficiency Solar Panels of JANUS-1 were also fully indigenized.

Innovation

The world's first satellite featuring both SAR and optical sensors on a single satellite is result of agreement between three Indian space leaders—GalaxEye, Ananth Technologies and XDLINX Labs and US-based satellite software provider Antaris. The four companies intend to solve a vexing legacy challenge for consumers of remote sensing data. Typically, satellite constellation operators have deployed specialized satellites to capture specific types of data. Each image or data point is captured at a unique time from a unique location, making it difficult to correlate data from separate satellites. The new multi-sensor satellite being developed under the MOU will capture, for the first time in history, both SAR data and optical data from the same satellite—improving the ability to correlate the data and its analytical utility. The resulting datasets will have tremendous value for environmental, insurance and defense applications.

Patents

Antaris cloud based platform – https://www.antaris.space/platform

Commercialisation

Since its establishment in 1992, Ananth Technologies has contributed towards manufacturing of 89 satellite and 69 launch vehicles built/launched by ISRO, including two satellites for European customers that ISRO had built in collaboration with Airbus, France. Ananth has extensive design, manufacturing and AIT facilities across India, and has been a key member of the Indian Space program. Learn more at www.ananthtech.com

Satellite Bus Technology – ISRO/ Alpha Design Technologies Pvt. Ltd, Bangalore

The Technology Transfer Documents were formally handed over by Shri. D Radhakrishnan, Chairman and Managing Director of NSIL to Col. H. S. Shankar (Retd.) VSM, Chairman and Managing Director of Alpha Design.(photo credits-indiaweb2.com).

Founded in 2003, by Col. H.S. Shankar, Akunuri Mohana Rao and Rakesh Dhar Jayal, Alpha Design Technologies is a leading aerospace and defense company based in India. With expertise in engineering, manufacturing, and system integration, ADTL has been a key player in various projects related to defense, space, and homeland security, contributing significantly to India's technological progress in these domains. Col. H. S. SHANKAR (Retd) VSM, graduated from University (of Mysore) and ME from IISC, Bangalore. After retirement from BEL in March 2003, he started (as

CMD) a new R&D and Manufacturing Defence Electronics Company called Alpha Design Technologies Private Limited in Bangalore.

Technology

Microsatellite has been considered as disruptive technologies in satellite engineering. Its development cost and time provide advantages for new kind of Earth observations, telecommunications, and science missions. University of Surrey is known as one of the pioneers in the design and build of microsatellite in the 1990s. It started launching microsatellite in 1991 with amateur radio missions. Technical University (TU) of Berlin had launched six microsatellites between 1991 and 2007. IMS-1, previously referred to as TWSat (Third World Satellite), is a low-cost microsatellite imaging mission of ISRO (Indian Space Research Organization). The overall objective is to provide medium-resolution imagery for developing countries for free. The data from this mission will be made available to interested space agencies and student community from developing countries to provide necessary impetus to capacity building in using satellite data. Launch.

Innovation

The IMS-1 (Indian Micro Satellite) satellite bus, developed by the U R Rao Satellite Centre (URSC/ ISRO), is a versatile and efficient small satellite platform designed to facilitate low-cost access to space. IMS-1 is an Earth observation satellite in a sun-synchronous orbit, and is the fourteenth satellite in the Indian Remote Sensing (IRS) satellite series built, launched and maintained by ISRO. The satellite bus serves as a dedicated vehicle for various payloads, enabling Earth imaging, ocean and atmospheric studies, microwave remote sensing, and space science missions while ensuring a quick turnaround time for satellite launches. IMS-1 bus, weighing about

100 kg, accommodates a 30 kg payload. Solar arrays generate 330 W power with a raw bus voltage of 30-42 V. It offers a 3-axis stabilized with four reaction wheels with a 1 N thruster that provides +/ – 0.1 degree pointing accuracy. It is a forerunner for IMS-2 bus technology, capable of improved features. IMS-1 bus is utilised in previous ISRO missions like IMS-1, Youthsat and Microsat-2D.

Patents

NASA has a wide range of advanced aerospace technologies that can be useful for both small companies seeking to introduce new solutions and large corporations looking to improve their capabilities. These technologies have the potential to transform the aerospace industry and drive the development of innovative solutions.

https://technology.nasa.gov/patents

Commercialisation

https://www.adtl.co.in/

Alpha specializes in development and production of Night Vision Thermal sights, Electronic Warfare equipment, Tactical Communications equipment, and major R&D Projects such as Software Defined Radios, Missile Seeker Systems (in collaboration with BRAHMOS), IFF, Simulators, Airframes for SU-30 air crafts, etc. In December 2021, Adani Enterprises, through its subsidiary Adani Defence Systems and Technologies, has made an acquisition of Alpha Design Technologies. According to a 2018 report by Business Standard, Alpha Design was acquired by Adani Enterprises for ₹400 crores. A venture capital (VC) fund managed by Elara Capital, Elara India Opportunities Fund (Elara IOF), is a promoter entity with the Adani Group in Bengaluru-based defence company Alpha Design

Technologies Pvt Ltd (ADTPL), as reported by the Indian Express (IE). ADTPL works closely with ISRO and DRDO. It also has a Rs 590 crore contract with the Union Ministry of Defence to upgrade Pechora missile and radar systems.

Solar Ultraviolet Imaging Telescope (SUIT) – IUCAA, Pune

Anamparambu Ramaprakash is Scientist 'H' (Professor); Head, Instrumentation; Dean, Visitor Programme, at Inter-University Centre for Astrophysics and Astronomy (IUCAA). He works on building instruments for astronomy both ground-based and space-borne. Observational interests are in polarization studies of a variety of sources like brown dwarfs, dark molecular clouds, blazars. Also interested in studying variables like GRB afterglows, T-Tauri stars, blazars etc.

https://www.researchgate.net/profile/Anamparambu-Ramaprakash

Technology

Aditya will be the First dedicated solar satellite for studying the atmosphere of Sun. This will be a Visible emission line space coronagraph capable of taking images close to the sun (from 1.1 solar radii) at very high cadence (one image every second). It will also have a multi-slit spectro polarimeter capable of making polarimetric observations in the corona.

Dr. George Carruthers, a scientist at the Naval Research Laboratory received a patent for a Far Ultraviolet Electrographic Camera, which obtained images of electromagnetic radiation in short wavelengths. Apollo 16 astronauts placed the observatory on the Moon in April 1972, where it sits today on the Moon's Descartes highland region, in the shadow of the lunar module Orion.

Innovation

The Solar Ultraviolet Imaging Telescope (SUIT) is an instrument onboard the Aditya-L1 spacecraft, the first dedicated solar mission of the Indian Space Research Organization (ISRO), which will be put in a halo orbit at the Sun-Earth Langrage point (L1). SUIT has an off-axis Ritchey–Chrétien configuration with a combination of 11 narrow and broad bandpass filters which will be used for full-disk solar imaging in the Ultravoilet (UV) wavelength range 200-400 nm. It will provide near simultaneous observations of lower and middle layers of the solar atmosphere, namely the Photosphere and Chromosphere. These observations will help to improve our understanding of coupling and dynamics of various layers of the solar atmosphere, mechanisms responsible for stability, dynamics and eruption of solar prominences and Coronal Mass ejections, and possible causes of solar irradiance variability in the Near and Middle UV regions, which is of central interest for assessing the Sun's influence on climate.

https://www.prl.res.in/~uso/SUIT_ISRO_Brochure_final.pdf

Patents

Open Astronomy – https://openastronomy.org/

Open Access Repository of the National Institute for Astrophysics – https://baas.aas.org/pub/2022n2i015/release/1

Commercialisation

https://instru.iucaa.in/

The instrumentation laboratory at IUCAA is involved in a variety of R&D activities aimed at finding applications for new technologies in astronomy. The three core areas which we specialize on are focal plane array controllers, optical fibres and adaptive optics for astronomy. The lab also has end-to-end design, development and delivery capabilities for both ground and space based instruments. Instruments and subsystems designed and built in the laboratory are being used in many facilities in India and abroad such as the IGO, 11m Southern African Large Telescope (SALT), 10.4m Gran Telescopio Canarias at La Palma, Spain, Palomar 60 inch telescope, Skinakas 1.3m telescope etc. IUCAA is also one of the lead partners of the TMT-India collaboration along with IIA, Bengaluru and ARIES, Nainital. TMT-India is responsible for India's involvement with the international consortium of institutions in Canada, China, Japan and the US.

Smart Policing – Staqu Technologies, Gurugram

Atul Rai is Co-founder & CEO at Staqu Technologies, graduate from APJ Abdul Kalam Technological University, Thiruvanthapuram with MS in AI from University of Manchester. Afterv working in Hungary and UK, He promoted startup with two others to work on Video Analytics Industry. Anurag Saini works in the hardware, which involves optimization of different AI models on the local hardware. He has worked with notable companies like Qualcomm before co-founding Staqu. The third co-founder is Pankaj Sharma and he has expertise in backend technologies. He has authored two research papers and is adept at cloud technologies. Awards – NATIONAL STARTUP AWARD, Emerge 50 award from NASSCOM, Tech Rocketship, FICCI Smart Policing etc.

https://www.linkedin.com/in/atul-rai-7501181b/

Technology

The U.S.' National Institute of Standards and Technology hosts an ongoing performance assessment of facial recognition systems, called the Face Recognition Vendor Test.

https://www.nist.gov/programs-projects/face-recognition-vendor-test-frvt

It was reported Delhi police were using 80 percent facial recognition confidence threshold. In ideal conditions, facial recognition systems can have near-perfect accuracy. Verification algorithms used to match subjects to clear reference images (like a passport photo or mugshot) can achieve accuracy scores as high as 99.97% on standard assessments like NIST's Facial Recognition Vendor Test (FRVT). ISO/IEC 19794-5 defines specifically a standard scheme for codifying data describing human faces within a CBEFF-compliant data structure, for use in facial recognition systems. Modern biometric passport photos should comply with this standard.

Innovation

JARVIS is an audio and video analytics software as well as an audio-video management technology platform that has changed the way people think about security cameras. JARVIS helps transform long CCTV video footage into meaningful information. The Video Analytics Software fueled with Artificial Intelligence, computer vision, deep learning, patented technologies, and unique capabilities, provides short and crisp real-time alerts that are actionable.

The startups AI's accuracy, 97.5% is monitored against the standard benchmarks on voxceleb data by vgg group (Visual Geometry Group) oxford which is one of the largest databases in terms of speaker identification.

Patents

Staqu has two patented technologies that have been used in developing JARVIS. Indian patent no 303927 LARGE SCALE IMAGE RETRIEVAL BASED ON IMAGE AND SKETCH BASED QUERIES, 2015 and Indian patent no 303742 SYSTEM FOR POSE-INVARIANT IDENTIFICATION AND SEARCH OF AN IMAGE OBJECT IN AN INPUT IMAGE, 2015

Commercialisation

https://www.staqu.com/what-is-jarvis/

Features of video analytics platform – JARVIS is camera agnostic, meaning it can be integrated with any make and model camera. The average bandwidth is 1 Mbps per camera. There are two types of video footage in the JARVIS dashboard. By selecting the type of camera, you can check the live video. You can also choose the DVR recording and check the hourly video footage which has backed up data from 30 days. You can have city, area, and region-wise access controls. You can create user access yourself. At the same time, even reports will be available according to role-based dashboards. Static IP is required but you can utilize our in-house technology to transfer data to our cloud storage.

The UP Prison Administration and Reform Services wanted to centralize 3000+ CCTV cameras for transparent visibility of over 70 prisons in a single platform. To achieve this, Staqu developed a Centralized Command Center interface of JARVIS at the headquarters in Lucknow to aggregate the video feeds from all the CCTV cameras across all prisons in Uttar Pradesh. As per the stakeholder's requirements, we also enabled insight-based analytics on visitors and inmates to review events such as perimeter security breaches, violence, overcrowding, unauthorized access, and more.

Other Indian companies in this space are – IDEMIA, NEC India, Vision-Box, INNEFU Labs.

Unmanned Autonomous Vessel – Sagar Defence Engineering, Pune

Lakshay Dang is National Award Recipient, Co-founder/Chief Technology Officer(CTO) at Sagar Defence Engineering. Mridul Babbar National Award Winner | NASA Awardee is Co-Founder. Both are engineers started working on prototyping, developed Nano satellites, 3D printers and honed their skills in `Mahindra Solar Spark the Rise' competition. Nikunj Parashar another Co-Founder, was a Master Mariner, worked with Maersk Tankers, a company that manages tanker. He is also CEO of Oceanos B.V.

The startup was selected for iDEX challenge 4 – Autonomous Underwater Swarm Drones and MOU entered with Indian Navy.

Technology

Simple remote control vessels/systems can be categorized as USVs. An ASV is a robotic marine vessel/boat that can monitor its status, position, and aspects of its operational environment to automatically navigate and acquire data without the need for continual operator oversight. ASVs are a subcategory of USVs (Uncrewed surface vessels). USV development began in 1993 at the MIT Sea Grant College Program. The first vehicle produced from the program was called ARTEMIS, a small-scale fishing trawler capable of testing navigation and control systems required by a USV.

Innovation

MSV developed with features such as: Tele-operated – Direct remote control of vessels throttle, gearboxes and rudders. Heading Hold – Direct control of vessels throttle, gearboxes and heading. Command control unit steers the boat on commanded heading. Semi-autonomous – Vessel follows a pre-programmed waypoint track. Mission planning software allows the track to be programmed ahead of the mission and for real time modification of the track to be undertaken as required. Constant speed can be maintained to compensate for wind and tidal conditions or the throttle and gearbox can be manually controlled from RCW. The vessel will return to a preset location as defined in the RCW on loss of communication or dead stop in existing position. All RCW safety functionality will still be present and will override external control if required. Auto speed – Pre defined speed in steps can be fed into the system. Our Unmanned Surface Vehicle

A new company from ESA's UK business incubator has developed an autonomous boat that is propelled by the waves and carries ocean sensors powered by solar energy. Sagar Defence developed a aimilar product – "AutoNaut". It works on Wave Propelled Technology.

Patents

List of patents in the Unmanned Surface Vehicle (USV) industry – https://golden.com/query/list-of-patents-in-the-unmanned-surface-vehicle-usv-industry-PD54Y

Commercialisation

https://www.sagardefence.com/

MSVs manufactured by Sagar Defence can Hover on a Point, In order to hover on a point the autopilot controls the position of the vehicle relative to a user-defined waypoint. Two modes are possible:Position Control by Maneuver (PCM), Dynamic Positioning (DP), Hovering within an Area, Within a set distance of a datum (waypoint), Within a defined boundary, Avoiding one or more defined danger zones.

Other developments from India:

Jalchar is Unmanned (Water) Surface Vehicle (USV) or Drone Boat designed by Dronobotics to assist Navy, Coast Guards, Disaster Management, Search & Rescue, Scientific Researches and Commercial & Personal needs – https://www.dronobotics.in/jalchar.html

Bangalore-based Tardid Technologies will be delivering three units of an unmanned surface vessel (USV) developed in partnership with Pune-based Accurate Industrial Controls to the Indian Navy.

AUV (Autonomous Underwater Vehicle) – 150 is an unmanned underwater vehicle (UUV) being developed by Central Mechanical Engineering Research Institute (CMERI) scientists in Durgapur.

Industrial Products

1. AI based Video Analytics Platform-DocketRun, Hubballi,
2. Ajit Microprocessor – Prof Madhav Desai, IITB
3. Automated Pencil Electrode Formation Pltform – Lanka Tata Rao, BITS Pilani, Hyderabad
4. Carbon Nanotubes – Nopo Nano Technologies, Bangalore
5. Carrier Ethernet Switch Routers – Prof Ashwin Gumaste, IITB
6. Cellulose based geotextile – Anasua Guha Ray, BITS Pilani Hyderabad
7. Drop-In Liquid Sustainable Aviation and Automotive Fuel – Dr Anil Kumar Sinha, CSIR-IIP
8. Electric Wheel Barrow-Technovos Machinery Pvt Ltd, Bangalore
9. Flow battery – Prof Kothandaraman Ramanujam, IITM
10. GigaMesh – mmWave wireless backhaul radio-Astrome Technologies, USA/India
11. Guided waves sensors – Prof Krishnan Balasubramanian, IITM
12. Horizontal boring machine for underground – CSIR-CBRI
13. Hot wire cutting machine – Prof Sathyan S, IITM
14. Induction Motor Stethoscope (MSCOPE) – CSIR – CSIO and Ai-DEA LABS
15. Li-Fi products-Velmenni, New Delhi

16. Microfluidic Electro-Viscometer – Dr. Sanket Goel, BITS Pilani, Hyderabad
17. Silver Nanowire – CSIR-NCL
18. Ultra Spinner – CeraTattva, IITM, Chennai
19. Ternary Content Addressable Memory (TCAM) in a network router – Prof. Krishna Moorthy Sivalingam, IITM
20. Wirelsss GPS Clock – Signals & Systems (India) Private Limited (SANDS)

AI based Video Analytics Platform- DocketRun, Hubballi

Ajay Kabadi & Shweta Shettar, are first-generation tech entrepreneurs with an eye for innovation and discovery in the AI and machine learning space, came up with the concept of DocketRun. He roped Chetan Kulkarni as co-founder responsible for marketing and product design. Incubated at Deshpande Startups, Hubballi, Karnataka. Ajay was an engineering graduate from SDM College of Engg& Tech, Dharwad with MS(Engg) from KLE Technological University, Hubbali. Sweta had Masters degree in Statistics from Karnataka University, Dharwad. Chetan Kulkarni was an Engineer from BMS College of Engineering. Gururaj Deshpande, the serial Entrepreneur was born in Hubli/Dharwad situated in Karnataka. He gave back to his place of birth, this incubator, see the portfolio of Deshpande Startups – https://deshpandestartups.org/portfolio

Technology

Currently almost all industrial facilities have centralized surveillance systems for the protection of materials and personnel. Due to the size of the facilities, there are many installed cameras that record a multitude of images that are difficult to analyze and discern in real time, mainly because the personnel assigned for review and analysis is limited. There are three distinct types of video analytics: fixed algorithm analytics, Artificial Intelligence learning algorithms and Facial Recognition. Each of these processes digital video signals via an algorithm to perform a security-related function. First generation video analytics worked by detecting pixel change in certain parts of the video, a door or tree blowing in the wind, or an animal passing by, could trigger an alarm and false alarms were common. The second generation of video analytics helped to reconstruct what happened; however, it was designed more as a forensic tool rather than a tool that exists to tell you where the van or person is right now, just moments after you heard about them.

Most cameras on the market today use what is termed 'edge analytics', which means that the analysis is performed on data at a sensor, network switch or other device (such as in the camera itself) instead of waiting for the data to be sent back to a centralised data store. With the development of AI-based analytics, machine learning and Deep Neural Networking (DNN) algorithms, the camera analysis has become more precise, with an ability to detect specific objects and distinguish between them.

Innovation

The DocketRun AI Edge Device is a video analytics device that leverage pre-existing CCTV-IP infrastructure to monitor a variety of SOPs. It is the only platform that can analyse the complete process of electrical and mechanical jobs in a steel plantas demonstrated at Tata Steel. The platform is also highly scalable, making it ideal for large-scale deployments.

System Details: The system includes a GPU-based server and DocketRun AI models and custom AI logics. The platform is easy to deploy and use, and it can be customized to meet the specific needs of each customer.

Patents

One of the many patents by others – https://patents.google.com/patent/US20100026802A1/en

Commercialisation

https://docketrun.com/product/#how-it-works

DocketRuns Smart Video Analytics Platform uses existing CCTV cameras to extract feeds from various cameras and perform real-time analysis of the following details: Panel number confirmation, Personal Protective Equipment (PPE) detection, Kool coat detection, No-entry zone detection, Lock detection, Colour change detection. The platform can process 10 to 10,000+ cameras without lagging in FPS (frames per second). In the event of a violation, the platform can trigger real-time IP67 graded feedback systems, such as: Hooter systems to alarm, Stopping moving machines via direct or PLC configuration using relay system, Voice announcement systems to announce violations in any regional languages with custom messages

Videos on steel plant – https://www.cronj.com/blog/ai-solutions-video-analytics-software-steel-manufacturing-industry/

Ajit Microprocessor – Prof Madhav Desai, IITB

Prof Madhav Desai working at IITB had his graduation from the same institute followed by MS and PhD from University of Illinois. He worked at Digital Equipment Corporation before joining IITB. He is co-founder of Powai Labs Technologies, started at SINE incubator. The company has developed an FPGA based simulation accelerator which can be used in a seamless manner to accelerate the simulation of VLSI designs described in VHDL/Verilog. AJIT is a part of the indigenous processor development effort championed by DeiTY. A proof-of-concept implementation of the AJIT processor in Silicon has been implemented at SCL Chandigarh in a 180nm technology.

https://www.ee.iitb.ac.in/wiki/faculty/madhav

Technology

A microprocessor is an integrated circuit (IC) that contains a few millions of transistors (semiconductor-based electronic devices) fused on a semiconductor chip. It is just a few millimetres in dimension and is used in almost every electronic device from the microwave and washing machine in homes to advanced supercomputers of a space station. In 1985, The world's first single-chip fully-32-bit microprocessor, with 32-bit data paths, 32-bit buses, and 32-bit addresses, was the AT&T Bell Labs BELLMAC-32A, with first samples in 1980, and general production in 1982.

SHAKTI is an open-source initiative by the Reconfigurable Intelligent Systems Engineering (RISE) group at IIT-Madras. The aim of SHAKTI is to produce production grade processors, complete System on Chips (SoCs), development boards and SHAKTI-based software platform. VEGA Microprocessors are a portfolio of indigenous processors developed by C-DAC. The portfolio includes several 32-bit/64-bit Single/Multi-core Superscalar In-order/Out-of-Order high performance processors based on the RISC-V ISA.

Innovation

AJIT is a medium-sized processor. It can be used inside a set-top box, as a control panel for automation systems, in a traffic light controller or even robotic systems. AJIT can run one instruction per clock cycle and can operate at clock speeds between 70-120MHz. Prof Desai and his team of students---C. Arun, M. Sharath, Neha Karanjkar, Piyush Soni, Titto Anbadan, Ashfaque Ahmed, Aswin Jith, Ch. Kalyani, Nanditha Rao---used a tool set called AHIR-V2, that can convert an algorithm to hardware and which was developed completely at IIT Bombay to design the microprocessor circuit.

Patents

The researchers have made the software tools associated with AJIT freely available to everyone. The processor is also available as a 'softcore', where vendors can buy a license to use the design of the microprocessor and fabricate it to use it in their system.

A system and method for emulating a logic circuit design using programmable logic devices", Patent Application No. 211/MUM/2005, Published 2005-06-04, Filed 2005-02-05, United States Patent Application Pub. No. US 2006/0247909 A1, Pub. Date Nov. 2, 2006. Madhav P. Desai, and Sachin B. Patkar(IITB) and Himanshu Sharma, Mitra Purandare(Powai Labs).

Commercialisation

Processor IP Core, AJIT is proven on silicon and is licenced to a number of System on Chip, products. Powai Labs works very closely with the client team building the System on Chip using AJIT; from Prototype to ASIC. AJIT licence is also available in a range of models for Industry, Research Labs and Higher Technical Education & Research. A digital SOC for implementing an IRNSS receiver (NAVIC) using an embedded AJIT processor has been implemented in 65nm CMOS technology, and is functional. An extension of the AJIT 32-bit processor to include 64-bit instructions and multi-core implementations. A four core, eight thread processor has been implemented and is being used to implement a network router.

http://www.powailabs.com/

Automated Pencil Electrode Formation Platform – Lanka Tata Rao, BITS Pilani, Hyderabad

Lanka Tata Rao completed his PhD at BITS Pilani Hyderabad campus and is now post-doctoral Researcher at Tel Aviv University, Israel. A mechanical engineer with graduation from Acharya Nagarjuna University and MTech from Andhra University, he worked on Membraneless Microfluidic Fuel Cell (MMFC) for his PhD and now working on Nanometric Biosensors for biomedical Applications at Tel Aviv University.

https://www.linkedin.com/in/lanka-tata-rao-2584881b1/

Technology

Microfluidic devices with integrated electrodes, or electromicrofluidic devices, have attained essential roles in diverse areas, including energy harvesting for portable applications and sensing devices.

Paper–pencil based microfluidic fuel cell is one of the most recent vital advancements to develop point of the source (POS) and point of care (POC) devices owing to the well-proven benefits of microfluidic environment and graphite electrodes. In recent years, graphite pencils are being used as electrodes and have shown encouraging outcomes and promising features of MPFCs when compared with the existing approaches.

Innovation

Most of the recent researches in the field of paper–pencil based microfuel cells employ manual deposition of graphite on the paper for fabricating the electrode. Evidently, the quantity of graphite deposited on the paper affects the performance of the fuel cell, which can be modified by varying the number of pencil strokes. The amount and quality of the graphite being deposited and adhered on the surface can vary from person to person and time to time depending upon the pressure applied.

The device from the researcher addresses the aforementioned problems and provides an integrated solution for economical, easy to use, uniform and, a portable, automated device for graphite electrode on for paper based devices. Such automated graphite electrodes have excellent uniformity, high efficiency, and can be fabricated inexpensively. Moreover, the quantity of force can also be identified at the time of graphite electrode fabrication time by force sensing resistor (FSR) sensor. The platform has been harnessed to be used to realize microchannel and electrodes of microfluidic paper fuel cell (MPFC) showing excellent power output. Overall, the platform is an accurate, fully-automated device for graphite electrode fabrication on porous cellulose paper for sensing, energy harvesting, and flexible electronics applications.

https://www.nature.com/articles/s41598-020-68579-x

Patents

Publications – Automated pencil electrode formation platform to realize uniform and reproducible graphite electrodes on paper for microfluidic fuel cells, Nature.Com

Performance optimization of microfluidic paper fuel-cell with varying cellulose fiber papers as absorbent pad, International Journal of Energy Research

Patent – A Device for Making Designs on a SubstrateA Device for Making Designs on a Substrate, IN 202011020964 · Issued May 20, 2019

Commercialisation

https://www.mmne.in/tech-4-transfer

MEMS, Microfluidics and Nanoelectronics Lab is a collaborative effort across the departments at BITS-Pilani, Hyderabad Campus. This technology and other technologies are available for transfer/commercialisation.

Collaborative project – Collaboration in Microbial Fuel Cell Research and Innovation Driven Graduate Education (Co-PI, PI from India), The Research Council of Norway, NOK 12.50 million (India NOK 1.24 million), 5 years (2022-2027). Collaborators: Prof. Rajnish Calay (UiT, Arctic University of Norway), Northern Arctic Federal University (Russia), IIT Kharagpur, CSIR-IICT, Lehigh University (USA), Drinkwell (USA), SINTEF (Norway) & Dr. Sanket Goel. Funding Agency: The Research Council of Norway, NOK

Carbon Nanotubes – Nopo Nano Technologies, Bangalore

Gadhadar Reddy is an inventor, entrepreneur who studied Electronics Engineering at BMS College of Engineering (Bangalore) followed by a master's degree in molecular sciences and Nanotechnology from Louisiana Tech University (USA). He studied various methods of producing Carbon Nanotubes and decided to pursue the extremely difficult and promising HiPCO® process. In 2011, he founded NoPo Nanotechnologies in Bangalore along with Dr.Robert Kelley Bradley who is designated as Director of Technology & Research – As co-inventor of the HiPCO reactor, serve as team leader, technical advisor and strategic decision maker surrounding construction and commercialization of an advanced HiPCO reactor, the NoPo reactor, supporting the company goal of being the premier manufacturer of SWCNTs.

https://www.linkedin.com/in/gadhadar/

https://www.linkedin.com/in/robertkelleybradley/

Technology

HiPCO® (High-Pressure Carbon Monoxide) is a chemical reaction to produce high purity Single-Walled Carbon Nanotubes. The reaction uses Metal Carbonyls as a catalyst, high temperature (~1000°C) and high pressure (~100 atmospheres) to produce Single-Walled Carbon Nanotubes of small diameter. Around 1991, at the Indian Institute of Science(Bangalore); researchers in Dr.C.N.R.Rao's lab were looking for ways to embed metals inside Buckyballs (Fullerenes). Dr.A.Govindaraj was carrying out these experiments using Ferrocene, Iron Carbonyl as catalysts and Carbon gases such as Methane and acetylene. While analyzing products of the reaction under an Electron Microscope he found tubular structures along with the fullerenes. The results were published a few months after Ijima's announcement of the discovery of Carbon Nanotubes. Similar experiments with Carbonyl were being carried out in Dr Richard Smalley's laboratory at Rice University. Robert Kelley Bradley joined Smalley as a PhD student and proceeded to work on building the first HiPCO® reactor as part of his thesis. These reactors were the first proof of concept to make use of High-pressure Carbon Monoxide and temperature to produce Carbon Nanotubes continuously. HiPCO® was promising due its ability to one day produce single chiral nanotubes. Smalley's influence and free samples, helped HiPCO® become one of the best-studied Carbon Nanotubes in history.

Innovation

The shutdown of the HiPco reactor at Rice University has resulted in a scarcity of HiPco material available to the research community, and a new source of similar SWCNTs is desperately needed. Continued research and development on the design, materials used, and the overall process have led to a new HiPco material, referred to as NoPo HiPCO®, as an alternative to the erstwhile Rice HiPco SWCNTs. Erstwhile members of the Smalley group at Rice

University, which developed the original HiPco process, helped start NoPo Nanotechnologies with the aim of updating the HiPco process, and produce what they call NoPo HiPCO® SWCNTs. Collaboration between scientists at Swansea University (Wales, UK), Rice University (USA), Lamar University (USA), and NoPo Nanotechnologies (India) has demonstrated that the latter's process and material design is a suitable replacement for the Rice method.

The startup developed single-walled carbon nanotubes (SWCNT) for applications ranging from electronics, sensors, semiconductors, EV batteries, medical, filtration and others. It is one of the few players globally to produce small diameter 0.8-1 nm nanotubes at scale.In 2019, NoPo's HiPCO Single Walled Carbon Nanotubes were ranked No.1 in Quality by Prof.Kataura (AIST, Japan) at the prestigious NT-19 conference held in Germany.

Patents

Publications – The State of HiPco Single-Walled Carbon Nanotubes in 2019, https://www.mdpi.com/2311-5629/5/4/65

A PRECISION CONTROLLED CARBONYL GENERATORA PRECISION CONTROLLED CARBONYL GENERATOR, IN 299675 · Issued Aug 3, 2018

Commercialisation

https://www.noponano.com/applications

There are several applications being pursued – HiPCO Purified for EV Battery Applications, HiPCO in Electronics Applications, HiPCO Water Filtration, HiPCO in Aviation, HiPCO in Medicine.

In the global market there are other producers – http://www.omoe.com/products.html

Carrier Ethernet Switch Routers – Prof Ashwin Gumaste, IITB

Ashwin Gumaste, Institute Chair Professor at IITB, is a renowned Technology creator, system & network architect, researcher. Credits/ honours include – 27 US patents granted; 5 national awards, – India's highest scientific award the S. S Bhatnagar prize (2018), Swarnajayanti Award (2013), DAE SRC Outstanding Research Investigator award (2010), Vikram Sarabhai award (2012), NASI Reliance Industries Platinum Jubilee award (2016).

Profile – https://www.linkedin.com/in/ashwing/

Video – https://www.cse.iitb.ac.in/~gnl/video.mp4

Technology

Carrier Ethernet is a set of services specified by MEF, an organization of service providers and equipment vendors that define services to connect Ethernet LANs within a metropolitan area. Service providers can use Carrier Ethernet to offer service-level agreements that guarantee higher data rates and quality of service (QoS) for voice, video, data and mobile services. Because defined services describe the service but not the underlying technology, service providers can choose from available wide area technologies to provide the level of service.

Innovation

CARRIER ETHERNET SWITCH ROUTERS: FROM CONCEPTS TO PRODUCTS, TO SALES, AND BEYOND:

From a technical perspective, the Internet was wired to support TCP/IP, Ethernet, SONET/SDH and WDM as a suite of protocols. Any new design had to be cognizant of the existing infrastructure, and be backward compatible with the history of protocols that existed.In this regard, we proposed the framework of Omnipresent Ethernet (OE for short), in 2009. The conceptual idea behind OE was to collapse multiple networking layers into a single layer, be backward compatible with existing technologies, make a strong impact on CAPEX and OPEX, and be able to support carrier-class services that generate revenue (essentially be deterministic). In OE, we took advantage of existing patterns in the Internet connection graph and manipulated such interconnection to meet our goal of end-to-end carrier-class services on a single layer. We built three products – a small box for your home/office environment that has 8 Ethernet copper ports a 2 Gigabit Ethernet Fiber/Copper ports with scalability built in, and a metropolitan network aggregator with 10×1 Gigabit Ethernet ports and 2×10-Gigabit Ethernet ports. Mumbai, MTNL provide the opportunity to demonstrate – their data-center using our CESR was its clocking of a mere 1 microsecond port-to-port latency across 3 layers of the networking stack. The two data-centers in Worli and Belapur work on 56 of our CESRs since May 2011.

(https://fundamatics.net/article/carrier-ethernet-switch-routers-from-concepts-to-products-to-sales-and-beyond/)

Patents

A LOW LATENCY CARRIER CLASS SWITCH-ROUTER – Patent No. WO2013051004A2, US patent 20120106555 – (https://iitb.irins.org/profile/155602)

https://patents.justia.com/inventor/ashwin-gumaste

Commercialisation

The technology is transferred to ECIL, which is manufacturing same under ECR-1000 series.

Cellulose Based Geotextile – Anasua Guha Ray, BITS Pilani Hyderabad

Dr. Anasua Guharay is Associate Professor Department of Civil Engineering, BITS-Pilani Hyderabad. She graduated with Bachelor of Engineering, from Jadavpur University followed by MTech and PhD from IIT Kharagpur. She is cross-Appointed Assistant Professor, Department of Civil Engineering, Hiroshima University, Japan for project under India-Japan Cooperative Science Programme between JSPS (Japan) and DST.She is also working with Australian PI under Asian Smart Cities Research and Innovation Network (ASCRIN).

https://universe.bits-pilani.ac.in/hyderabad/guharay/Profile

Technology

Polymeric geo-synthetics in the form of geotextiles are widely used for reinforcing soil, improving drainage, controlling soil erosion, and embankment construction. However, these geotextiles are costly as well as non-biodegradable in most cases. Existing research provides recommendations on improving the soil in an economic and eco-friendly manner by using biodegradable and ecofriendly geotextiles. However, these biodegradable and eco-friendly fibers have a tendency to degrade in the acidic and/or alkaline environment of the soil. Some tried jute geo-textiles with durability and strength obtained by treating jute with selective non-metallic and fibre/fabric retainable antimicrobials. The treatment with antimicrobial chemicals improves the durability of jute geotextile but the coating of fibres leads to leaching and thus, may potentially cause groundwater pollution. Other innovations include an improved process of forming geotextile comprising a mixture of two component polyurethane resin and one or more fillers. There is a need to arrive at an economic technique to improve the durability 10 of geotextile fiber, without compromising on its strength.

Innovation

The researcher developed a process for treating a cellulose based geotextile fiber by preparing an aqueous alkaline solution, reacting coal combustion byproduct with the solution to obtain a polymerized blend and applying the blend obtained to the geotextile fiber. The cellulose based geotextile fiber is selected from jute, coir, hemp and flax. The coal combustion byproduct comprises the alumino-silicate byproduct from thermal power plants. In an embodiment of the invention, the aqueus alkaline solution comprises an aqoueus solution of Group III metals. Preferably, the solution is an aqueos mix of sodium hydroxide and sodium silicate. The coal combustion byproduct reacts with the aqueous alkaline solution to form a polymerized blend. This improves durability of natural geotextiles used for sustainable construction of reinforced foundation beds, slope stability etc.

Patents

Publications – Received IGS – Dr. M.D. Desai Memorial YGE Biennial Award 2022 for best paper in the category of "Geosynthetics and Natural Fibers" for the paper titled "Effect of Natural Fiber Reinforcement on Strength Response of Alkali Activated Binder Treated Expansive Soil: Experimental Investigation and Reliability Analysis" by Mazhar Syed and Anasua GuhaRay published in Construction and Building Materials, Elsevier, 273 (2021) 121743.

Indian Patent No: 201711033016, Filed on 18 September 2017, Treatment process for cellulose based geotextile and geotextile obtained therefrom, A. GuhaRay, A. Kar and S. Gupta.

Commercialisation

For Technology Transfer, contact Rajnesh Kumar, BITS Pilani, Pilani Campus Vidya Vihar, Pilani 333031, Rajasthan, India,Phone: +91-1596-55515, E-mail: tto.office@goa.bits-pilani.ac.in

For sponsored Research, contact Prof. Sanket Goel, BITS Pilani, Hyderabad Campus Jawahar Nagar, Kapra, Hyderabad 500078, Phone: +91 – 40-6630-3686, E-mail: dean.srcd@hyderabad.bits-pilani.ac.in

Drop-In Liquid Sustainable Aviation and Automotive Fuel – Dr Anil Kumar Sinha, CSIR-IIP

Dr Anil Kumar Sinha is Chief Scientist at IIP, Dehradun. He had PhD from NCL, post-doctoral fellow at NI-AIST, Osaka, Researcher at Toyota Central R & D Labs Inc., Japan before joining IIP. The Scientist received CSIR Technology Award for innovation, 2021. The Dr Anil Kumar Sinha's team carries out innovative patentable research in catalytic conversion of renewables into fuels, bio-lubricants, and chemicals and dissemination of knowledge through high impact publications. The team closely works with the government and industry, for excellence and leadership in catalysis research of industrial relevance in the area of cleaner energy. Commercial implementation of the hydrocracking of renewable oils are some of the high impact research activities. The team also focuses on catalyzing renewable feedstock augmentation. The team work for the approval of standards for in-house developed biofuels and bio-lubricants.

Technology

Biojet fuels have already been successfully tested and used in commercial aviation. They have the advantage of being drop-in fuels, meaning they can be used without significant modifications to existing aircraft or infrastructure. This makes them a viable option for transitioning towards more sustainable aviation. Several airlines, including British Airways and Virgin Australia as well as industry stakeholders, have initiated projects and collaborations to explore and promote the use of biojet fuels. Sustainable Aviation Fuel (SAF) initiatives have gained momentum globally, with targets set to increase the percentage of biojet fuels in aviation fuel blends.Bio-Jet produced at CSIR-IIP from the single-step process contains aromatics, thus meeting the stringent ATF standards (Annexure I). The biojet available in the market has no aromatic content, because of which additional aromatics are required to be added to meet the desired specification at additional cost.

Innovation

CSIR-IIP process is a single-step non-precious metal-based catalytic process for conversion of plant-derived oils to produce drop-in biofuel. Currently, available two-step processes use precious metal as a catalyst in the second stage. Catalyst developed at CSIR-IIP is stable; reusable and has performed well even after regeneration. On the process side the reaction conditions have been so optimized as to maintain the desired amount of aromatics and cycloalkanes produced in the process.

Single step catalytic HEFA process for converting lipids to SAF, first in the world. Properties and composition of product (SAF) is similar to those required for Jet A / Jet A-1. Technology is feed flexible: Tree borne oils such as jatropha, pongamia, sapium; derived lipids such as palm stearin, palm fatty acid distillate (PFAD), Used Cooking Oil (UCO), algal oils demonstrated to yield SAF directly meeting ASTM D1655. The product (SAF) contains aromatics in the typical ATF range (~6-15% by weight). Flight demonstrations have been done on the produced SAF, both on civilian and military aircrafts (AN-32).

Patents

i. An improved process to produce aromatics-rich aviation fuel along with other c1 – c24 hydrocarbons; US 2017 / 0253808 A1, Appl. No.: 15 / 510, 598

ii. H2 and biofuels production from renewable feedstocks, US 2018 /0010052 A1, Appl. No: 15 / 645, 629

iii. A catalytic process to convert renewable feedstock into aromatics rich aviation Fuel; WO 2014049621 A1; Application number PCT/IN2013/000596

iv. An improved process to produce aromatics rich aviation fuel along with other C1-C24 hydrocarbons; WO2016038633A1; App. number PCT/IN2015/050109

v. single step catalyst and process to convert triglycerides and free fatty acids directly into isomerized hydrocarbons. Indian Patent 3196DEL2012

vi. A process to prepare inorganic microporous materials and hierarchical porous materials from natural clay materials. Indian Patent 2418DEL2011

Commercialisation

The commercial plant at MRPL 70 tons per day feed processing is being implemented along with Engineers India Limited.

Electric Wheel Barrow-Technovos Machinery Pvt Ltd

Entrepreneur couple Archana Ramprasad and Bharath Anantha Srinivas founded Technovos. Archana is a dentist while Ananthat is an engineer with graduation from KS Institute of Technology and PG from University of Texas.

Technology

The humble wheelbarrow was first invented in In 231 A.D, Zhuge Liang of Shu Han in China created a single wheel cart for an efficient way of transporting food and supplies to the front lines of battle. In the 1970s, British inventor James Dyson introduced the Ballbarrow, an injection molded plastic wheelbarrow with a spherical ball on the front end instead of a wheel. Compared to a conventional design, the larger surface area of the ball made the wheelbarrow easier to use in soft soil, and more laterally stable with heavy loads on uneven ground. The Honda HPE60, an electric power-assisted wheelbarrow, was produced in 1998.

Innovation

Gaade-3 is India's first electric wheelbarrow. Designed for easy transportation of materials, provides an excellent platform from being inclusive and connecting to the entire value chain The machine is based on modular platform. Ensures safety in handling materials and productivity of workforce. Pollution and noise free operation– Environmentally friendly Provides for 'last-mile' delivery solution, that reduces the dependence on fossil fuels. Can carry upto 500Kg, fitted with Heavy Duty Drive Axle, Max Torque: 800Nm, Rated Power:2.2kW. Swappable battery Compatible with Lithium Ion Battery – 30 Km/Charge. It is IOT enabled for real time monitoring.

Patents

The common product at construction sites still attract many patents: https://patents.justia.com/patents-by-us-classification/280/653

Commercialisation

http://www.gaade.world/products

The products include Electric Wheel Barrow, GaadE and Mini Excavator Novo MX 20. Mini excavator market in India is currently around 4-5% of the overall excavator market and has been growing year on year. The present mini excavator manufacturers in the 2.3 ton class are importing the machines. For optimised dynamic machine performance, Engine RPM is controlled electronically by the Operator. Heat dissipation is enhanced through distributed layout. It also improves performance by improving the air suction for engine thereby increasing the life of engine. Extendable track frame for improved stability and versatile machine operation. Good all-round visibility. Rubber tracks are provided for all round performance. Also available with steel track on demand. Swing offset track frame design provided for easy to operate in tight working spaces. Low and High-speed travel option. Extendable dozer blade also available.

Product Designer Ravi Kiran has few concepts to offer – https://www.coroflot.com/RaviKiran_kabadi/Electric-Wheelbarrow

Flow Battery – Prof Kothandaraman Ramanujam, IITM

Kothandaraman Ramanujam, FRSC is Professor, Department of Chemistry, Indian Institute of Technology Madras. His academic research pursuits under the broad headings of (i) Lithium/Sodium/Zinc/Vanadium based batteries; (ii) Organic Dyes for Solar Cells; and (iii) Sensors have enabled delivery of " translatable research". He is incubating a startup "Electrobasics" at IIT Madras, which deal with the custom materials related to electrochemistry related science and engineering. After his PhD in IISc he worked as Post-Doctoral Researchers at Michigan State University and at National Research Council of Canada, Ottawa on Fuel Cells.

https://chem.iitm.ac.in/wp-content/uploads/2020/10/ECS-resume_raman.pdf

https://www.linkedin.com/in/kothandaraman-ramanujam-8565a217/

Technology

In flow batteries, energy is stored in two liquid electrolytes in separate tanks. When you charge, the energy supplied urges electrons from the electron-poor side to move to the electron-rich side like taking water uphill creating a potential difference. During discharge, the reverse happens electrons flow from the electron-rich side to the electron-poor side. (The flow of electrons is electricity. Gaining electrons is a 'reduction reaction', losing electrons is 'oxidation', hence 'redox'.) The conversion of energy from chemical to electrical happens in a cell, which is split into two half-cells by a membrane. Of course, you need electrolytes that are electron-rich and electron-poor to start with that is the science of preparing electrolytes. Usually, vanadium is used as an electrolyte, as the metal exists as four ionic species with two, three, four or five (positively charged) protons more than the number of (negatively charged) electrons.

Innovation

Prof Kothandaraman Ramanujam of IIT-Madras has developed a flow battery based on lead. in the 'soluble lead redox flow batteries', the big challenge was the growth of dendrites, which are filament-like spikes, or extrusions, that could create short-circuit by connecting the two electrodes and giving the electrons a less-resistance pathway. Ramanujam's team has been able to "successfully circumvent" the dendrite growth problem. "Using additives, dendrite growth has been mitigated up to 50 mAh per sq cm of areal capacity, when the battery was cycled at 50 mA per sq cm of current density. The achieved capacity is nearly five times that of lead-acid batteries.

Video https://youtu.be/vIVmtdIfX8M

Patents

A new 'multilayer sandwich design' of a Redox Flow Battery Cell, Kothandaraman R. and Varadaraju UV (Indian Patent, Year: 2013, App. No.: 3713/CHE/201).

Organic materials capable of suppressing H 2 evolution and oxidizable by V 5+ (VO2+) for redox balancing in vanadium redox flow battery. Kothandaraman R and Vasudevarao P (Indian Patent, Year:2016, App.No. 201641030008).

Organic catholyte materials for aqueous organic flow battery. Kothandaraman R, Indrapal Singh Aidhen,Raja M and Jagadeeswari S (Indian Patent, Year: 2020, IDF NO. 2067)

Commercialisation

A 300 W/1kWh VRFB system was built and demonstrated to DST-SERI . He was awarded a consultancy project from ONGC, to build 10kW/10kWh VRFB capable of operating at current density > 100 mA cm-2 at 1.2 V per cell.

Flow batteries are in early-commercialisation phase and just starting the manufacturing scale-up. The flow battery technology is being sharpened elsewhere in the world, too. Vanadium, the active material for storing energy, has been sought to be replaced with iron (Yang Shi, The Chinese University of Hong Kong), manganese (Prof Ingo Krossing, University of Freiburg), and manganese and sulphur (Dr Barun Chakrabarti, University of Warwick).

GigaMesh – mmWave Wireless Backhaul Radio-Astrome Technologies, USA/India

Neha Satak graduated from University of Rajasthan, continued with MSc – Aerospace engineering at IISC and PhD in Aerospace Engineering from Texas A&M University. She worked as a postdoctoral research associate with the Air Force Research Lab in the US. She is also one of two Indian women to win the prestigious Karman Fellowship for space tech innovators this year. She is co-Founder and CEO of Astrome Technologies. Prasad HL Bhat is Co-founder and CTO.

Astrome, which was incubated at IISc, announced that it had raised $3.4 million in funding from IAN Fund, Urania Ventures and Cognizant Technology Solutions, Co-founder Lakshmi Narayanan, Impact Collective of South Korea, ARTPARK (AI and Robotics Technology Park—backed by IISc, AI Foundry and the government of India), and a consortium of US-based angels. It is the first 5G startup to be selected for a Qualcomm and Verizon sponsored 5G Accelerator by EvoNexus in San Diego, US.

https://www.linkedin.com/in/nehasatak/

Technology

The E-band (71 GHz to 86 GHz) supports transmission of high-speed data (~10 Gbps) over short distances (2 km to 3 km). They have developed India's first E-band backhaul hardware that telecom services providers can use to take their 4G and 5G wireless to large swathes of the country. E-band refers to very high-frequency signals, and backhaul, simply put, is the connectivity between the core of a telecom network and the cell towers that send signals to our phones. Major OEMs like Ericsson, Siklu, Huawei and NEC have developed E-band products. All of these products can only do Point-to-Point communication, requiring a large number of devices to make star or mesh topologies required to distribute fibre-capacity in 5G networks, which leads to a large CapEx (capital expenditure) cost of deployment. Astrome is the only company that has a product which features Multiple-Point-to-Point communication in E-Band, resulting in a much lower CapEx than the competition.

Innovation

GigaMesh is World's first Multi-beam E-band Radio that is able to communicate from one tower to multiple towers simultaneously while delivering multi GBPS throughput to each of these towers. This product has the power of software over hardware. The developed proprietary algorithms enable Automatic link alignment and dynamic power alignment. Astrome is Cisco's development partner. Astrome and Cisco offer a quickly deployable, high bandwidth integrated Backhaul and Access solution comprising of: Cisco's router and Access solutions – Astrome's E-band, fibre-like Multiple-Point-to-Point backhaul solution. This solution in its different forms can be used for Enterprise LAN network, Service Provider to Enterprise connection and Tower to Tower backhaul and fronthaul connectivity.

Patents

WO2018037424A1

System and method for integrated optimization of design and performance of satellite constellations

Commercialisation

https://astrome.co/products/gigamesh/

Astrome, headquartered in Bengaluru, India and with offices in the U.S. and France, provides gigabit speed wireless solutions to telecom service providers, Private Networks/Enterprises, and Defense organizations. Astrome is focused on delivering GigaMesh, a multi-gigabit wireless X-haul radio to accelerate the deployment of 5G in suburban areas and broadband in rural areas.

SatixFy's PRIME 1 beamformer chip will power Astrome's Next-Gen GigaMesh product, which is one of the only point-to-multi-point E-band high-speed link for terrestrial 5G in the world. The PRIME 1 beamformer chip, initially developed as a key building block for SatixFy's satellite antenna systems, supports up to 32 antenna elements and can be digitally connected to other PRIME chips to rapidly build a range of antennas. The PRIME 1 chip was developed with the support of the UK Space Agency via the European Space Agency's ARTES Core Competitiveness Programme.

https://www.satixfy.com/news/satixfy-signs-deal-partnership-mou-with-astrome-to-develop-5g-gigamesh-2-0-terrestrial-backhauling-product/

Guided Waves Sensors – Prof Krishnan Balasubramanian, IITM

Krishnan Balasubramaniamn is Institute Professor at IIT Madras and Evanglising Lab to Market Transitions in India. Prof. Krishnan Balasubramaniam has been involved in the field of Non-destructive evaluation for more than 33 years, with 480 technical publications, 30 patents filings and instrumental in the incubation of several startups including Dhvani Research, Playns Technologies, Detect Technologies, Maximl Labs, Trotix Robotics, HyperVerge, and Solinas Integrity. He also was conferred the DRDO Academy Excellence Award for 2015. In 2018, bestowed with the prestigious ABDUL KALAM National Technology Innovation Fellowship by the Indian National Academy of Engineers and the Life Time Achievement Award by the Indian Institute of Technology Madras.

https://www.linkedin.com/in/krishnan-balasubramanian-534145157/

Technology

Ultrasonic waveguide based measurement methods have been extensively used for developing sensors for level, density, temperature, and rheology measurement of the surrounding fluid. While using as a sensor, the material property of the waveguide (density and elastic moduli), as a function of temperature, were assumed to be known. Consequently, if the waveguide is surrounded by a fluid, with known properties (such as air), then the material properties of the waveguide can be obtained as a function of temperature. The ultrasonic waveguide sensors have several advantages over the conventional thermocouples. This includes the inherent property of higher reliability, since there is no junction that can fail. Also, as described in this paper, many notches along the waveguide can ensure multiple temperature measurements using a single waveguide.

https://www.ndt.net/article/wcndt2016/papers/mo2g4.pdf

Innovation

XYMA Analytics is a spin-out from Centre for NDE, IIT Madras and incubated by IIT Madras Incubation Cell. XYMA provides novel ultrasonic sensors and Industrial-IoT solutions to industries using high temperature processes such as refineries, power plants, steel plants and other manufacturing industries. Their sensors provide dense measurements across a unit, improving performance and asset life, which is coupled with AI-powered physical models for intelligent support.

µTMaps and µSTMaps are robust high temperature sensors which are capable of multi-point temperature measurement using a single waveguide sensor. PoRTS is a our multi-parameter sensor which measures the Viscosity, Temperature and Level of a fluid using a single ultrasonic waveguide with higher reliability and precision.

Ztar is a waveguide based ultrasonic level sensor which provides accurate measurement even at higher temperatures. It has both contact and non-contact variants.

https://pubs.aip.org/aip/rsi/article-abstract/90/4/045108/283216/Ultrasonic-waveguide-based-level-measurement-using?

Patents

Prof. Krishnan Balasubramaniam and Prof Prabhu Rajagopal. IITM Licensed 8 patented technologies and one Trademark in the field of "Sensor-Based Technology for Process Efficiency In Industries".

Video – https://youtu.be/dFcDdvZDRBY

Commercialisation

https://xyma.in/products.php

Dr. Nishanth Raja is the Chief Executive Officer of XYMA Analytics – an IIT Madras incubated company. He was a Senior Research Fellow in Fluid Control Research Institute, Palakkad in Kerala and later joined as the project officer in Centre for Non-Destructive Evaluation (CNDE) – IIT Madras. Mr.Aswin Kumar Kathirvel is the Chief Technical Officer of XYMA Analytics. He completed his Bachelor's degree in the field of Mechanical Engineering at IIT Madras.

Horizontal Boring Machine for Underground – CSIR-CBRI

Dr. Soraj Kumar Panigrahi is Sr Principal Scientist at CSIR-CBRI working in Acoustics, Instrumentation and Mechanical Systems (AIMS) Group. A mechanical engineering graduate from UCE Burla, Mtech REC, Rourkela and PhD from IIT Roorke. His team on this development included Mr. Narendra Kumar, Mr. R.S Bisht and Mr. Sameer.

https://cbri.res.in/scientific-profiles/group-iv/senior-principal-scientist/s-k-panigrahi-2/

Technology

Presently, the installation, repairs and replacement of underground facilities involve open trench excavation methods. Trenchless construction is a method of laying underground facilities without disturbing the surface structure. Big capacity crawler mounted Underground Horizontal Directional Drilling Rigs are available (US Patents US4474252A, US6932171B2, US6736219B1). The machines are of large capacity,very expensive and suitable for big projects. They require large space on the road side and works on the principle of wet boring. All the said machines are power operated and require heavy hydraulic systems. Small capacity boring machines are also available in international market (Model:140 EW, Praire Dog Boring Equipment Inc. & Tunnel Rat, Porta-Mole Underground Boring Systems).

Innovation

A small capacity Boring Machine developed previously at the Institute is based on hydraulic system, costly and requires a very big pit on the road side and capable of boring upto 8 m length only. To fulfill the requirements of construction industry a small capacity boring machine capable of making horizontal bores under the ground at required depth economically and effectively has been developed at CSIR-CBRI. The machine is suitable to make bores for installation of sewer pipe lines, conduits, electrical cables, water lines, other transmission products under the buildings, roads and allied constructions.

The salient features of the developed boring machine are as follows;

Boring diameter : Up to 200 mm

Boring length : Up to 25.0 m

Depth of Boring : Up to 1.0 m (under surface)

Required Pit Size : 1m X 0.75m

Power requirement Hent : 3 HP (Single/three Phase)

Patent

Publications – Narendra Kumar, Panigrahi S K, Sameer, Gautam D K (2016), Boring machine for making horizontal bores under the ground-Trenchless technology, New Building materials & Construction World, Vol. 21(12), p126-130.

A small capacity prototype underground horizontal boring Machine (Boring capacity of 160 mm dia. Upto 8m length) has been developed previously at CSIR-CBRI (patent Appln. No. 448/DEL/2009). It requires a large pit as the complete machine is required to be placed inside the pit. It is hydraulically operated, heavy and costly.

Commercialisation

This technology is available for transfer.

Video – https://youtu.be/hJV41AyRMtk

Other technologies ready for transfer –

https://cbri.res.in/technologies-available/

Institute transferred several technologies in the past –

https://cbri.res.in/the-institute/performance-indicators/technologies/

Training in trenchless Construction: http://www.indstt.com/

Hot Wire Cutting Machine – Prof Sathyan S, IITM

Sathyan Subbiah, professor in the Department of Mechanical Engineering at IIT Madras, graduate from same institute followed by M. S from University of Illinois and Ph. D., from Georgia Institute of Technology. Research revolves around the area of machining currently sponsored by Saint Gobain Research India, Reliance Petrochemical, Micromatic apart from DST, DHI. Earlier worked at Rolls Royce Singapore for about 6 years.

https://home.iitm.ac.in/sathyans/about.htm

Technology

A hot wire cutter is a tool used to cut polystyrene foam. The device consists of a thin, taut metal wire, often made of nichrome alloy, which is heated via electrical resistance to approximately 200°C.

Innovation

CNC Hot wire can cut Thermocol upto 40kg/m3 automatically by using multiple strings (NiCr wire). It can cut cursive letter, Dome arrays, Pillar arrays, Pipe section, Corner patti etc. Lite model CNC Hot wire can cut Thermocol upto 40kg/m3 automatically by using a single string (NiCr wire).It can cut cursive letter, Dome arrays, Pillar arrays, Pipe section, Corner patti etc.

Videos: https://youtu.be/PQVLUgbcB8s, https://youtu.be/Ser3j6mebPM

Patents

SVP Laser Technologies has been recognized as the Top IP Driven SSI Industry in India by CII during International Conference on IPR held in October 2018.

METHOD OF POWER CONTROL IN CNC HOT WIRE MACHINES, Srinivasan Viswesh | Subbiah Sathyan | Chitikena Hareesh, INDIAN INSTITUTE OF TECHNOLOGY MADRAS,IN, Patent No. IN201841035019A, 2020

The company has 7 granted patents and 5 trademarks and 10+ international patent pending-applications in this Digital manufacturing domain.

Commercialisation

https://www.greacnc.com/cnc-thermocol-eps-cutting

Mr.Viswesh is the Co-Founder and Managing Director of SVP Laser Technologies, Chennai. He is a B.Tech (Mech) from IIT Madras and MS from University of Minnesota USA with 15 years work experience in Advanced Manufacturing Industry. He started his entrepreneurial jorney in 2008 after working in the technology division of comapany like Siemens and has been successfully focussing on developing products related to Low Cost Automation & CNC Digital Manufacturing.The team has developed several products like the MULTICNC.IN (Multi-purpose Substractive prototyping machine and software), RoboCNC.in (Vision guided educational robot), AutoCAM2D.com (CAM software), ECNCshop.com (Online Machine shop) etc. With multipl patented technologies, SVP Laser has been developing mission critical Digital Manufacturing technologies such as the MultiCNC® CNC controller, AutoCAM2D CAM software, and other CNC controlled machines for applications such as jewelry manufacturing, PCB, furniture, and foam fabrication.All of these products are shipped to nations such as Canada, the United States, the United Kingdom, the United Arab Emirates, Oman, and the Philippines, among others. CNC LHK (Long Hot Knife), OLOM

Induction Motor Stethoscope (MSCOPE) – CSIR – CSIO, Chennai

Dr G S AYYAPPAN is Sr. Principal Scientist, Energy Management Technologies (Chennai Centre) of CSIR-CSIO. He started with a Diploma in Electrical & Electronics Engg. from PACR Polytechnic, Rajapalayam, followed with B.E from Anna University, and M.E Sathyabama University. He received PhD on Condition monitoring of motors from Academia of Scientific & Innovative Research, CECRI, Karaikudi.He worked on DST funded project – Design & Development of cost in situ intrusive Motor Stethoscope (MSCOPE) for Monitoring the Health of Induction Motor using the Latest art of Instrumentation.

https://icsio.csio.res.in/csio.ems/emp_profile.aspx?id=309

Technology

The problem of failures in induction motors is a large concern due to its significant influence over industrial production. Therefore a large number of detection techniques were developed detection using three methods: motor current signature analysis (MCSA), surface vibration (SV), and instantaneous angular speed (IAS). Induction motor faults often generate particular frequency components in the electric current spectrum. The abnormal harmonics contain potential information of motor faults. Therefore, the frequency analysis approach is used to diagnose induction motor faults.

Innovation

MSCOPE is an instrument used to diagnose the health of Induction Motors. This Instrument employs Hybrid techniques like Motor Current Signature Analysis (MCSA), Vibration Analysis (VA) and Temperature Analysis (TA) to detect the Motors faults On-site, On – line and In-situ.The MSCOPE detects the faults and their severity level without removing the motor from the existing setup. The system uses hybrid algorithm for both diagnosis and detection of faults.

Features: Capable of detecting 16 different faults present in an induction motor. Highlights the faults detected and also displays the severity of the faults detected. Hybrid Measurement(Vibration, Voltage, Current, Temperature). Hybrid Analysis(Vibration Analysis, Motor Current Signature Analysis, Temperature. Analysis). Hybrid Decision Making algorithm for severity & location of fault (Fuzzy Logic, Machine learning and Artificial Neural Network). Three levels of diagnosis namely Basic, Intermediate, Advanced Diagnosis

■ Induction Motor Stethoscope (MSCOPE) – CSIR – CSIO, Chennai ■

Patents

Publications – Mathematical Modelling and IoT Enabled Instrumentation for Simulation & Emulation of Induction Motor Faults, https://www.researchgate.net/profile/Ayyappan-Gs

Patents – A SYSTEM AND METHOD FOR NON INTRUSIVE LOAD MONITORING OF IDENTICAL ELECTRICAL UTILITIES, Application Number: PCT/IN2021/050145 Date of Filing: 16-02-2021, Inventor(s): KUMAR MUKESH, GOPINATH R., SRINIVAS KOTA, AYYAPPAN G S, P ANAND V

Commercialisation

This technology and other technologies in energy management are available for transfer – Induction Motor Efficiency Monitoring System (IMEMS), Induction Motor Stethoscope (MSCOPE), Power Quality Analyser (PQA), Portable Energy Audit Tool (PEAT), Pump Efficiency Monitoring System (PEMS), Energy Management System (EMS), Smart Energy Meters for Mass Housing, Building Energy Management System (BEMS), Air Conditioner Efficiency Meter (ACE Meter).

https://www.csio.res.in/CommonNew.php?ds=273&page=1

Li-Fi Products-Velmenni, New Delhi

Deepak Solanki Founder & CEO at Velmenni is a researcher at heart, participated in various projects from academic institutions like IIIT – Hyderabad & Sine IIT – Bombay while alongside publishing multiple research reports on mobile robotics. Recently he remedied one of the biggest Road Traffic Control issues in Delhi NCR, India. Started with an engineering degree from Lovely Professional University, worked as research intern at IIIT Hyderabad & ikalogic and worked few months Thinklabs Technosolutions Pvt. Ltd. (an IIT Bombay Alumni Venture). Conducted training programs in robotics and embedded systems for engineering students at various prestigious institutes including IIT Bombay, BITS Pilani – Hyderabad, NSIT Delhi, SRM University among others. Ujjwal Minocha a tech entrepreneur and investor is Co-Founder. Another co-founder Nikhil Bhulabhai comes with decades of business experience in Africa.

https://www.linkedin.com/in/deepaksolanki64/

Technology

Light communication is a bi-directional wireless communication network enabling the transmission of data by leveraging the unlicensed visible or invisible part of the light spectrum. Light communication refers to all types of wireless communications where optical/light wavelengths are used. VLC(Visible Light Communication), FSO(Free Space Optics), LiFi(Light Fidelity), Infra-red Remote Controls, etc. are all examples of LC. In Li-Fi the data is transmitted from a light access point to a user's smart device (laptops/ PCs/ Smartphones). It enables user mobility and can offer smooth handover in case a user moves from one light access point to another.

Professor Harald Haas coins the term LiFi at TED Global in 2011. LiFi is demonstrated for the first time in public. In 2018 pureLiFi demonstrate the world's first integrated Laptop and mobile phone sleeve at Mobile World Congress. Global leaders in communications, lighting, infrastructure, and device manufacturing industries have come together to form Light Communications Alliance – an open, non-profit association, with the aim to promote light communications technology with an efficient and result-oriented approach. The major collaborators include PureLiFi, Velmenni, Orange, Nokia, and Zero.1, Fraunhofer HHI, du. Velmenni is now a part of the Cisco LaunchPad program that nurtures co-development, co-creation, new business models and joint GTMs.

The world's first mountain-top LiFi laser 5G internet was demonstrated in Ladakh–https://youtu.be/Rw-QZuGVP3o?si=Un9Pi-H3BUB3caWQ

Innovation

Data input from the router is transferred to the LiFi Access Point (attached to the LEDs) over POE/Ethernet cable. That same data is then encoded, modulated, and transmitted using LEDs. The

LiFi Dongle (attached to the smart device) does demodulation and decoding of the data and sends it to the user's smart device using USB. Reversing this process, LiFi Dongle then performs the necessary encoding and modulation for uplink communication of data. NIR LEDs integrated into LiFi Dongle act as a medium for uplink communication enabling bi-directional communication.

Patents

OPTICAL WIRELESS COMMUNICATION SYSTEM AND ADAPTIVE OPTICAL WIRELESS COMMUNICATION NETWORK, Publication number: 20200195343, Inventor: Deepak SOLANKI, 2020

Commercialisation

https://www.velmenni.com/lifi-dongle-access-points

Velmenni has been working on LiFi Technology for the past 5 years. It has achieved multiple research and development milestone within Optical Wireless Communication including development of Optical Wireless Mesh Network.

Techshlok, New Delhi demonstrated LiFi at LiFi at India Electronics Week 2020. ERNET India executed LiFi pilot project jointly with IIT Madras. IIT Delhi, we are developing a LiFi network at 100 Mb/s.

Microfluidic Electro-Viscometer – Dr. Sanket Goel, BITS Pilani, Hyderabad

Prof Sanket Goeal is Principal Investigator, MEMS, Microfluidics & Nanoelectronics Lab, BITS Pilani, Hyderabad campus. A researcher with BSc from Ramjas, MS (Physics) from IITD an PhD (Microfluidics and Photonics) worked at UPES, Dehradun before joing BITS. He is Founding Director, Cleome Innovations. Dr SB Punnet completed his PhD from MMNE Lab, BITS Pilani, Hyderabad Campus

Technology

Viscometers are broadly employed in a wide range of sensing and monitoring applications, such as biochemical optimization, biomedical diagnostics, pharmaceuticals, and various adulteration detections. When realizing them in a microfluidic environment, the viscometers can potentially be used in an automated and robust point-of-care setting. In recent times, micro viscometers have been exploited for widespread and diverse detection applications such as sensing adulteration in various fluids used in day-to-day life, diagnostics in the biomedical domain involving human bodily fluids, pharmaceuticals, and biochemical analysis.

Innovation

Measurement of viscosity is quintessential in chemical & biochemical processes. While important to sustain processes, viscosity can also be an indicator of abnormal behavior. Conventionally the process is cumbersome with the need for elaborate laboratory setup and expensive equipment. To provide an alternative methodology, A microfluidic viscometer was developed using a 3D printer on chromatograph paper. The viscometer consisted of a micro-channel with a defined boundary made of a hydrophobic substance, which was formed using 3D printing technology. This hydrophobic boundary ensured that the fluid being tested flows within the micro-channel. To measure the viscosity of the fluid, a pair of micro-electrodes were integrated into the micro-channel using the screen-printing method. The arrangement of electrodes allowed for direct contact between the electrodes & the flowing fluid. The other portion of each electrode extended beyond the hydrophobic boundary & was designed to establish contact with a microcontroller through a connector. In addition to detecting the electronic contact between the fluid & the micro-electrodes, the microcontroller was responsible for accurately measuring the time interval between the two electronic senses. This measurement was achieved by recording the timestamps corresponding to the moment each electronic contact was established.

- Microfluidic Electro-Viscometer – Dr. Sanket Goel, BITS Pilani, Hyderabad

Patents

Indian Patent Filed (201911049248, November-2019)

Commercialisation

https://www.cleome.in/

Trials conducted on milk, and automobile fuel Samples. Potential Application include monitoring adulteration of various fluids.

https://www.mmne.in/research/%C2%B5-fluidic-viscometer

Dr Sanket Goel and Dr Satish K Dubey, founded Cleome Innovations in April 2021 to work in tandem with MEMS, Microfluidics & Nanoelectronics Laboratory towards commercialization of under development futuristic biomedical sensors, smart sensors and miniaturised energy harvesters. Over the course of time, Cleome Innovations has engaged in the development of µ-fluidics assisted technologies for diagnostics device development.Cleome Innovations is incubated at Technology Business Incubator, BITS Pilani, Hyderabad Campus

Dr Amol Kulkarni is Senior Principal Scientist at CSIR-National Chemical Laboratory, with Ph.D.from Institute of Chemical Technology, Mumbai, 116 publications, 3235 citations with expertise in Multiphase reactors and Microreactors. Kulkarni's team comprised of Prachi Kate and Suneha Patil. BLV Prasad and Nandini Devi also contributed to this challenging interdisciplinary work.

https://ncl.irins.org/profile/245733

http://academic.ncl.res.in/aa.kulkarni/profile

Technology

Silver Nanowires have caught significant attention of both academia as well as industry over last decade because of inherent extraordinary thermal and electrical properties of its base metal.

The performance of the material gets enhanced even further at the Nano-scale due to increase in the surface area of the material by about 1000 times, which leads to lesser consumption of the material without compromising the quality of the end application.

Silver nanowires are raw materials used in manufacturing conducting inks and flexible transparent conductive films (cost effective alternative to indium tin oxide (ITO) films). These applications require large quantity of silver nanowires with precise control on dimensions.

Innovation

NCL scientists have developed a continuous process for manufacturing silver nanowires with precise control on diameter and length. Silver nanowires of the following specifications can be achieved:ü Length: 50-200 ¼m ü Purity: >99.5%ü Diameter 3 ranges: 30-40/50-60/80-100 nmü Appearance: Gray suspension in solvent (Water/ Ethanol/Iso-propyl alcohol) § The process technology is continuous and scalable process that recycles unreacted reactants efficiently.

The process has a temperature of over 130 degrees Celsius (Fahrenheit). In the series of four Multistage Multiphase reactors, reactants are preheated and supplied to utilities connected to the reactors for accurate temperature control. Condensers are mounted on top of the reactors and are used to collect the condensed reaction vapors. After passing through four multiphase reactors, the reactant mixture is cooled, collected, and delivered for further purification at the fourth multiphase reactor's outlet in the product tank.

Patents

Publications: https://www.sciencedirect.com/science/article/abs/pii/S1385894721003090?via%3Dihub

Patents: WO2019049172, EP18778570.4, US16/644597, CN201880057937.9, IN201711031533

Commercialisation

CSIR-NCL has demonstrated this technology at 500 gm/day. It can be scaled up easily to 5 kg/day and further. The demand of silver nanowires as replacement to expensive ITO films to make flexible transparent conductive films (used in touchscreen displays) which are used in touchscreen is expected to cross USD 200 Million by 2025.

Applications include – Flexible transparent conductive films: High-intensity LEDs, touchscreens, conductive adhesives, solar, sensors. Conductive silver ink: Printed electronics (PE), flexible electronics (FE). Antimicrobial: Paint, cosmetics, bandages, clothing, water purification. Others: catalysts, adhesives, polymers.

CSIR-NCL has already signed a material transfer agreement with an Indian company Nanorbital Advanced Materials Pvt Ltd and another is in progress. The technology is available for licensing.

http://www.nclinnovations.org/pdfs/available_knowhow/056_Silver-Nanowires_OnePager.pdf

Ultra Spinner – CeraTattva, IITM, Chennai

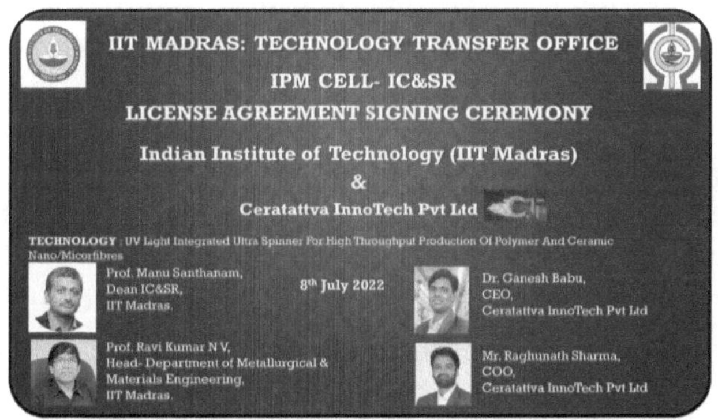

Dr. Ganesh Babu is Founder & CEO, CeraTattva InnoTech and Senior Project Officer at IIT-Madras. Raghunath Sharma Mukkavilli Doctoral Candidate at IIT Madras is Co – Founder. Prof Ravi Kumar, IITM is their mentor. Ganesh Babu had PhD from Cochin University of Science & Technology while Raghnath Sharma completed his doctoral work at Department of Metallurgical and Materials Engineering, IITM. The startup is incubated at IITM Research Park in March 2022. Dr.Ganesh Babu and Mr. Raghunath Sharma, members of the HighPerformance Ceramic lab at the MME Department,

https://www.linkedin.com/in/raghunath-sharma-mukkavilli-16242668

https://www.linkedin.com/in/dr-ganeshbabut/

Technology

Ceramic fibers include all non-metallic inorganic fibers (oxide or non-oxide) except for fibers manufactured via solidifying glass melts. Fibers spun by an electrospinning process are classified according to their structure (micro/nano) and properties, fibers morphology, and chemical structure. These fibers can be used in many applications. The superficial oxide ceramic fibers, such as TiO_2, Al_2O_3, and ZnO, and complex oxide ceramic fibers, such as $CaCu_3Ti_4O_{12}$ and $Li_{1.6}Al_{0.6}MnO_4$, are produced by the electrospinning method. Further, ZrC and Cu_2ZnSnS_4, which are non-oxide ceramic fibers, are made via the electrospinning process.

Innovation

The spin-off developed high quality ceramics and preceramics through the novel, economical, and sustainable precursor-derived ceramic (PDC) route. The 'Ultraspinner', a device developed and patented by Ceratattva, allows sustainable laboratory-scale production of PDCs and aids research work. Strategic and functional non-oxide ceramics are candidates for applications in aerospace, energy, electronics, and defence sectors, to name a few. Indian industries produce commonly used monolithic non-oxide ceramics such as silicon carbide and aluminum nitride. However, these ceramics are created via an energy-intensive powder route. India also lacked the ability to produce unconventional, more impactful ternary and quaternary ceramics such as hafnium and zirconium boride carbides which have an unprecedented ability to boost the avionics and defence technology of a country. The PDC route allows the production of such complex formulations, including amorphous ceramics, at low energy-utilization rates.

The 'Ultraspinner' was developed in order to overcome the disadvantages of the conventional electrospinning technique. The electrospinning machine uses extremely high voltage to produce ceramic fibers and it has a very low rate of production. 'Ultraspinner' is a much safer and better method as it produces the same amount of material in a fraction of the time and utilizes a regular voltage supply. A functional model has already been set up at the Department of Physics, IIT Madras. Ultraspinner can obtain polymer/preceramic fibers with higher yield and safer operating conditions compared to other contemporary technologies. Coupled with a UV curing facility and a pen type microscope, our Ultraspinner is beyond just fiber production and is a perfect "guide-mate" to assist in analysis on the spot providing flexibility to the user for quick modifications and/or immediate validation of result.

Patents

Publication – Large-scale synthesis of centrifugally spun tantalum oxynitride fiber electrocatalysts for hydrogen evolution reaction, https://ceramics.onlinelibrary.wiley.com/doi/10.1111/jace.19274

Video – https://youtu.be/BcY6PPJ5DyY?si=OyBilZODwRrWwvjz

Commercialisation

PDCs are multifunctional materials – their uses range from coatings for hypersonic vehicles to fibres used in biomedical sciences. They have the incredible advantage of being easily produced as coatings, films, fibers, or any other necessary form. Ceratattva produces both precursor-derived preceramics and ceramics.

https://ceratattva.com/portfolio/ceramic-processing-technologies/

Ternary Content Addressable Memory (TCAM) in a Network Router – Prof. Krishna Moorthy Sivalingam, IITM

Krishna Sivalingam Graduate from Anna University with Ph.D. (Computer Science) from State University of New York at Buffalo is Institute Chair Professor at Indian Institute of Technology, Madras. He worked n the USA as Assistant Professor (University of North Carolina) Associate Professor (Washington State University) and Professor (University of Maryland) before joining IITM. He has 63 journal publications with 4291 citations.

https://iitm.irins.org/profile/50716

Technology

The route lookup function typically involves performing the longest prefix match on an ordered set of entries carefully configured on a ternary content addressable memory (TCAM) hardware. TCAM consumes a lot of power & currently routers perform route lookup based on longest prefix match & using the TCAM for the route lookup consumes lot of power.

Innovation

Before search begins all entries when entered inside TCAM are closing the circuitry on TCAM word entry and show "true" at encoder side. All entries are temporarily in the match state. When parallel search is done it will brake all entries that have at least one bit that does not match the searched entry. This also explains why TCAM memory is so power hungry. It needs to power on all circuits to be able to make a search not only the matched ones. Limited memory space and power consumption associated with a large amount of parallel active circuitry are the main issues with TCAM.

The TCAM hardware is specially designed for parallel search to locate a matching entry across the entire TCAM in a single cycle, & which is a de-facto hardware used for route lookup on high-end network routers. reduces power consumption of high-end router by up to 18%.

Patents

PCT Application No.PCT/IN2019/050072, Inventors SANKARAN, Ganesh Chennimalai, SIVALINGAM, Krishnamoorthy.

Present disclosure relates to a method and system for performing route look-up for routing data in a network router. First router shares a direct index with one or more neighboring routers. A second router of the one or more neighboring routers encodes the direct index as part of a packet header and sends the packet header with encoded direct index to a next hop router of the one or more neighboring routers. The next hop router then decodes the encoded direct index and locates one or more route look-up results based on the decoded direct index. In an embodiment, an outgoing interface index of a second hop router is added to a packet header of a data packet at the first router. Further, the data packet is forwarded to one or more hop routers based on the outgoing interface index by the second hop router.

Commercialisation

This technology is transferred to Agalsearch Systems Private Limited promoted by IITM faculty Chakkaravarthy Ramachandran and Balaji Srinivasan.This technology and many more patented technologies are available for transfer from IITM.

https://ipm.icsr.in/ipm/our-technologies

Wirelsss GPS Clock – Signals & Systems (India) Private Limited (SANDS)

Dr.L R Rajagopal, Founder & CEO, has a graduate degree in Electrical Engineering, and obtained Masters and Doctoral degrees from Indian Institute of Technology, Delhi, in 1984 and 1987 respectively. In recognition of his work, he was awarded Prof. M N Saha award by Institute of Electronics and Telecommunication Engineers (IETE), India. He has also worked as collaborating scientist with Indian Institute of Technology, Delhi, for about eight years, and for about a year with Indian Institute of Technology, Madras. Dr L R Rajagopal has been actively involved in promoting communication protocol standards Electronic Meters in India, and has served as the Chairman of the subcommittee on Protocol Standards, Central Board for Irrigation and Power (CBIP). He was actively involved in Best Practices Committee of Ministry of Power, which conducted national seminars in promoting loss reduction programmes for various electric utilities in India.

Technology

GPS (global positioning system) is a network of orbiting satellites that provide navigation and communication information to earth. One feature embedded in the GPS signal is time, which is synchronized with the atomic clock at the National Institute of Standards and Technology in Boulder, Colorado. The atomic clock serves as the United States' primary time and frequency standard, and synchronization via satellite makes GPS clocks extremely accurate and reliable. These clocks do not receive a signal directly from the GPS. A controller receives the time signals from the GPS, and then the controller distributes the correct time to clocks by way of a direct connection or wireless transmission. While clocks do not need to be outdoors, it is important that clocks receiving the incoming signal be within range of the transmitter. There are several different styles of clocks that get their time from GPS-signaled controllers: analog and digital, powered by batteries or by AC power.

Innovation

GPS Clock offers an easy, cost-effective solution for accurate, synchronized time displays without expensive, disruptive installation procedures. Because there are no wiring requirements, installation times are drastically reduced. It is ideal for renovation projects, as there is no need to worry about installation work, as well as new construction. The GPS clock can be synchronized through GPS Antenna or Wireless Antenna. The display can be wall/ panel / tabletop mountable. It can be used as a wireless clock to synchronize many wireless slave clocks in and around the buildings.

Patents

History and patent on Atomic clock – https://ethw.org/Milestones: First_Atomic_Clock,_1948

Commercialisation

https://www.sandsindia.com/Home/

SANDS is primarily a technology company manufacturing niche products using embedded technology for the Generation, Transmission & Distribution segments of the Power Industry. On the Services front, we specialize in Meter Data Analytics for Power Distribution companies, to curb Energy thefts and fraud management. We also undertake testing of Energy meters at the site on behalf of the utilities as part of the regulatory guidelines.

ARGUS: VIBRATION-BASED MACHINE CONDITION MONITORING SYSTEM: Online Vibration monitoring is an effective condition monitoring tool where the sensors are mounted on the bearing points of the asset permanently and are configured to collect vibration data on a real-time basis. It can be programmed to provide alerts or alarms to users in case of any breach of the preset threshold values. The Manual/offline vibration analyzers are used for regular/periodic vibration data collection and the collected data indicates machine health in the current situation. The challenge with manual/offline data collection is that critical and large-size equipment health condition continuously evolves. To monitor that condition, vibration spectrum analysis and diagnostic studies need to take place continuously on a 24/7 basis. By leveraging smart sensors and wireless connectivity, online condition monitoring systems make it possible to perform vibration analysis safely, continuously, and economically.

Consumer Products

1. AC Helmet – Jarsh Innovations, Hyderabad
2. Board games – Mozaic Games, Bangalore
3. Burst Preventive Puncture Tyres – TJ Tyres, Faridabad
4. Mouseware – dextroware devices,Chennai
5. Piezoelectric microphone – Anand Richard Lobo, Goa
6. Robotic Scrubber Dryer – Aubotz Labs,Pune
7. Saline water lamp – Dr PURNIMA JALIHAL, NIOT, Chennai
8. Siddu Jackfruit-ParameshaS.S and IIHR Karnataka
9. Stay Warm (Hand, Body, Foot and Sleeping Bag Warmers) – Parisodhana Technologies, Hyderabad
10. Walnut cracker – Mushtaq Ahmed Dar, Kashmir

AC Helmet – Jarsh Innovations Pvt Ltd, Hyderabad

Kausthub Kaundinya is Founder & CEO at Jarsh Safety, a graduate from VNRVJIET and incubated at VJ Hub, he was mentored by Dr DN Rao. Anand Kumar MS from Bits Pilani is Co-Founder and CPO. Sreekanth Kommula also from Bits Pilani is another co-founder and CTO. Jarsh Innovations received a funding of Rs. 5 lakh from their college's startup incubator VJ-Hub in July 2016. The Ministry of MSME pitched in with Rs. 1.5 lakh along with Indian Institute of Science, Bengaluru, initially and later sanctioned another Rs. 15 lakh in grants. The product has won several awards – Gold Medal (TCS), Gold Medal (XLR8 AP), National Winner (GITR), Gold Medal (ISTE), National Winner (CII), and Silver Medal (IIA Fair).

https://www.linkedin.com/in/yskkjarsh/

Technology

Solid-state cooling relies on a phenomenon known as the Peltier effect, discovered in 1834 by French physicist Jean Charles Athanase Peltier. The Peltier effect occurs when an electric current is passed through a junction of two dissimilar materials, resulting in a temperature difference. Thermoelectric coolers (TECs), also known as Peltier devices, are the primary components used in solid-state cooling systems. TECs consist of an array of semiconductor materials, typically composed of bismuth telluride, connected in series and sandwiched between two ceramic plates. When a direct current (DC) is applied to the TEC, electrons in the semiconductor material move from the hot side to the cold side, carrying heat with them and causing one side of the device to cool down while the other side heats up. Thermal management is also a concern for solid-state cooling systems. Efficiently dissipating the heat generated on the hot side of the thermoelectric cooler is crucial for maintaining optimal performance. Advanced heat sink designs and materials are being developed to tackle this issue and further enhance the overall efficiency of solid-state cooling systems.

Innovation

The latest development to football helmets has been to add air conditioning, with the Louisiana State University football team to use these new models in the 2023 NCAA season. The air flow will last for five hours, meaning that players can benefit from the cooling effect throughout an entire game.

Indian firm Jarsh developed air conditioned helmet based on solid-state cooling technology, Cool up to $\Delta - 15°C$ and heat up to $\Delta + 10°C$, provided with rechargeable Li-ion battery. The helmet has an operating temperature range of $- 5°C$ to $55°C$. Jarsh-NIA AC

Helmet, designed for the outdoor workforce and field executives was launched in Dubai.

Patents

Design of Air Conditioned Helmet IN 304557 · Issued Feb 8, 2019IN 304557 · Issued Feb 8, 2019

Method of cooling and air-circulation inside a Helmet IN 6499/CHE/2015 · Filed Nov 16, 2015IN 6499/CHE/2015 · Filed Nov 16, 2015

Commercialisation

https://jarshsafety.com/ac-helmet/

Board Games – Mozaic Games, Bangalore

Mozaic Games (previously Dice Toy Labs) was founded in 2018 in Bangalore, India by Phalgun Polepalli and Shwetha Badarinath, husband and wife duo. Phalgun was an engineer from BMS College of Engineering with PGDBM from XIME while Shwetha was an engineering graduate from JSSATE. Both worked in Software companies for limited period before starting DICE Toy Labs Private Limited.

Technology

By 2010, over 250 million sets of Monopoly® had been sold since its invention and the game had been played by over half a billion people making it possibly the most popular board game in the world. Lizzie Magie patented the original version of her board game (US patent #748,626). "The Landlord's Game" had a square pathway where players started on a corner featuring a map of the world with the phrase "Labor Upon Mother Earth Produces Wages". Darrow earned a patent for Monopoly in December 1935 (US #2,026,082), and neither he nor Parker Brothers mentioned The Landlord's Game. Since that day, it has been translated into 37 languages and evolved into over 200 licensed and localized editions for 103 countries across the world. The game of capitalism, competition and business strategy has firmly established itself as a significant piece of popular culture. The game's name remains a registered trademark of Parker Brothers, as do its specific design elements; other elements of the game are still protected under copyright law.

Innovation

Modern strategy board games are an excellent investment for anyone looking for a fun and challenging way to spend their free time. These games are designed to challenge your mind and test your strategic skills. Not only are they fun, but they also help to improve critical thinking, problem-solving, and decision-making skills. Mazaic product line-up of modern strategy board games includes popular titles such as Indus 2500BCE, Chai Garam, Startups & Beyond, Yudhbhoomi and our latest game Karigar-e-Taj. These games are suitable for players of all ages and skill levels, making them perfect for a wide range of players. In addition, these games are designed with Indian culture and history in mind, giving players a unique and immersive gaming experience. For example, Yudhbhoomi is a game based on epic wars in Indian history, the game comes with a story based campaign where we have to collaborate to help Rani Abbakka Chowta reclaim her fort in Ullal from the Portuguese colonists.

Patents

Board games are protected under Trademark, Copyright and Design registration. In case of Scrabble it was held:

No copyright protection can be given to the expression of an idea, which can be expressed only in a very limited manner, because doing so would confer monopoly on the ideas itself.

Word 'Scrabble' was given a Trade Mark protection.

In respect of designs capable of registration under the Designs Act the copyright in design shall cease as long as any article to which the design has been applied, has been reproduced more than 50.

https://indiancaselaw.in/mattel-inc-and-others-v-jayant-agarwalla-and-others/

Commercialisation

https://mozaicgames.com/en-us

STARTUPS & BEYOND | 2 – 4 PLAYERS | MEDIUM-HEAVY STRATEGY – Start with developing your business model (D2C or Offline) and build a revenue engine. Maximise your revenue by deploying your product planning, inventory planning, marketing, sales, and forecasting skills. Watch out for Competitors because they can eat into your market share. Check if your business model can thrive even during a pandemic or any economic crisis coming your way!

Video: https://youtu.be/m2TNt4JlncM?si=6LQj9pZWKKr7kLc-

Other games:

VALLAMKALI | 3 – 6 PLAYERS | LIGHT STRATEGY FAMILY FUN PARTY

INDUS 2500BCE | FLIP & WRITE STRATEGY GAME

KARIGAR-E-TAJ | 1 – 4 PLAYERS | LIGHT-MEDIUM STRATEGY

YUDHBHOOMI | 1 – 4 PLAYERS | LIGHT-MEDIUM STRATEGY

CHAI GARAM | 2 – 4 PLAYERS | MEDIUM STRATEGY

NEW BOARD GAME DESIGN KIT

BULK BUY (3) INDUS 2500BCE | FLIP & WRITE STRATEGY GAME

-382-

Burst Preventive Puncture Curative (BPPC) Tyres – TJ Tyres, Faridabad

Sameer Panda PhD from VSSUT, Burla is CEO & Founder of TJ Tyres. He earlier worked at Tata Motors IPR group. TycheeJuno (TJ) Tyres is an innovation and technology-driven start-up working that developed BPPC tyres. XLr8 AP is a joint venture with the Innovation Society of the Government of Andhra Pradesh and the Federation of Indian Chambers of Commerce and Industry (FICCI). It was led by Managing Director Glenn Robinson of the IC² Institute. Beginning with a pool of 430 applicants from across India, XLr8 AP selected the cohort of 33 startups to receive training and mentoring. Of these, 25 companies received technology validation and market assessment using the IC² Institute's Quicklook® methodology, and four of the competing companies were selected to receive advanced commercial acceleration for a period of up to one year. TJ Tyres is one of the four. BPPC Tyre technology of TJ Tyres had won NASA Tech Brief award and had featured in NASA's official publication and subsequently they received Gold Medal in IIGP (DST-Lockheed Martin) in 2016, Gold Medal in International Innovators Fair 2017 organised by Indian Innovators Association.

Technology

A run-flat tire is a pneumatic vehicle tire designed to resist the effects of deflation when punctured, allowing the vehicle to continue to be driven at reduced speeds for limited distances. First developed by tire manufacturer Michelin in the 1930s. These tires contain an extra lining within the tire that self-seals in the event of a small hole due to a nail or screw. In this way, the loss of air is prevented from the outset such that the tire is either permanently self-repairing or at least loses air very slowly. A tubeless tire becomes a run-flat when the walls are reinforced enough to help support the tire when deflated. The Mild RFT is a Multi-chambered Tubeless tyre with sealant inside the chamber to take care of puncture in tread and side wall.

Innovation

The start up developed Brust Preventive and Puncture Curative multi chambered tubeless tyre which prevents bursts and cures punctures. The patented tyre technology with many trade secrets is a Multi-chambered Tubeless tyre with sealant, coolant, and balancers inside it, to take care of punctures and prevent blow-outs. The sealant seals the puncture and automatically heals the tyre. The coolant inside the chamber keeps the temperature of the tyre at an optimal level preventing localized overheating and thus preventing blow-outs. The balancer inside the chamber balances the tyres in the run-time. Due to the application of technologically upgraded materials and structure, the pressure retention for both air and nitrogen filling is almost three times more as compared to the conventional material used for normal tubeless tyres.

Patents

Multi-chambered Tubeless tyre or tubeMulti-chambered Tubeless tyre or tube IN 559/Del/2005 · Issued Mar 1, 2016.

MANUFACTURING PROCESS OF ENVELOPE(S) INTEGRATED IN TUBELESS TYRE AND PRODUCT MADE BY SAME PROCESS, Indian Patent number 408131, 2022

Commercialisation

TJ Tyres who has invented BPPC Tyre (Burst Preventive, Puncture Curative) have entered into 2 wheeler market segment with Investment from CIIE (IIM Ahmedabad) and backing from NITI Aayog.

https://tjtyres.com/bike-tyre.html

Mouseware – Dextroware Devices, Chennai

Pravin Kumar is Founder of Dextroware Devices, an assistive tech start-up at IIT-M Research Park. It was his student project at Rajalakshmi Engineering College,Chennai. Finalists in the Google – Build for Digital India contest. The startup is accepted for incubation by IIT-M and Digital Impact Square, a TCS Foundation Initiative, and the startup got support and grants from both TCS and IIT Madras, which helped it design and develop Mouseware for commercial use. IITM incubated 233 startups in deep tech – http://rtbi.in/incubationiitm/home.html.

Technology

A head mouse is a type of mouse where the user controls the cursor by moving their head. It makes use of head movements as cursor commands. Since the traditional computer mouse is only suitable for operation using hands, a head-controlled mouse can be considered a great alternative for people who are unable to use their upper limbs. In short, it is more convenient for people with limited mobility to use this instead of a conventional mouse. A Head mouse is a device that takes your head movement as input and helps your control the mouse cursor on your smart device. This head mouse is ideal for people with physical disabilities including those who suffer from Repetitive strain injury (RSI), Carpet tunnel syndrome, spinal cord injury, cerebral palsy, multiple sclerosis, muscular dystrophy, or quadriplegia. Head mouse helps you with the hands-free operation of smart devices. These smart devices can be your smartphone, tablet, TV, or Laptop. With the help of a head mouse, users can easily send emails, access the internet, play games, check social media, watch videos online and do so much more. Using a head mouse, with the help of the onscreen keyboard, users can easily use their keyboard to type messages, add comments and send emails to their loved ones.

There are different types of head mouse to help with the various types of disablities. Some of more common head mouse includes: Software-based head mouse, Optical head mouse, Sensor-based head mouse.

Innovation

Mouseware is a head mouse that is made keeping in mind the usage restrictions of Persons with Disability. The innovative product Mouseware is a head-wearable device that enables hands-free control of computers & smartphones with simple head movements. This eliminates the requirement of user's hands to operate the smart devices, and is specifically designed for people with upper-limb disabilities or injuries. The product's main objective is to provide a virtual hand for people who are unable to use their hands to interact with the technology and also aims to provide them with equal job opportunities. Users can wear it as a cap, spectacles, headset, or head strap. The mouse click is performed using a switch with can be connected with the 3.5 mm jack present in the receiver. The Receiver is plugged in via the USB port on your computer. The mouse pointer or cursor is controlled using the head movement of the user. The received is placed on the user's head and when the user moves their head, the signal is transmitted wirelessly to the receiver, and the mouse cursor moves.

Patents

Indian patent – SIMPLE HEAD OPERATED MOUSE FOR DISABLED PERSONS (HAND DISABILITY), Arun Dattatraya Sonar, https://www.quickcompany.in/patents/simple-head-operated-mouse-for-disabled-persons-hand-disability Sony patent on Head Mounted Display – https://patents.google.com/patent/US20140361956

Publication: http://www.cs.clarku.edu/~jmagee/papers/MageeEtal-UAHCI2011.pdf

Commercialisation

https://dextrowaredevices.com/

The product is available for Rs 15,000/-

Video: https://youtu.be/pbgqirbsmAA?si=9v0Uh6MQumxrxxay

Piezoelectric Microphone – Anand Richard Lobo, Goa

Anand Richard Lobo Studied Bachelor of Electrical Engineering at Old Dominion University, Violist at Bombay Chamber Orchestra and Mandolinist, Violist, Singer, Sound Engineer at Lemongrass Acoustic Trio and founder of Lobo Project.

Kishore Shah is the mentor with many accomplishments. HOPE (Habitat for Passionate Entrepreneurs) a platform to retain the art, build a sustainable Business model for Goan Artist entrepreneurs is one such intitiave.

Technology

The sound to voltage conversion is not noted for its high quality – most piezo contact mics are tuned speaker elements used in reverse. The brass disc on which the element is glued is designed to resonate at the design frequency of 2-4kHz so that a large audio output is achieved with a small power input. This will tend to lead to a peakiness at mid-frequencies, However, the main reason these have gotten a bad rap is that many people couple them into a standard audio load, which loses low frequencies. The reason why these devices often sound tinny is because the piezo sensor presents its signal through a series capacitance which is small, typically 15nF or less. When wired to a normal 50 kilohm line input this forms a 200Hz high-pass filter, which eliminates the bass.

https://www.richardmudhar.com/blog/using-piezo-contact-mics-right/

Innovation

Piezoelectric microphones (piezo pickups) are generally frowned upon in the professional audio industry because they are known to sound 'tinny'; generally associated with a sharp, high-pitched audio signal with no 'body' or 'warmth' i.e. almost no low-frequency content. Even so, many brand-name manufacturers still create many varieties of piezoelectric microphone, and while cheaper ones do nothing to help matters, even expensive, branded piezo pickups have some of the same problems, despite seemingly different designs.

This piezoelectric microphone is designed to be a significant improvement over existing products, thanks to different design of the piezoelectric element, and a better design of preamplifier circuit. The microphone design was originally built for acoustic musical instruments, and as a bonus it can, in fact, be used on almost any surface from which the user wants to record mechanical(acoustic) vibration. This can be extended to also record sounds underwater, if the piezoelectric transducer and its connections can be suitably waterproofed.

The piezoelectric disc, and the circuit inside the preamplifier, is arranged in such a way as to reduce electrical interference (EMI) through a widely-used configuration known as 'differential signal' or 'balanced audio'. This provides a clear, powerful sound, while minimizing the 'hum' of electrical noise. In addition, powering the preamplifier circuit uses an industry standard called 'phantom power' which is available on practically all professional audio equipment. This avoids the need for constantly buying and maintaining batteries, reducing e-waste.

Listen – https://ohnoitsalobo.github.io/pickup/

Patents

Piezophone™ is registered trademark.

Commercialisation

The innovator has been using the microphone continuously for over 2 years since coming up with the design, and sold a few prototypes to other musicians who are also using it regularly with good success.

Lobo Projects, H No 1202/2, Murida, Plot 38, Fatorda, Goa 403602, Contact Number: 7507648215, Contact Email ID: anandrlobo@gmail.com

Robotic Scrubber Dryer – Aubotz Labs Pvt Ltd, Pune

Runal Dahiwade is Founder & CEO Peppermint Robotics. A graduate from Visvesvaraya Technological University (VTU), earlier he co-founded Carkhana, online marketplace for Automobile Accessories and sold it to Topwheelz. Miraj C. Vora, from Christ University, Bangalore is co-founder Chief Business Officer. Harshal Khamankar from G.H.Raisoni College of Engg. Nagpur is their Sr.Deign Engineer. The startup one of top 12 startups to the 2020 Cohort of Qualcomm Design in India challenge, participant in Virtual Incubation Program of Nasscom 10000 Startup and funded under Nidhi Prayas of DST with incubation at SINE, IITB.

Technology

Autonomous devices that clean and treat surfaces vacuum cleaners, mopping devices, polishers and lawn mowers are just a few are becoming more and more popular. As these devices move across the surface they are cleaning or treating, determining the most energy-efficient path for the device is a key element in reducing operating costs. The devices also need to completely cover the surface they are treating if they are to complete the tasks they were employed to perform. Finally, these devices need to access hard-to-reach areas in corners and behind doors. A robotic floor scrubber Dryer is a form of robot that cleans floors with brushes. Suction is used by the machine to remove dirt, debris, and wastewater. These robots are often battery-powered and move around cleaning the floors and large spaces. They also have a specific path mapping feature that allows them to easily and efficiently travel across the floor's surface.

Innovation

Peppermint's robotic scrubber dryer is an intelligent and connected robot. It provides real-time data and analytics with 100% accuracy. The Peppermint dashboard provides automatic reports with an interface that is easy to customize to your requirements. The robotic floor scrubber dryer has 11 levels of safety which include 4 different types of sensors and cameras that integrate with its intuitive MINT-OS to navigate safely and conveniently around the surroundings. It detects human movement and dynamic as well as static obstacles through its intelligent obstacle detection system. The robot comes with dynamic pressure for different types of floors. It cleans with 99.99% harmful bacteria removal and also neutralizes oil on the floor. Its triple-action-clean technology delivers deep and efficient cleaning.

Patents

Received Indian Patent for Robotic Cleaning Device Patent no: 411156, in 2022, innovator-Harshal Khamankar.

Patents for sale – https://ipofferings.com/patents-for-sale-robotics-automation.php

This portfolio consists of two U.S. Patents and one U.S. Patent Application, one European Patent and one European Patent Application, and a Chinese Patent Application.

U.S. Patent No. 10,037,027: System and method for determining an energy-efficient path of an autonomous device, European Patent 3264212: System and method for determining an energy-efficient path of an autonomous device, U.S. Patent No. 10,335,003: System and method for an autonomous cleaning apparatus, European Patent Application 16161810: System and method for an autonomous cleaning apparatus, U.S. Patent Application 20180164826: A surface processing device and a method for processing surface areas, European Patent Application: 16204026: A surface processing device and a method for processing surface areas, Chinese Patent Application 108227700: Surface processing equipment and the method for handling surface region.

Commercialisation

https://getpeppermint.co/scrubber-dryer/

Video: https://youtu.be/fJzUZ7eA97U?si=ELLPHEwU7eR3QOSo

Peppermint's best-in-class fully autonomous robotic floor scrubber dryer is designed to handle both industrial and commercial floor cleaning spaces with ease & efficiency. It's the perfect floor cleaning solution for pharmaceutical spaces, warehouses, manufacturing plants, airports, and shopping malls, amongst others. It is an amazing companion for housekeeping operators to collectively keep the facility at the top of its cleanliness and hygiene standards. GMR Innovex launches the Robotics Center Of

Excellence for Airports and has recently signed a Memorandum of Understanding (MOU) with Peppermint Robotics, SINE IIT Bombay, and Flo Mobility to explore the potential of robotic technology and identify its use cases for airports and related business.

-395-

Saline Water Lamp – Dr Purnima Jalihal, NIOT, Chennai

Purnima Jalihal, works as Scientist G at National Institute of Ocean Technology (NIOT), Chennai currently Heading the Renewable Ocean Energy and Fresh Water program.. She was a graduate in civil engineering from Bombay University followed by MS and Ph.D from, Duke University,Durham, NC, USA. She was awarded the VISHWAKARMA MEDAL for the year 2006 by the Indian National Science Academy for work on Desalination in Kavaratti. Dr. Purnima Jalihal of NIOT was awarded the 2019 Uehara Prize on September 26, 2019 at the 7th International OTEC Symposium in Busan.

Among her many research achievements – Have played a major role in the analysis, design, deployment and retrieval of HDPE pihpes for all desalination projects of NIOT. Have several years of experience in design of floating wave powered devices, offshore platforms, risers and moorings, ocean current turbines, and optimization of heat exchangers and demisters for ocean energy and thermal desalination systems. Working towards scaling up and commercialization of desalination technologies for power plants using condenser reject heat and floating large capacity plants for the mainland.

https://www.researchgate.net/scientific-contributions/Purnima-Jalihal-2107485213

Technology

Times Best Innovation 2022 includes Saline Water Lantern designed by Colombian renewable-energy startup E-Dina, WaterLight harnesses a chemical reaction between abundant resources salt water and magnesium to create an electrical current for generating light or charging mobile devices. Just a half-liter of saltwater can provide light for up to 45 days.

https://www.wundermanthompson.com/work/waterlight

Innovation

Dr Jitendra Singh has launched India's first Saline Water Lantern which uses seawater as the electrolyte between specially designed electrodes to power the LED lamps. ROSHNI stands for Renewable Ocean System for Harnessing Novel Illumination. This lantern works on the principle of ionization. Electrical energy is produced when salt water electrolytes react with magnesium inside the device. The lantern works continuously up to 12 hours for every replacement of saline water. Electrodes used in lantern have a life of 500 hours of usage. Lantern can be charged using brine water prepared from common salt (10 g) and water (about 300 ml).

Patents

Publication-Stable, high-performance, dendrite-free, seawater-based aqueous batteries

https://www.nature.com/articles/s41467-020-20334-6

Expired patent on Saline Water lantern – https://patents.google.com/patent/US5963009A/en

More patents with description – https://www.bananaip.com/ip-news-center/patents-bright-idea/

Commercialisation

Many technologies available for transfer from NIOT – https://www.niot.res.in/niot_tech_transfer.php

The lamp is licensed thru NRDC – M/s Pournima Water Technology Private Limited, Point of contact: Mr. Ajit Kadam; Mobile: +91 7709151229 / +91 9822858488

Siddu Jackfruit-Paramesha S. S and IIHR Karnataka

Framer inventor S. S. Paramesha with his father S, K, Siddappa. The fruit was named Sidhujack. He was supported by Dr. G. Karunakaran, the Principal Scientist of Central Horticultural experiment Station, Hirehalli of ICAR-IIHR.

Technology

The jackfruit (Artocarpus heterophyllus Lamk.) is highly heterozygous and cross pollinated tree and as such seedlings exhibits a wide range of variations which aid in the selection of superior desirable types. Due to cross pollination and predominance of seed propagation over long period of time, there is high degree of genetic diversity within the species. Improvement in yield and quality of highly cross-pollinated crops like jackfruit is generally achieved by selecting genotypes with desirable character combinations existing in nature. The improvement of jackfruit is required to make it amenable for intensive cultivation and make it suitable for a variety of value-added products. There is a significant variation for various traits such as plant phenology, leaf shape, leaf size, fruit shape, fruit size, number of fruits per plant, flake colour, number of flakes per fruit etc. The jackfruit crop has long juvenility, high clonal heterozygosity, recalcitrant type of seeds make it difficult to improvement of jackfruit varieties or hybrids, but on the other hand ease of vegetative propagation of hybrids or varieties is advantageous for the jackfruit breeder. The development of jackfruit is again based on the selection of clones especially for small-sized quality fruits, dwarf, less gum type, disease and pest resistance etc.

Innovation

Siddu Jack jackfruit is famous, elite, highly nutritious jackfruit variety from Karnataka. It is highly suitable for homesteads and commercial cultivation. The Indian Council of Agricultural Research (ICAR), New Delhi awarded Siddu as the best jackfruit variety in India. The Siddu halasu is an exotic jackfruit variety. (Halasu in Kannada[1] language).

The mother tree of 'Siddu Jack' was planted by S K Siddappa. 'Siddu Jack' is promoted by the Indian Institute of Horticultural Research (IIHR) since 2019, lakhs of seedlings of 'Siddu Jack' have been sold, thanks to the efforts by the Indian Institute of Horticultural Sciences, Bengaluru. IIHR Scientists helped in identifying and authenticating the uniqueness of the variety.

Patents

SidduJack is now (21" day of April 2023) registered (PPVFRA- Protection of Plant Varieties and Farmers' Rights Act – REG/2020/348) jackfruit variety as an intellectual property. Mr. Paramesha S. S. have the exclusive right to produce, sell, market, distribute, import or export the variety and of authorizing any other person to do so.Piracy & unauthorized cultivation, grafting, promotion, selling is violation of PPVFRA which would invite legal prosecution.

Commercialisation

Health Benefits of Sidhu Jack : A rich source of vitamin C, potassium, dietary fiber, and some other essential vitamins and minerals. Jackfruit seeds may help reduce levels of low-density lipoprotein (LDL) cholesterol. Raw jackfruit helps in type 2 diabetes. Jackfruit is a rich source of antioxidants, that are essential for a healthy immune system. It contains substances with anti-inflammatory, antibacterial, and antifungal properties that may also help promote wound healing.

https://siddujack.com/shop/

Check many other varieties developed by the institute: https://www.iihr.res.in/success-stories

Stay Warm (Hand, Body, Foot and Sleeping Bag Warmers – Parisodhana Technologies, Hyderabad

Dr. Satyanarayana Kuchibhatla, Metallurgy engineer from Andhra University moved on for advanced training at IIT Bombay and University of Central Florida, returned to India in the year 2011 from Pacific Northwest National Laboratory, USA. He contributed to multiple projects related to energy, environment and health using state of the art tools and technologies during a rewarding tenure before returning to India. He co-founded Parisodhana Technologies in the year 2016 with Ajay Karakoti materials Scientist from IITB and University of Central Florida. The startup is supported by Grand Challenges Canada, WIN Foundations, IKP Knowledge Park and BIRAC, DBT of Govt. of India.

http://scholar.google.co.in/citations?hl=en&user=_tG6ccEAAAAJ&view_op=list_works

https://www.linkedin.com/in/satyanarayana-kuchibhatla-0866a818/

https://www.linkedin.com/in/ajay-karakoti-2920a116/

Technology

Hand warmers are small, often disposable, packets that produce heat to warm cold hands. They are used throughout the world in a variety of ways, including outdoor recreation, manual labor, and homelessness. The first commercially produced hand warmer was created by Japanese inventor Niichi Matoba. Matoba received a patent for applying the principle of an oxidation reaction that produces heat by means of platinum catalysis. Air-activated hand warmers contain cellulose, iron, activated carbon, vermiculite (which holds water) and salt. They produce heat from the exothermic oxidation of iron when exposed to air. The oxygen molecules in the air react with iron, forming rust. Salt is often added to catalyze the process.

https://www.scienceiq.com/Facts/WarmerHands.cfm

Innovation

Latent Heat2Comfort Technologies (H2C) specializes in instant, portable and non-electric products that provide heat for comfort and convenience. Proprietary heating technology is a unique blend of electrochemistry, heat transfer and packaging concepts. Products based on this platform technology are manufactured using environment friendly ingredients and are safe to discard after use along with dry domestic waste. And products are simple to use

– Just tear open the external packet, expose the inside pouch to air, shake it and experience the warmth. StayWarm, the first product launched by H2C, provides lasting and comfortable warmth without any need for power supply or batteries. Palm-size pouches, that conveniently fit in pockets, gloves, or shoes provide 6-8 hours of warmth. The product performs well in all kinds of situations: at home, office or outdoors, whether it is going to office or having fun and adventure at a ski resort. StayWarm helps you beat the chill and assists you travel/work with ease.

Patents

Air-activated Device-warming Systems And Methods https://uspto.report/patent/app/20210131704

Commercialisation

Using the fundamental aspects of materials, Dr. Kuchibhatla and his team indigenously developed instant, portable, non-electric heating and cooling technologies with applications spanning from protecting defence personnel working in harsh ambient conditions, high altitudes to providing instant first aid and pain relief on demand. On the civilian side, heating technology based products are used to prevent hypothermia in newborn babies & empowering adolescent girls by providing relief to menstrual cramps. The instant, non-electric cold packs which do not require a refrigerator increase the ease of cold therapy offered by Physiotherapists and dental surgeons. Together these products are targeted to positively impact lakhs of lives across India and other low and middle income countries, create employment and targeted to generate INR 100 Crore revenue by 2026.

https://www.parisodhana.com/

https://www.heat2comfort.com/

H2C is your one stop shop for portable products to address your heating/warming needs.

Walnut Cracker – Mushtaq Ahmed Dar, Kashmir

Mushtaq Ahmed Dar from Anantnag, J&K is the innovator hails from the village of Kreri, Anantnag. In this village, most of the residents are engaged in horticulture and agriculture. His idea was incubated at GIAN J&K in Kashmir University, Srinagar.

http://risingkashmir.com/-mushtaq-dar-kashmirs-serial-innovator

Technology

n a garden or orchard setting, it is essential to remove the green pericarp from freshly harvested walnuts. This can be achieved through various methods, including mechanical peeling machines or manual techniques. Removing the green pericarp helps prevent mold growth and allows for proper drying of the walnuts. After the green pericarp is removed, the walnuts need to be dried to reduce their moisture content. Drying can be done using natural methods such as air drying or with the help of specialized walnut drying equipment. Calibrating or sizing the walnuts is an important step in the processing journey. Once the walnuts are properly dried and calibrated, they are ready for cracking and sorting. Cracking machines are used to break open the shells, allowing access to the kernels inside. After cracking, the kernels go through a sorting process to remove any remaining shell fragments or damaged kernels.

Innovation

In traditional methods of cracking and in other devices, there is a risk that the shell upon manual cracking using hand-held device may crack and fly, thereby endangering user's eye. This cracker overcomes such scenarios.

Walnut Cracker that we witness in market today, was not the same always. Initially, it was in a very crude form. However, the Value Addition and Research Development (VARD) and Business Development (BD) groups at NIF converged the efforts, In-situ, at Anantnag by sharing and implementing inputs, attracting regular feedback from target end users; implementing the feedback in a disciplined manner (since walnut cracking happens during specific parts of year and not entire year). NIF with its existing professional expertise decided to amalgamate expertise of fabricators and entrepreneurs available locally who could readily comprehend and implement user feedback, and also engage youth from B-School, and with a team effort this innovation is now an ambitious start-up of India.

In terms of technology, the cracker has a hopper as a feed-in section, a cracking unit and the outlet. Walnuts to be cracked are placed in the hopper which automatically passed it through the cracking unit consisting of two specially designed twin rollers with specific geometries to grip the walnut and deliver impact action.

The gap between rollers can be adjusted from outside to a range between 0.5 to 2.5 cm depending on walnut size and shape. Wooden Rollers can be attributed as an Innovative mechanism in the process which crack the walnut effectively and efficiently such that its useful fruit (kernel) is separated.

https://nif.org.in/innovation/walnut-cracker/758

Patents

Patent Application # 2347/DEL/2006, Patent granted: 407967

Commercialisation

With assistance of NIF the innovator has transferred the technology to Mohd Rafiq Ahanger, an innovator turned entrepreneur and director, Rafiq Innovations Pvt Ltd, now a start-up recognized by Department of Industrial Policy and Promotion (DIPP) – incubated by NIFientreC, with the objective of triggering the scale up of this much needed innovation by local people. Start-up Certificate # DIPP8028.

https://www.facebook.com/p/Rafiq-Innovations-Private-Limited-100063703037679/

Young Innovators

1. ReMat Filament Machine – Siddhant Panjikar, Goa
2. Converting plastic waste bottles to 3d printing filament – Vailan De Souza, Goa
3. Child Safety Solution – Maniksha Dubey, Dehradun
4. Design of Precise Roller Bearings based Peristaltic Pump with Integrated Real-Time Data Acquisition System – Avinash Kumar Akela and Dr. Ameet Chavan VIT-AP University, Amaravati, AP
5. Evyam new gen solution-, Pragada Satwik, Sreenidhi Institute of Science and Technology, Hyderabad
6. Happy – The Smart Desk Companion Robot – Dhruv Jha, VIT-AP University, Amaravati, AP
7. IOT BASED PROTECTIVE DEVICE TO PREVENT ELECTROCUTION – Dr. P. Sadanandam Vaagdevi College of Engineering, Vaagdevi Incubation and Business Accelerator
8. Magneto-Rheological Clutch for a commercial vehicle – LOYAD JOSEPH LOSAN, JITHIN VIJAYAKUMAR, SADDALA REDDY THARUN, MOOD RAHUL, MURTHI RAMCHANDRA REDDY, NIT Calicut
9. Plastic Collecting Device Makara – Varun Saikia, Navrachana School, Sama Gujarat
10. TCS CodeVita season 10 global coding competition – Kalash Gupta, IITD

Rapid Prototyping Lab

The Rapid Prototyping Lab at the Goa State Innovation Council (GSInC) is a state-of-the-art facility that provides a platform for innovators, entrepreneurs, and researchers to turn their ideas into tangible prototypes. Equipped with advanced machinery such as 3D printers, laser cutters, CNC machines, and electronics workstations, the lab offers a range of prototyping services to support the development of new products, services, and solutions. The lab is open to anyone with a creative idea and provides access to specialized equipment, tools, and expertise to help bring their concepts to life. The ultimate goal of the Rapid Prototyping Lab is to foster innovation and entrepreneurship in the state of Goa by providing a collaborative space for prototyping and testing new ideas.

https://goastateinnovationcouncil.com/downloads/annual-reports/GSInC_AnnualReport_2022-2023.pdf

Project 1

ReMat Filament Machine

Name of innovator/s: Siddhant Panjikar

Name of School/College/Start-up/Organisation: Makers Sutdiio

Address: Usgao, Ponda-Goa.

Contact no. 7276347926

Objective: waste generated from 3d printers is crushed and used again.

Abstract:

3D Printing is a rapidly growing industry. 3D printing machines are used in many areas, including automobiles, medicine, architecture, and sculpture. Prominent material used are PLA, ABS, PETG, TPU. So as the use of 3D printer is on the higher scale consumption of raw material (filament) is also high. According to the reports, approximately 20% of the filament is wasted in the 3D Printing industry.

To recycle this filament this machine is introduced. The working is pretty simple, load the waste filament or 3D models in hopper. The machine will shredder, melt, and make it into a new filament wire. This filament wire can be again used for the 3D Printer. Fabrication of this machine took around 1 year. This machine got a grant from FIIRE's Nidhi EIR Scheme. Later care out the assembly and testing the machine in the Prototyping Lab of Goa State Innovation Council.

Project 2

Converting Plastic Waste Bottles to 3d Printing Filament

Name: Vailan De Souza

Name of School/College/Start-up/Organisation: Prototyping Lab

Address: Fatorda-Goa.

Ph. No.: 9881253391

Project Objective:

A machine for turning PET bottles into printable filament.

Project Abstract:

PETamentor is an innovative solution aimed at addressing the environmental challenges posed by plastic waste while simultaneously promoting sustainable manufacturing practices. This abstract provides an overview of PETamentor, focusing on its ability to convert plastic bottles into 3D printing filaments, thereby contributing to the circular economy and reducing the ecological footprint of plastic waste.

The exponential increase in plastic consumption has led to a significant rise in plastic waste, causing severe environmental pollution and resource depletion. PETamentor seeks to tackle this issue by harnessing the potential of discarded plastic bottles and transforming them into high-quality 3D printing filaments.

The process involves collecting plastic bottles and subjecting them to a series of mechanical and chemical treatments to break them down into smaller, recyclable components. The resulting material is then processed into filaments suitable for 3D printing applications. PETamentor incorporates advanced recycling technologies and quality control measures to ensure the production of filaments that meet industry standards and exhibit desirable properties.

By converting plastic bottles into 3D printing filaments, PETamentor offers several advantages. Firstly, it reduces the reliance on virgin plastic materials traditionally used for filament production, thus conserving valuable resources. Secondly, it provides a sustainable alternative to single-use plastic bottles by transforming them into useful products with extended lifespan and functionality. Additionally, PETamentor contributes to waste reduction and promotes a circular economy model by reintroducing plastic waste back into the production cycle.

Project 3

The Ultimate Child Safety Solution

Name: Maniksha Dubey

https://www.linkedin.com/in/manishka-dubey-871a65202/

Manishka Dubey the (YOUNGEST) WINNER(Cheque of 10 lakh) OF THE INVENTOR CHALLENGE BY COLORS INFINITY TV also the YONGEST INNOVATOR who WON GOLD MEDAL IN INEX INDIA INTERNATIONAL INNOVATION AND INVENTION EXPO GOA FOR the PROTOTYPE "SAFETY BAND" INEX INDIAINTERNATIONAL INNOVATION AND INVENTION EXPO GOA Nov 2022 and 2nd prize winner (CHEQUE OF 15K) WitBlox Young Inventor partnership with Techfest, IIT Bombay 2022.

The Child Safety Band provides a comprehensive solution for keeping track of children and ensuring their safety at all times. Suitable for all ages: The band is designed for children of all ages, providing a level of safety and security for children of all ages. Easy to use: The band is easy to use and can be worn comfortably by children. The alarm button and location tracking features are easy to activate in case of emergency. Real-time information: The location tracker and upgraded version with GSM and GPS modules provide real-time information, so parents and caregivers can always know where their child is.

Features:

Automatic Night Mode Light: Utilizing an LDR sensor, the light will automatically turn on in low-light conditions, making it easy for parents or caregivers to locate their child in the dark. Emergency Alert Switch: Triggers an alarm sound when activated, providing a reliable alert system in case a child wanders out of a safe zone or gets lost. Location Tracker: Alerts parents when the child moves 20m away from them, eliminating limitations of limited range and lack of real-time tracking. Upgraded Version: GSM and GPS modules for precise and real-time tracking of the child's location. In case of emergency, an SMS message with the child's current location is sent to the parents, enabling them to respond quickly and locate their child.

Project 4

Design of Precise Roller Bearings Based Peristaltic Pump with Integrated Real-Time Data Acquisition System

Inventors – Avinash Kumar Akela and Dr. Ameet Chavan VIT-AP University, Amaravati, AP

The invention is a Single-channel peristaltic pump that comprises a dimensionally stable support frame and a tube retainer connected to it through a locking connection. Multiple roller bearings is mounted on the support frame which is rotated with help of a miniature stepper motor. The tube retainer has a tube bed body with a tube bed inside and two legs at the end. Flexible tube sections are placed in the tube bed and can be squeezed by the roller bearings to deliver a medium peristaltically. The two legs are resiliently elastic and can be clipped into the support frame radially. The tube bed body has a substantially omega-shaped design and features a continuous inlet and outlet area that ensures smooth peristaltic delivery of the medium with minimal pulsations.

This system offers several advantages

- Highly flexible and can be used for a wide range of applications
- Robust design, ensuring durability and reliability
- Roller Bearing are suitable for applications requiring high pressures and precision
- Ensure high purity in the pumped media since the fluid only comes into contact with the flexible tubing, preventing contamination
- Offer accurate metering of fluids, making them suitable for dispensing, metering, and transfer applications
- Easy to maintain, resulting in reduced downtime
- Compatible with various liquids, making them versatile for different applications
- Gentle Pumping Action: The pumping action of peristaltic pumps is gentle, ensuring minimal damage to the pumped fluid
- Variable Speed Options: These pumps offer variable speed options, allowing for precise control over the flow rate
- Easy Tubing Replacement: Tubing replacement in peristaltic pumps is easy, facilitating quick maintenance and minimizing downtime
- Prevention of Backflow: Peristaltic pumps prevent backflow of fluids, ensuring efficient and controlled pumping
- Integrated control enables real time monitoring of fluid flow

Project 5

Evyam New Gen Solution

Innovator: Pragada Satwik, Sreenidhi Institute of Science and Technology, Hyderabad

https://www.linkedin.com/in/satwik-pragada-629a8b26b/

Evyam New Gen Solutions pvt.ltd that focuses on building innovative product in the hardware sector Evyam new gen faucet is a unique integrated tap with features of a sop dispensers,water dispenser and hand dryer in a single unit with gesture control the tap developed with smart technology help in saving water and reduces the spread of germs and viruses with touch less system the tap comes with the app to get notifications regarding any issues in the system manufacturing a touch-less faucet The problem we identified in the present market is quick germ and virus dissemination due to physical touch of taps, even if we have a touch less tap in the market that is not halting virus spread since the soap is being physically touched by speedy individuals. And spreading the virus, therefore Evyam developed a product in such a manner that the sop dispenser, saving water and hot blower are all combined into a single unit where we can replace the old tap and install the new gen tap that is entirely touchless in a very simple and unique design. it Is best solution we brought into the market for stopping the most rapidly spreading of germs and virus.

Project 6

Happy – The Smart Desk Companion Robot

Inventor – Dhruv Jha, VIT-AP University, Amaravati, AP

https://www.linkedin.com/in/dhruv-jha-2002/

Happy was developed as part of an engineering clinic project, Happy is more than just a machine; it's a friend, an assistant, and a source of joy. With a compact footprint, Happy sits gracefully on your desk, ready to engage. Its arms and head, gracefully manipulated by SG90 180-degree mini servos, bring a unique charm to its presence. The 3.5-inch TFT LCD embedded in its head is a window to its soul, displaying expressions and information.

At the core of Happy resides a Raspberry Pi, making it more than just a robot – it's a versatile computer. This little genius houses a Raspberry Pi camera and a microphone module, elevating its interaction capabilities. Happy's abilities extend beyond the ordinary. It tracks your face and transforms your spoken words into text, enhancing its understanding of you. Two touch sensors on its head respond to your affectionate pats, adding a touch of warmth to the connection.

But what truly sets Happy apart is its emotional depth. Expressive eyes and sounds reminiscent of Wall-E allow it to communicate with you on a whole new level. It's not just a desk accessory; it's a companion that brightens your workspace and your day. Happy's sensitivity goes beyond the digital realm. Equipped with a vibration sensor, it doubles as an earthquake detector, demonstrating its potential for real-world applications. It can be your personal assistant, a vigilant child monitor, or your reliable video call companion. What makes Happy even more special is its commitment to openness. Every part, meticulously designed and 3D printed with PLA+, is freely available for the community to explore and improve upon. Soon, it will be fully open-source, inviting enthusiasts and creators to participate in its evolution.

The story behind Happy is one of compassion and hope. Its creator was inspired by a desire to make a positive impact on someone's life during a challenging period. Though in its early stages, Happy's potential to bring smiles and solace is undeniable. It's a testament to the power of innovation driven by empathy. Happy is a simple bot with grand aspirations, a work in progress fueled by an unyielding passion for learning and improving. As it evolves, it promises to become an even more invaluable addition to your desk, your life, and your heart.

Design and Development of an Iot Based Protective Device to Prevent Electrocution

Innovator: Dr. P. Sadanandam Vaagdevi College of Engineering, Vaagdevi Incubation and Business Accelerator

Dr. P. Sadanandam and his Team with the prototype from Vaagdevi College of Engineering, Vaagdevi Incubation and Business Accelerator, Warangal, Telangana, India.

Every year in India, about 11,000 agricultural workers are dying due to electric current. On average 50 people are dying every day. This is due to non-compliance with the standards in wiring, cut, and fallen transmission lines, aging, corrosion, and the formation of conductive paths on motor casings and control boxes under damp conditions. Whatever the reason, it is very sad that our farmers, the food providers of our country, are dying in performing their daily routine honesty. Death due to electrocution demands close attention not only to document the true cause of death of the unfortunate victim but also to detect defective conditions which should prevent future electrocution. The main motive of this project is to reduce rate of electrocution. Electrocution injuries can be quick but often deadly. This project deals with prevention of electrocution with the help of IOT Whenever short-circuit occurs, at this instance the current sensor will sense the short-circuit current and compare with reference current with the help of Arduino controller. Based on this comparison, the controller sends the signal through the IOT communication to the actuator which is placed at distribution transformer. Now the actuator will drive the motor and isolates the circuit with the help of auto-recloser. During this process the information is passed to the respective lineman in the form of message.

Project 8

Design, Fabrication and Testing of Low-Cost Innovative Magneto-Rheological Clutch for a Commercial Vehicle

Innovators: Loyad Joseph Losan, Jithin Vijayakumar, Saddala Reddy Tharun, Mood Rahul, Murthi Ramchandra Reddy, NIT Calicut

The invention alludes to Magneto-rheological fluid-based devices in general and their configuration. The inventors have devised an efficient design capable of torque transmission and related features of temperature control and magnetic flux control, along with fluidic mixing of the smart material, which guarantee laminar/turbulent flow enhanced heat transfer as well as proper stir for annihilating sedimentation problems. This project aims at developing a novel MR clutch device that suits the new age automotive requirements and has the scope for commercialization.

The input rotor has a set of shear surfaces which aids in torque transmission. In the present disclosed design, there exists two separate shear surfaces with modified topology which enhances both conductive and convective heat transfer and the pumping impetus over to the fluid shearing in contact with it. An output rotor (Disc) is rotatably mounted along the axis of the input rotor (housing) for rotating along its common axis. The present invention has achieved this with the help of standard deep groove ball bearings. This output rotor shall transmit the required transmission capability to the system under application. The output rotor (Disc) also consists of a set of shear surfaces on both sides of the disc. The first set of shear surfaces of the input rotor shall be separated from the first set of shear surfaces from the output rotor by a combination of annular and radial surfaces. This separation has been achieved in this invention by the introduction of steps above and below the bearings to constrain its motion and thus ensure the presence of the required combination of annular and radial spaces.

Patent applied.

Contact: Dr. Jagadeesha T, Associate Professor, 8547193373

Project 9

Plastic Collecting Device Makara-

Innovator: Varun Saikia, Navrachana School, Sama Gujarat

Varun Saikia, studies in the eighth grade and has developed a cost-effective machine that can remove litter, especially plastic items from different water bodies like lakes, seas and rivers. Before developing the device, Varun made several models and finally came up with a miniature version of the model by reusing plastic items like spoons, bottles and bucket and cardboard paper. He used two drinking bottles as the main body and attached the spoons as the wings of the body. He then placed a battery on the bottle and finally attached the cardboard box at the end of the two bottles. He tested the device in a baby pool and got a positive result.

With the help of his teachers and parents he then started to make the device. The innovative device, named as Makara, is fully battery-operated machine that aims to reduce manual cleaning and focuses more on time management and effective cleaning. The machine, that costs Rs 12,000, consists of a paddle wheel operated by a motor and a pulley and can be controlled using a remote. The paddle wheel pushes the vessel ahead as it navigates through the floating garbage. The force of the wheel pushes the garbage inside the net tail bin which is attached to a basket. Once the basket is full, it can be detached to unload the garbage collected. After testing it in a pool, Varun took the machine to the Gotri pond in the city to clean a patch of it. With the help of the municipal staff, he tested the machine. Garbage including floral waste, coconuts and plastic items were removed from the pond.

He recently won an Outstanding Achievement award from the Initiative for Research and Innovation in STEM (IRIS) National Fair 2021. He is the first teenager from his state to win the award, which is granted by the American Meteorological Society, Massachusetts, for excellence in atmospheric and related sciences. The IRIS Fair is a collaboration with the Department of Science and Technology, Government of India. The award is granted to young people who design outstanding innovations.

Media links: https://connectgujarat.com/navrachana-student-wins-prestigious-american-meteorology-award-at-the-iris-national-fair-2021/

Project 10

TCS CodeVita Season 10 Global Coding Competition

Winner: Kalash Gupta, IITD

CodeVita, a coveted coding contest, also holds the Guinness World Records title as the world's largest computer programming competition. CodeVita has been designed to promote programming as a sport. It aims to encourage participants from all over the world to pit their skills against each other. They all face real-life challenges.

Kalash Gupta, a computer science and engineering student at the Indian Institute of Technology Delhi, has been named the winner of the TCS CodeVita season 10 global coding competition, which drew over 100,000 contestants from 87 countries.

CodeVita is the world's largest computer programming competition, according to Guinness World Records. Coders from Chile and Taiwan were the contest's first and second runners-up, respectively. The contest was held by Tata Consultancy Services. Gupta won prize money of $10,000. The first runner up, Mauricio Andres Cari Leal of Pontificia Universidad Catolica de Chile, received $7,000, and the second runner up, Jeffrey Ho from National Tsing Hua University, received $3,000. The third runner up, Michal Stanik from Czech Republic, received $2,500. All four winners earned an internship opportunity with TCS' Research & Innovation organization.

Inter-Collegiate Programming Contest (ICPC) is the Olympics of competitive programming. Teams first qualify for the regionals by giving preliminary contests, then qualify for the world finals from there. Team "Cheese_Maggi" representing the Indian Institute of Technology, Guwahati secured the 4th Rank in the Asia-West Region (3rd in India, 52nd Globally) in the ICPC World Finals 2022 held at Dhaka.

Hash Code is a team programming competition, organised by Google, for students and professionals around the world. You pick your team and programming language and they pick an engineering problem for you to solve. Google's longest running global coding competition, Code Jam, calls on programmers around the world to solve challenging, algorithmic puzzles against the clock. Microsoft Imagine Cup is full of opportunities to gain new skills, access exclusive training, unlock mentorship opportunities, and have a chance to win great prizes and make a difference in the world.